Scott Foresman

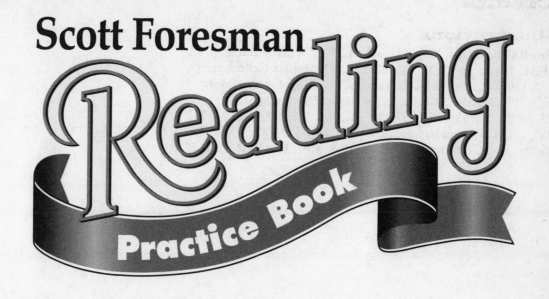

Reading Practice Book

Scott Foresman

Editorial Offices: Glenview, Illinois • Parsippany, New Jersey • New York, New York
Sales Offices: Parsippany, New Jersey • Duluth, Georgia • Glenview, Illinois
Carrollton, Texas • Ontario, California

D1279204

Credits

Illustrations

Rondi Collette: pp. 139, 149 (bottom), 179, 279; **Nelle Davis:** p. 49;
Waldo Dunn: pp. 37, 38, 68, 122, 232, 297; **Morissa Geller:** pp. 39,
172, 180, 242, 249; **Vickie Learner:** p. 199; **Mapping Specialists:**
pp. 9, 271; **Laurie O'Keefe:** pp. 59, 98; **Joel Snyder:** pp. 2, 7, 8, 12,
22, 28, 67, 112, 138, 152, 157, 158, 182, 192, 212, 217, 218, 237, 252,
282, 292; **TSI Graphics:** pp. 29, 79, 149 (top), 159, 187, 273; **N. Jo
Tufts:** pp. 88, 128; **Jessica Wolk-Stanley:** p. 62; **Lisa Zucker:** p. 239.

ISBN: 0-328-02250-0
ISBN: 0-328-04054-1

Copyright © Pearson Education, Inc.

All Rights Reserved. Printed in the United States of America. The
blackline masters in this publication are designed for use with
appropriate equipment to reproduce copies for classroom use only.
Scott Foresman grants permission to classroom teachers to reproduce
from these masters.

12 V011 09 08
12 13 14 V011 09

© 2004

Table of Contents

Unit 4

The Way We Were—The Way We Are	Comprehension	Vocabulary	Selection Test	Phonics/ Word Study	Research and Study Skills
Spring Paint	151, 153, 157	152	155–156	158	159–160
A Brother's Promise	161, 163, 167	162	165–166	168	169–170
from Catching the Fire	171, 173, 177	172	175–176	178	179–180
The Seven Wonders of the Ancient World	181, 183, 187	182	185–186	188	189–190
The Gold Coin	191, 193, 197	192	195–196	198	199–200

Unit 5

Into the Unknown	Comprehension	Vocabulary	Selection Test	Phonics/ Word Study	Research and Study Skills
To the Pole	201, 203, 207	202	205–206	208	209–210
from El Güero	211, 213, 217	212	215–216	218	219–220
Destination: Mars	221, 223, 227	222	225–226	228	229–230
The Land of Expectations	231, 233, 237	232	235–236	238	239–240
The Trail Drive	241, 243, 247	242	245–246	248	249–250

Unit 6

I've Got It!	Comprehension	Vocabulary	Selection Test	Phonics/ Word Study	Research and Study Skills
Noah Writes a B & B Letter	251, 253, 257	252	255–256	258	259–260
Louis Braille	261, 263, 267	262	265–266	268	269–270
The Librarian Who Measured the Earth	271, 273, 277	272	275–276	278	279–280
Tyree's Song	281, 283, 287	282	285–286	288	289–290
Cutters, Carvers, and the Cathedral	291, 293, 297	292	295–296	298	299–300

Sequence

- **Sequence** refers to the order of events in both fiction and nonfiction. Sequence can also refer to steps in a process.

- Clue words such as *when, first, then,* and *next* will help you follow the order in which events happen. Dates and times of day are other clues to the order of events.

First

↓

Next

↓

Last

Directions: Reread "Jerry Takes Off." Then complete the flow chart. Write the story events from the box in the flow chart in order.

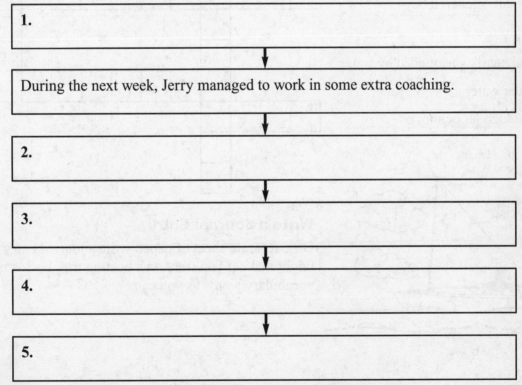

Story Events

Tanya and Tony churned up water as Jerry demonstrated his backstroke.

After Jerry perfected his flip turn, he learned how to dive properly.

When Jerry touched the opposite edge of the pool, Wayne Cabot shouted down to the three of them.

When Tony arrived at the shallow end, Coach Fulton described the way he wanted Jerry to practice his turns.

Then Jerry demonstrated how well he learned to start off in a backstroke race.

During the next week, Jerry managed to work in some extra coaching.

1.

↓

During the next week, Jerry managed to work in some extra coaching.

↓

2.

↓

3.

↓

4.

↓

5.

Notes for Home: Your child read a story and listed events from the story in the order in which they happened. *Home Activity:* Have your child describe five things that he or she did today in the order in which they happened.

© Scott Foresman 6

Vocabulary

Directions: Choose the word from the box that best completes each sentence.
Write the word on the line to the left.

_____ **1.** Michelle's boat had to change direction
in order to sail around the longest side
of the _____.

_____ **2.** Finally, she sailed the boat into a
small _____.

_____ **3.** With a _____, the boat hit something
hard.

_____ **4.** It was a _____ rock just under the
surface of the water.

_____ **5.** Luckily, the rock did not harm the boat,
and Michelle avoided a _____!

Check the Words You Know
__ cove
__ disaster
__ jolt
__ peninsula
__ submerged

Directions: Choose the word from the box that best matches each clue.
Write the word in the puzzle.

Down

6. a very unpleasant event

8. a small, sheltered bay

Across

7. land nearly surrounded by water

9. under water

10. a sudden jar or shock

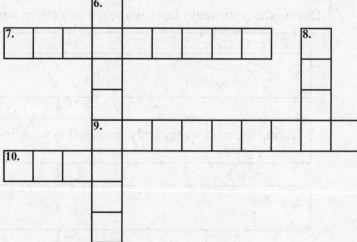

Write a Journal Entry

On a separate sheet of paper, write a journal entry you
might make if you were on a boating trip. Use as many
vocabulary words as you can.

Notes for Home: Your child identified and used vocabulary words from "Tony and the
Snark." *Home Activity:* Together, make up a story about troubles on board a ship. Encourage
your child to suggest ways the vocabulary words can be used in the story.

2   Vocabulary

© Scott Foresman 6

Sequence

- **Sequence** is the order in which things happen or characters perform actions.

- **Sequence** can also refer to the steps in a process.

- Sometimes events happen at the same time. Clue words like *while, as,* and *during* signal two events happening at the same time.

Directions: Reread what happens in "Tony and the Snark" when the boat capsizes. Then answer the questions below. Notice that some story events happen at the same time.

The mast careened. Tony, frightened, let go of everything. The next second the boat capsized.

As Tony hit the water he lost his breath. Struggling, he began to sink. Even as he did he felt the upward pull of his life jacket.

Spitting, flailing arms and legs, he broke through to the water's surface.

"Let your jacket hold you!" he heard Chris shout. "Don't fight! Get your breath!"

Tony stopped thrashing. And when he realized the jacket would hold him, he relaxed.

Reprinted with the permission of Simon & Schuster Books For Young Readers, an imprint of the Simon & Schuster Children's Book Division, from WINDCATCHER by Avi. Copyright © 1991 by Avi Wortis.

1. What happened when Tony hit the water?

_____

2. What happened as he struggled and began to go under?

_____

3. What happened while he was spitting and flailing his arms and legs?

_____

4. When was Tony finally able to relax?

_____

5. On a separate sheet of paper, list what you consider to be the five main events of "Tony and the Snark." Check to be sure that your events are in the right sequence.

Notes for Home: Your child read a story and used details to understand sequence—the order of events in the story. **Home Activity:** Encourage your child to make a schedule of his or her evening activities on a typical school night. Help your child list the events in sequential order.

© Scott Foresman 6

Name _____

1.	Ⓐ	Ⓑ	Ⓒ	Ⓓ
2.	Ⓕ	Ⓖ	Ⓗ	Ⓙ
3.	Ⓐ	Ⓑ	Ⓒ	Ⓓ
4.	Ⓕ	Ⓖ	Ⓗ	Ⓙ
5.	Ⓐ	Ⓑ	Ⓒ	Ⓓ
6.	Ⓕ	Ⓖ	Ⓗ	Ⓙ
7.	Ⓐ	Ⓑ	Ⓒ	Ⓓ
8.	Ⓕ	Ⓖ	Ⓗ	Ⓙ
9.	Ⓐ	Ⓑ	Ⓒ	Ⓓ
10.	Ⓕ	Ⓖ	Ⓗ	Ⓙ
11.	Ⓐ	Ⓑ	Ⓒ	Ⓓ
12.	Ⓕ	Ⓖ	Ⓗ	Ⓙ
13.	Ⓐ	Ⓑ	Ⓒ	Ⓓ
14.	Ⓕ	Ⓖ	Ⓗ	Ⓙ
15.	Ⓐ	Ⓑ	Ⓒ	Ⓓ

© Scott Foresman 6

Selection Test

Directions: Choose the best answer to each item. Mark the letter for the answer you have chosen.

Part 1: Vocabulary

Find the answer choice that means about the same as the underlined word in each sentence.

1. Homes on that <u>peninsula</u> are very expensive.
    A. steep hill
    B. cleared land in a forest
    C. low, grassy land near a stream
    D. land almost surrounded by water

2. Diane practiced sailing in the <u>cove</u>.
    F. a small, sheltered bay
    G. a small pond
    H. a lake
    J. a slow-moving river

3. Watch out for the <u>submerged</u> rocks!
    A. under the surface of the water
    B. floating on the water
    C. falling
    D. overhead

4. Sam thought his first date was a <u>disaster</u>.
    F. a surprise
    G. an event that causes much suffering
    H. a sad moment
    J. a joyous event

5. The car stopped with a <u>jolt</u>.
    A. loud noise
    B. gradual slowing
    C. jerk or sudden jarring movement
    D. smell of something burning

Part 2: Comprehension

Use what you know about the story to answer each item.

6. Before Tony's parents said he could buy the *Snark*, they—
    F. went to the Mart to see it.
    G. bought a life jacket.
    H. discussed it with his grandmother.
    J. made him clean and wax the car.

7. At the beginning of the story, Tony had money saved up from—
    A. selling a motor scooter.
    B. having a birthday party.
    C. opening a bank account.
    D. delivering newspapers.

8. Tony promised his parents that whenever he sailed, he would—
    F. wash and wax the car.
    G. wear a life jacket.
    H. go with a teacher.
    J. take swimming lessons.

9. Where does most of this story take place?
    A. at Tony's house
    B. at the Mart
    C. on the Connecticut shore
    D. in Jamal's driveway

10. Why did Tony's face get hot after he capsized the *Snark?*
    F. He scraped his face on a rock.
    G. His face felt hot compared to the cold water.
    H. He was embarrassed.
    J. He was scared.

11. What happened after Tony and Chris got all the water out of the *Snark?*
    A. Tony sailed it back to the harbor.
    B. Tony's father drove them to the harbor.
    C. They waded back to the harbor.
    D. Chris and Tony went swimming.

© Scott Foresman 6

GO ON ▶

12. Chris most likely started the sailing lesson by explaining words like "port" and "dagger board" so that Tony would—
   F. sound like a sailor when he talked to other people.
   G. lose his confidence and listen to her.
   H. realize that sailing is not easy.
   J. understand her directions when she told him what to do.

13. Which words best describe Chris?
   A. loud and bossy
   B. confident and encouraging
   C. daring and pushy
   D. shy and unsure

14. When Tony first arrived at Carluci's Fish Store, he assumed that—
   F. Chris was a boy.
   G. sailboats were faster than speedboats.
   H. Chris knew where treasure was buried.
   J. he could learn to sail in one afternoon.

15. You can tell that Chris thinks Swallows Bay Harbor is—
   A. too dangerous for sailing.
   B. a boring place to live.
   C. too crowded with people.
   D. a good place to learn sailing.

STOP

© Scott Foresman 6

Cause and Effect

Directions: Read the story. Then read each question about the story. Choose the best answer to each question. Mark the letter for the answer you have chosen.

The Dark Day

Mira woke with a jolt. Dad was shaking her by the shoulder, saying, "Mira, wake up! You overslept."

"Oh, no," groaned Mira. "I'm going to be late for school. I'll miss math review. This day is a disaster already!"

Her father looked concerned. "I'm sorry, honey. How quickly can you get ready? I'll drive you to school. I'm sure I can get you there in time."

Mira jumped into her blue jeans and raced to the kitchen, buttoning her shirt as she ran. She put two frozen waffles—her favorite breakfast treats—into the toaster. She flipped the light switch as she gulped down her juice, but nothing happened. "Everything's going wrong today. Now the light has burned out too."

Mira popped up her waffles, planning to eat them on the way to school. They were as cold and pale as before. "Hey, wait a minute!" She dashed to the window. No lights shone from other houses. The cars were still, buried under mounds of snow.

Then she saw her father shaking his head and smiling.

Mira could see tomorrow's headlines now:

MAJOR SNOWSTORM CAUSES **POWER FAILURE!!** LINES DOWN, TRAFFIC HALTED!

1. Mira is going to be late for school because—
   A. she overslept.
   B. she made waffles for breakfast.
   C. she'll miss math review.
   D. it was a dark morning.

2. Mira's waffles are pale and cold because—
   F. she's late for school.
   G. she likes them that way.
   H. she can't see their color in the darkened kitchen.
   J. there's no electric power.

3. The kitchen light doesn't work because—
   A. it burned out.
   B. she didn't turn it on.
   C. the snowstorm caused a power failure.
   D. everything's going wrong that day.

4. What was the first cause that set off the chain of effects in this story?
   F. a snowstorm
   G. no electricity
   H. Mira oversleeping
   J. Mira's father oversleeping

5. What was the storm's most serious effect?
   A. The morning was gray, and Mira overslept.
   B. Mira's waffles were cold.
   C. There was no electricity, and people couldn't travel.
   D. People needed shovels and boots.

Notes for Home: Your child read a story and noted the causes and effects of events in the story. **Home Activity:** Watch a television news program with your child. Ask her or him to explain what happened and why. See if your child can identify more than one cause or effect.

© Scott Foresman 6

Phonics: Common Word Patterns

Directions: Read each word below. Some words have a word pattern **consonant-vowel-consonant-e (CVCe)** as in **gave.** Most CVCe words have a **long vowel** sound. Other words have a word pattern **vowel-consonant-consonant-vowel (VCCV)** as in **pocket.** Often, the first vowel in VCCV words has a **short vowel** sound. Sort the words according to their word patterns. Write each word in the correct column.

listen	drove	bladelike	fifteen	home
smile	history	windows	life	jacket

CVCe
gave

1. _____
2. _____
3. _____
4. _____
5. _____

VCCV
pocket

6. _____
7. _____
8. _____
9. _____
10. _____

Directions: You can use word patterns to help you pronounce words. Read each sentence. Say the underlined word to yourself. Which pattern do you see and hear? Circle the correct pattern in ( ). Some words might have both.

11. Learning a new skill makes us feel confident <u>inside</u>. (CVCe/VCCV)

12. It is not always easy to avoid <u>disaster</u> when trying something new. (CVCe/VCCV)

13. Even though the boat <u>capsized</u>, the sailing student did not give up. (CVCe/VCCV)

14. It is probably best not to be <u>alone</u> when trying something new for the first time. (CVCe/VCCV)

15. History shows us that only those who take a chance come out a <u>winner</u>. (CVCe/VCCV)

Notes for Home: Your child sorted and wrote words based on letter patterns such as *gave* (CVCe) and *pocket* (VCCV). **Home Activity:** Write *gave* and *pocket*. Take turns changing one letter of each word to make a new word without changing the *CVCe* or *VCCV* patterns.

© Scott Foresman 6

Map/Atlas

A **map** is a drawing of a place. A **map key** shows what the symbols used on a map mean. A **compass** shows the directions north, south, east, and west. The **scale** shows distances. An **atlas** is a book of maps.

Directions: The map below shows the route taken by the explorers Meriwether Lewis and William Clark from 1804 to 1806. President Thomas Jefferson believed it was possible to sail across North America from the Mississippi River to the Pacific Ocean, and he sent Lewis and Clark to look for this water route. Use the map to answer the questions on the next page.

Lewis and Clark Exploration of the Northwest, 1804–1806

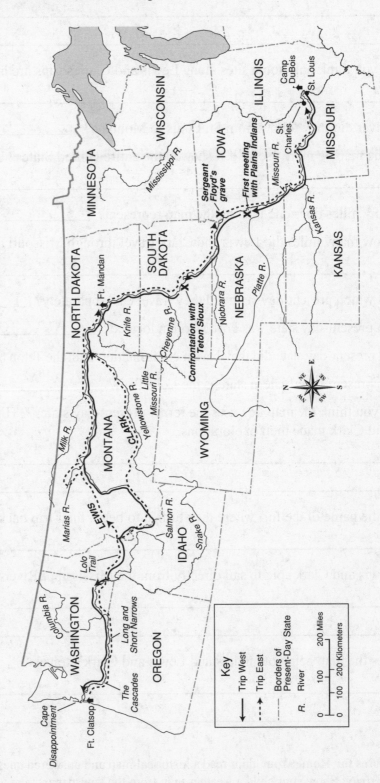

© Scott Foresman 6

Name _____

1. How does the map key help you understand the map? _____

_____

2. What do the dashed lines with arrows represent? What do the solid lines with arrows represent?

_____

_____

3. Why do you think only some sites along Lewis and Clark's trips are labeled?

_____

4. Which river did they follow from St. Louis to Montana? _____

5. Would the map be more useful if it showed the entire United States? Explain.

_____

6. How many miles does one inch on the map represent? _____

7. About how many miles did Lewis and Clark travel through Missouri as they went west?

_____

8. Through which present-day state did they travel east separately? _____

9. In which present-day state was Fort Mandan located? _____

10. In which present-day state did they have a confrontation with the Teton Sioux? _____

11. In which present-day western state is the Lolo Trail? _____

12. Why do you think the map key uses the term "present-day states"? Hint: Think about when Lewis and Clark made their explorations.

_____

_____

13. What is the name of the fort where they turned to begin their trip back east?

_____

14. Were Lewis and Clark able to sail directly from the Mississippi River to the Pacific Ocean?

_____

_____

15. How does the map help you understand Lewis and Clark's travels? _____

_____

_____

Notes for Home: Your child read a historical map and answered questions about it. *Home Activity:* Show your child a weather map from the newspaper. Take turns asking one another questions about it, such as: *Where is it going to rain? What does this symbol represent?*

© Scott Foresman 6

Author's Viewpoint

- An **author's viewpoint** is the way an author looks at the subject he or she is writing about.
- An author's viewpoint may be one of anger, admiration, pity, or some other feeling.
- You can identify an author's viewpoint by thinking about the words an author uses to describe a subject.

Directions: Reread "Play Ball!" Complete the table by providing phrases from the story that reveal the author's viewpoint about the main character. Then identify the author's viewpoint about the story's subject using details given in the story.

Character or Subject	Phrases that Describe Character/Subject	Author's Viewpoint
Kenny	Kenny hops up.	The author admires Kenny. He thinks that Kenny is quick, alert, and responsible.
	1.	
	2.	
	3.	
	4.	
Baseball	The team's three doctors are also in the dugout, watching how the players' bodies are working during the game.	5.
	. . . that sacred moment. . . .	
	. . . a tense batter throws his helmet and bat. . . .	

Notes for Home: Your child read a story and used words from the story to identify the author's viewpoint. *Home Activity:* Describe a person, place, or thing. Then ask your child to describe how you feel about that person, place, or thing, based on your description.

© Scott Foresman 6

Vocabulary

Directions: Choose the word from the box that best matches each definition.
Write the word on the line.

_____ 1. showing or causing hate

_____ 2. rough or cruel treatment

_____ 3. very great; enormous

_____ 4. devotion to a purpose

_____ 5. unfounded dislike

Check the Words You Know

__ abuse
__ dedication
__ hateful
__ hostility
__ prejudice
__ racial
__ tremendous

Directions: Choose a word from the box that best matches each clue.
Write the word on the line to the left.

_____ 6. During the Civil Rights movement of the 1950s and 1960s, many men and women were working and fighting for _____ equality for all Americans.

_____ 7. These Civil Rights workers often had to face the _____ of angry crowds.

_____ 8. Despite these obstacles, the _____ of the workers paid off as unfair laws were overturned.

_____ 9. Since the 1950s, there have been some _____ changes in the way people of different races relate to one another.

_____ 10. Although _____ against others still exists, the Civil Rights movement was successful in getting laws passed to protect against unfair treatment of others based on their race.

Write an Opinion

Think about a time you felt others had treated you unfairly because you were "different" from them. How did this make you feel?
On a separate sheet of paper, write an opinion on how prejudice affects the way people treat one another. Use as many vocabulary words as you can.

 Notes for Home: Your child identified and used vocabulary words from the story *Teammates*.
Home Activity: Select five words from a story you and your child read together. Take turns telling each other what the word means and using it in a sentence.

© Scott Foresman 6

Author's Viewpoint

- **Author's viewpoint** is the way an author thinks about the subject of his or her writing.

- An author's viewpoint may be one of fear, admiration, pity, amusement, or other feeling.

- You can identify an author's viewpoint by thinking about the words an author uses to describe a subject.

Directions: Reread the part of *Teammates* in which Pee Wee Reese takes a stand. Then answer the questions below. Think about how the author shows his viewpoint.

With his head high, Pee Wee walked directly from his shortstop position to where Jackie was playing first base. The taunts and shouting of the fans were ringing in Pee Wee's ears. It saddened him, because he knew it could have been his friends and neighbors. Pee Wee's legs felt heavy, but he knew what he had to do.

As he walked toward Jackie wearing the gray Dodger uniform, he looked into his teammate's bold, pained eyes. The first baseman had done nothing to provoke the hostility except that he sought to be treated as an equal. Jackie was grim with anger. Pee Wee smiled broadly as he reached Jackie. Jackie smiled back.

Stepping beside Jackie, Pee Wee put his arm around Jackie's shoulders.

Excerpt from TEAMMATES by Peter Golenbock, copyright © 1990 by Golenbock Communications, reprinted by permission of Harcourt Brace and Company.

1. How does the author signal that Pee Wee is going to do something important?

_____

2. Why is it difficult for Pee Wee to listen to the taunts of the crowd?

_____

3. How does the author show his opinion of the crowd?

_____

_____

4. What is the author's opinion of Jackie Robinson?

_____

_____

5. What does the author think of Pee Wee Reese? Explain your thinking on a separate sheet of paper. Give examples from the selection to support your answer.

Notes for Home: Your child read a selection and used its details to identify the author's viewpoint. *Home Activity:* Read a newspaper or magazine letter to the editor with your child. Ask your child to tell you the writer's viewpoint.

© Scott Foresman 6

Name _____

1.	Ⓐ	Ⓑ	Ⓒ	Ⓓ
2.	Ⓕ	Ⓖ	Ⓗ	Ⓙ
3.	Ⓐ	Ⓑ	Ⓒ	Ⓓ
4.	Ⓕ	Ⓖ	Ⓗ	Ⓙ
5.	Ⓐ	Ⓑ	Ⓒ	Ⓓ
6.	Ⓕ	Ⓖ	Ⓗ	Ⓙ
7.	Ⓐ	Ⓑ	Ⓒ	Ⓓ
8.	Ⓕ	Ⓖ	Ⓗ	Ⓙ
9.	Ⓐ	Ⓑ	Ⓒ	Ⓓ
10.	Ⓕ	Ⓖ	Ⓗ	Ⓙ
11.	Ⓐ	Ⓑ	Ⓒ	Ⓓ
12.	Ⓕ	Ⓖ	Ⓗ	Ⓙ
13.	Ⓐ	Ⓑ	Ⓒ	Ⓓ
14.	Ⓕ	Ⓖ	Ⓗ	Ⓙ
15.	Ⓐ	Ⓑ	Ⓒ	Ⓓ

© Scott Foresman 6

Selection Test

Directions: Choose the best answer to each item. Mark the letter for the answer you have chosen.

Part 1: Vocabulary

Find the answer choice that means about the same as the underlined word in each sentence.

1. The hostility between them is obvious.
   - A. cooperation
   - B. dislike; unfriendliness
   - C. respect
   - D. strong affection

2. Jack wished he could take back his hateful comments.
   - F. showing strong dislike
   - G. clever
   - H. not correct
   - J. silly

3. Marty has the dedication needed to win the award.
   - A. lack of interest
   - B. ill will
   - C. determination to reach a goal
   - D. talent

4. That law has put a stop to the abuse of animals.
   - F. movement
   - G. cruel treatment
   - H. housing
   - J. daily care

5. The truck carried a tremendous load.
   - A. important
   - B. very old
   - C. huge
   - D. valuable

6. Margo talked about her racial background.
   - F. of or about jobs
   - G. related to history
   - H. of or about art
   - J. of or about a race of people

7. I'll never understand Daisy's prejudice.
   - A. way of expressing oneself
   - B. interest in something
   - C. dislike without a reason
   - D. attraction to something

Part 2: Comprehension

Use what you know about the selection to answer each item.

8. Before Jackie Robinson tried out for the Dodgers, he—
   - F. became friends with Pee Wee Reese.
   - G. played in the Negro Leagues.
   - H. played against the Cincinnati Reds.
   - J. played in the Major Leagues.

9. African Americans gathered in crowds to watch Jackie Robinson at his first tryout with the Dodgers because they—
   - A. hoped he would become the first African American player in the Major Leagues.
   - B. thought he should play in the Negro Leagues.
   - C. did not know if he was a very good player.
   - D. wanted to protect him from people who threatened him.

10. The author most likely wrote this selection to—
    - F. persuade readers to learn more about baseball.
    - G. describe the people of the 1940s.
    - H. inform readers about a hero.
    - J. compare Jackie Robinson and Pee Wee Reese.

© Scott Foresman 6

GO ON

11. Branch Rickey and Pee Wee Reese both thought that Jackie Robinson—
   A. could end segregation in America.
   B. should not play for the Dodgers.
   C. might take their jobs.
   D. could help the Dodgers win games.

12. What is the main idea of this selection?
   F. There were many extraordinary baseball players in the Negro Leagues.
   G. Branch Rickey was not afraid of change.
   H. Pee Wee Reese and Jackie Robinson played on the same team.
   J. Jackie Robinson overcame prejudice to become the first African American player in Major League baseball.

13. Which sentence states a generalization that is valid?
   A. Everyone in the Major Leagues supported racial segregation.
   B. Many players in the Negro Leagues were good baseball players.
   C. Everyone hoped Jackie Robinson would become a star player for the Dodgers.
   D. Most players in the Negro Leagues became famous.

14. The author of this selection believes that all baseball players should be—
   F. treated equally, regardless of race.
   G. paid exactly the same salary.
   H. made famous throughout the world.
   J. yelled at by fans.

15. The author of this selection would most likely agree that—
   A. people should not be concerned about racial problems.
   B. Jackie Robinson's skills were more important to Branch Rickey than his self-control.
   C. Branch Rickey was a smart and courageous man.
   D. Pee Wee Reese was just like the rest of Robinson's teammates.

STOP

© Scott Foresman 6

Main Idea and Supporting Details

Directions: Read the passage. Then read each question about the passage. Choose the best answer to each question. Mark the letter for the answer you have chosen.

A Sport Unlike Any Other

Baseball is a sport unlike any other. It is a team sport that depends largely on individual effort. The pitcher must make his pitch and get it in the spot he wants to hit—until he releases the ball, his teammates can do nothing to help him. Teammates back one another up on all plays, but each fielder has to catch the balls within his reach and make accurate throws to get runners out. Each player is responsible for covering his own territory.

In no other sport does the defense hold the ball. The idea of basketball, football, and hockey is to take the ball (or puck) away from the opponent; the two teams fight for possession of the ball throughout the game. In baseball, the point is to cross home plate more often than the other team.

When the first batter comes up in a game, he is his team's only active player, against the nine active players in the field for the other team. In no other sport are the sides designed to be uneven at all times. The greatest number of active players on the offensive team is four—if the bases are loaded and a man is up to bat.

Professional baseball teams play a 162-game season—more than twice as many games as basketball teams, and more than ten times as many as football. The season lasts for six months, with a game almost every day.

1. What is the main idea of the passage?
   A. Baseball is the best sport.
   B. Baseball is just like any other sport.
   C. Baseball is unlike any other sport.
   D. Baseball is duller than any other sport.

2. The main idea of the first paragraph is that—
   F. the pitcher's teammates cannot help him until he throws the ball.
   G. baseball depends on individual effort.
   H. outfielders cover a lot of territory.
   J. fielders have to make accurate throws.

3. The main idea of the second paragraph is—
   A. that football is similar to basketball.
   B. that baseball is not a battle for possession of the ball.
   C. that hockey is played with a puck.
   D. that a football has a shape all its own.

4. The main idea of the third paragraph is—
   F. that there are never more than four offensive players at one time.
   G. that there can never be more than three runners on base.
   H. that the first batter faces nine opponents.
   J. that in baseball, the sides are never even.

5. Which of the following is **not** a supporting detail of the last paragraph?
   A. Baseball is the most popular sport.
   B. Professional basketball has fewer games in a season than baseball.
   C. Teams play every day for six months.
   D. Professional baseball has a 162-game season.

Notes for Home: Your child has identified the main ideas of a passage and the details that support those ideas. *Home Activity:* Review a magazine advertisement with your child. Challenge him or her to identify the main idea and supporting details.

© Scott Foresman 6

Phonics: Vowel Digraphs

Directions: The **long e** sound heard in **feet** can be spelled: **ea, ee, ei,** or **ie.** The **long a** sound heard in **wait** can be spelled **ai.** Read the newspaper story below. Say the underlined words to yourself. Match each underlined word with a word to the right that rhymes. Write the word on the correct line.

SPORTS

Yesterday was an amazing day in sports. Athletes from all over the world took the <u>field</u>. If the athletes were <u>afraid</u> of the competitions that were about to begin, it never showed. They <u>received</u> thunderous applause from the fans who had come to <u>see</u> them compete. Indeed, everyone who attended the games <u>believed</u> they were about to witness performances by the world's greatest athletes. They couldn't wait for the sports <u>series</u> to begin.

1. wearies _____
2. heaved _____
3. be _____
4. relieved _____
5. pealed _____
6. stayed _____
7. bead _____

Directions: Read each sentence. Say each underlined word to yourself. Listen for the word with the **long e** sound as in **feet,** or the **long a** sound as in **wait.** Write the word with the long vowel sound on the line.

_____ 8. <u>When</u> playing a <u>team</u> sport, everybody is responsible for a win or a loss.

_____ 9. The <u>pain</u> of losing is bearable if you <u>have</u> the thrill of winning too.

_____ 10. A dedicated athlete could, if she or he <u>wished</u>, play a sport during each <u>season</u>.

_____ 11. Often communities have local sports <u>leagues</u> for <u>amateur</u> athletes.

_____ 12. It is an <u>unbelievable</u> feeling when all players work <u>together</u> on a team.

_____ 13. <u>Often</u> athletes <u>aim</u> to be number one in their sport.

_____ 14. Most athletes <u>love</u> the challenge they <u>feel</u> from competing against others.

_____ 15. Many <u>consider</u> playing sports to be their <u>field</u> of dreams.

Notes for Home: Your child worked with words with long *e* (*see, sea, field, receive*) and long *a* (*wait*) vowel sounds. ***Home Activity:*** Read a sports story with your child. Try to find other words with these vowel sounds and spelling patterns.

© Scott Foresman 6

Technology: Newspaper

You can find current **newspapers** and **news magazines** online using a computer and the Internet. When you connect to the Internet, you may see a welcome screen with choices such as "news" or "newsstand." If you click on this kind of button, you might get a screen like the one below. The underlined words at the bottom of the screen are links to other web pages. If you click on a link, you'll get a new web page.

Directions: Use the computer screen to answer the questions that follow.

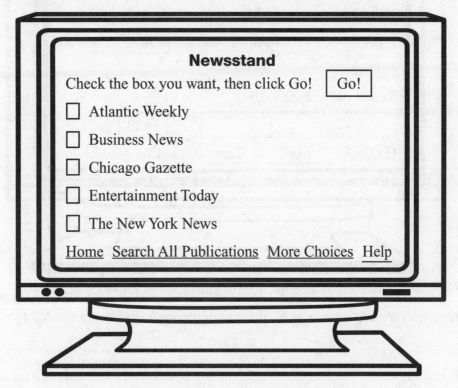

Newsstand

Check the box you want, then click Go!   Go!

☐ Atlantic Weekly

☐ Business News

☐ Chicago Gazette

☐ Entertainment Today

☐ The New York News

Home   Search All Publications   More Choices   Help

1. Explain how you can get to the web page for *The New York News*. _____

_____

2. How might you be able to get to other newspapers not listed on this screen? _____

_____

3. What should you do if you need help? _____

_____

4. How is an online "newsstand" similar to a real newsstand? How is it different?

_____

_____

_____

_____

© Scott Foresman 6

After you get to an online newspaper or magazine, you may be able to search by a specific section of the newspaper, such as sports. There will probably also be a search box in which you can type key words. Use "AND" between each key word.

Directions: Use the computer screen to answer the questions that follow.

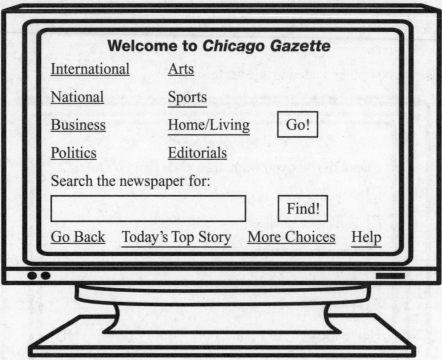

Welcome to *Chicago Gazette*

International   Arts

National   Sports

Business   Home/Living   Go!

Politics   Editorials

Search the newspaper for:

[   ]   Find!

Go Back   Today's Top Story   More Choices   Help

5. In which section would you search for information about a museum exhibit? _____

6. In which section would you search for information about current news about Europe?

_____

7. In which section would you search for information about the people running for mayor?

_____

8. In which section would you search for information about decorating your living room?

_____

9. Give two ways to find a list of upcoming baseball games. _____

_____

10. If you wanted to find an article that had been printed in the newspaper a few months ago, would you search an online newspaper or go to the library to look for a print newspaper or a microfilm of a newspaper? Explain.

_____

_____

Notes for Home: Your child answered questions about finding infomation in a newspaper or magazine on the Internet. *Home Activity:* Look through your local newspaper with your child or search for one on the Internet. Discuss the different sections of the paper.

© Scott Foresman 6

Cause and Effect

- An **effect** is something that happens. A **cause** is why something happens.

- To find an effect, ask yourself, "What happened?" To find a cause, ask yourself "Why did it happen?"

- An effect may have more than one cause, and a cause may have more than one effect.

- Sometimes an author does not state a cause, and you need to draw your own conclusions about why something happens.

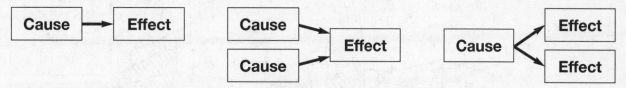

Directions: Reread "Leaving Home." Then complete the table. Provide each missing cause or effect.

Cause (Why did it happen?)	Effect (What happened?)
1.	Pa felt it was too crowded where they lived.
2.	Pa decided to move the family out West.
They would have to leave family and friends behind.	3.
4.	Mama's friends gathered to say farewell.
Mama was sad to leave.	5.

Notes for Home: Your child identified causes and effects in a story. **Home Activity:** Ask your child to relate the events of the day. Discuss the events together, encouraging your child to identify any cause-effect relationships among the day's events.

© Scott Foresman 6

Vocabulary

Directions: Choose the word from the box that has the same or nearly the same meaning as each word or words below. Write the word on the line.

_____ 1. building mixture of crushed stone, sand, cement, and water

_____ 2. real

_____ 3. changed

_____ 4. usual

_____ 5. traditions

Check the Words You Know

__ adobe
__ authentic
__ concrete
__ converted
__ heritage
__ normal

Directions: Choose the word from the box that best completes each sentence. Write the word on the line to the left.

_____ 6. With hard work, the Pueblo people _____ clay, straw, and water into a place to live.

_____ 7. They made _____ bricks to build the walls.

_____ 8. It was _____ for them to use these natural materials for building their homes.

_____ 9. It was part of the _____ passed down from their elders.

_____ 10. There are still people today who would much rather live in an _____ adobe home than in one built with newer materials.

Write a Description

On a separate sheet of paper, write a description of something a family member taught you to do or make. It could be a skill like woodcarving, playing an instrument, or cooking a special meal. Use as many vocabulary words in your description as you can.

Notes for Home: Your child identified and used vocabulary words from "April's Mud." *Home Activity:* Challenge your child to make up a story about building a place to live, using the vocabulary words listed above.

© Scott Foresman 6

Cause and Effect

- An **effect** is something that happens. A **cause** is why something happens.

- An effect may have more than one cause, and a cause may have more than one effect.

- Sometimes you need to draw your own conclusions about what happens and why.

Directions: Reread the passage of "April's Mud" that describes what happens when the Ellises try to make adobe bricks. Then answer the questions below. Look for effects that have more than one cause.

At the end of the day they were all so sore and tired they could hardly move. But they forgot to cover the finished adobes, and when a rainstorm came up suddenly during the night, the adobes melted right back to mud again. Then, because the clay was so dense and Tom hadn't mixed in enough straw, their next batch cracked.

"April's Mud" from RIO GRANDE STORIES, copyright © 1994 by Carolyn Meyer, reprinted by permission of Harcourt Brace and Company.

1. Why are the Ellises hardly able to move?

_____

2. Name two causes of the adobes melting back into mud.

_____

_____

3. Name two causes of the adobes cracking.

_____

_____

4. What might the family do next time to save the adobe bricks from melting?

_____

5. On a separate sheet of paper, list the causes and effects of Tom's decision to build an adobe house. Remember that the author may not always state causes and effects directly.

Notes for Home: Your child read part of a story and used its details to identify causes and effects. *Home Activity:* Read a story or watch a TV drama or comedy with your child. Take turns challenging each other to identify what happens (effects) and why (causes).

© Scott Foresman 6

Name _____

1.	Ⓐ	Ⓑ	Ⓒ	Ⓓ
2.	Ⓕ	Ⓖ	Ⓗ	Ⓙ
3.	Ⓐ	Ⓑ	Ⓒ	Ⓓ
4.	Ⓕ	Ⓖ	Ⓗ	Ⓙ
5.	Ⓐ	Ⓑ	Ⓒ	Ⓓ
6.	Ⓕ	Ⓖ	Ⓗ	Ⓙ
7.	Ⓐ	Ⓑ	Ⓒ	Ⓓ
8.	Ⓕ	Ⓖ	Ⓗ	Ⓙ
9.	Ⓐ	Ⓑ	Ⓒ	Ⓓ
10.	Ⓕ	Ⓖ	Ⓗ	Ⓙ
11.	Ⓐ	Ⓑ	Ⓒ	Ⓓ
12.	Ⓕ	Ⓖ	Ⓗ	Ⓙ
13.	Ⓐ	Ⓑ	Ⓒ	Ⓓ
14.	Ⓕ	Ⓖ	Ⓗ	Ⓙ
15.	Ⓐ	Ⓑ	Ⓒ	Ⓓ

© Scott Foresman 6

Selection Test

Directions: Choose the best answer to each item. Mark the letter for the answer you have chosen.

Part 1: Vocabulary

Find the answer choice that means about the same as the underlined word in each sentence.

1. Luke does not lead a <u>normal</u> life.
   - A. healthful
   - B. special
   - C. usual; like most other people's
   - D. exciting; filled with interesting events

2. The bed was a <u>converted</u> sofa.
   - F. changed into another form
   - G. expensive
   - H. decorated with bright colors
   - J. repainted

3. Dad has an <u>authentic</u> 1956 race car.
   - A. one of a kind
   - B. fake; copied
   - C. in the latest style
   - D. real; genuine

4. It was cool inside the <u>adobe</u> house.
   - F. made of wood
   - G. building material made of baked clay
   - H. new
   - J. shaded

5. Mr. Alvarez made <u>concrete</u> stairs.
   - A. mixture of sand, cement, and water
   - B. wood
   - C. plaster that sets in a hard coat
   - D. dried mud

6. Sam wanted to learn about his <u>heritage</u>.
   - F. neighborhood
   - G. friends from school
   - H. childhood
   - J. beliefs and traditions handed down from earlier generations

Part 2: Comprehension

Use what you know about the story to answer each item.

7. The first adobes that April's family made were ruined because they—
   - A. dried out too fast.
   - B. were washed away by rain.
   - C. baked in the sun.
   - D. did not have enough straw.

8. In this story, April learns that—
   - F. her parents are hippies.
   - G. she is going to attend a new school.
   - H. her classmates think her father is interesting.
   - J. she has classmates who live in old buses.

9. Which event from the story happened before April saw the floor plan?
   - A. April's father taught her class to build a *horno*.
   - B. April's family made adobe bricks.
   - C. April's father visited her class at school.
   - D. April decided to invite her classmates to visit her home.

10. In his plans for the house, Tom seems to feel that it is most important to—
    - F. make sure April and Susan have their own rooms.
    - G. make the house bigger than Mr. Flores's house.
    - H. make the house very much like houses of the old days.
    - J. make the house as modern as possible.

© Scott Foresman 6

GO ON

11. Compared to the beginning of the story, at the end April is more—
    A. embarrassed.
    B. shy.
    C. lonely.
    D. confident.

12. The finished shape of the *horno* is like the shape of—
    F. an igloo.
    G. a bus.
    H. an adobe house.
    J. a teepee.

13. Why did April feel better about the school project by the end of the story?
    A. She always enjoyed working with her father.
    B. Her classmates did not know she lived in a bus.
    C. Her friends already knew how to work with adobe mud.
    D. Her classmates enjoyed making the *horno*.

14. The author's main purpose in this selection is to—
    F. tell an entertaining story about April.
    G. explain how to make adobe bricks.
    H. persuade people not to build adobe houses.
    J. compare adobe houses with wooden houses.

15. When their adobe house is built, April will most likely—
    A. decide to build a room for herself.
    B. feel proud of her family's work.
    C. be embarrassed by the dirt floor.
    D. try to keep people from seeing it.

STOP

© Scott Foresman 6

Making Judgments and Plot

Directions: Read the story. Then read each question about the story. Choose the best answer to the question. Mark the letter for the answer you have chosen.

Undercover Artist

No one paid much attention to the new kid, Max. Who would? He didn't talk much. At lunch, Max just about disappeared. Some of his new classmates thought he was homesick. Others just thought he was boring.

One morning a cartoon of Mr. Foley's sixth grade class appeared on the chalkboard. You could easily identify people in it. The artist had caught the personalities of everyone in the class. It showed Joey gazing out the window. Kathy was waving her hand to answer a question. Keisha was shown taking lots of notes. It captured Mr. Foley perfectly with his glasses on top of his head and chalk marks all over his suit.

Almost everybody laughed and praised the drawing. Mr. Foley didn't erase it. Max said nothing. He didn't seem very interested.

By lunch time, the class was dying to discover who the mystery artist was. No one in the sixth grade had such talent.

Then Rosa remembered that Max always doodled while the rest of the class talked and joked. She went to look over Max's shoulder. Sure enough, he was deep into a funny drawing of their last baseball game.

"I guess the cat's out of the bag now," said Max.

"It sure is," said Lou, "and we're glad. We need you on the class newspaper!"

1. The rising action of this story begins when—
   A. we first read about Max.
   B. the cartoon appears on the board.
   C. the class is at lunch.
   D. the newspaper comes out.

2. The climax of the story occurs when—
   F. Lou says, "We need you on the class newspaper!"
   G. Max just about disappears at lunch.
   H. the class sees the drawing on the chalkboard.
   J. the class realizes that Max is the artist.

3. At first, the class assumed Max was
   A. very talented.
   B. an athlete.
   C. very involved in schoolwork.
   D. uninteresting or homesick.

4. By the story's end, the class
   F. thinks Rosa is very smart.
   G. wants to frame a picture by Max.
   H. wants to print the next issue of the newspaper.
   J. has new ideas about Max.

5. Max was quiet because—
   A. he didn't like his classmates.
   B. he was always busy drawing.
   C. he didn't know the answers.
   D. he was doing his homework.

Notes for Home: Your child read a story and used its details to identify important characters and events and to make judgments about them. *Home Activity:* Ask your child to outline the main events of a story you both know. Talk together about your judgments of the main characters.

© Scott Foresman 6

Phonics: Diphthongs and Digraphs

Directions: Each sentence contains an underlined word with the letter combination **au, aw, ew,** or **ou.** Say the underlined word to yourself. Listen to the sounds that the letters **au, aw, ew,** and **ou** represent. Circle the word in ( ) that has the same vowel sound as the underlined word.

1. The class <u>knew</u> that building the playhouse would be a lot of hard work. (knee/new)

2. It takes many people to build a <u>house</u>. (hound/hoot)

3. They <u>paused</u> to inspect the land on which the house would be built. (pace/paw)

4. The builders showed the plans they had <u>drawn</u> to their supervisor. (author/away)

5. The carpenter tried to figure out <u>about</u> how much wood she would need. (soup/round)

6. Then she made a list of other <u>raw</u> materials she needed to get. (say/sauce)

Directions: Read the sentences below. Each sentence contains a word with a vowel sound heard in **saw, new,** or **loud.** Underline this word and write it on the line.

_____ 7. Today, some people still live in authentic adobe homes.

_____ 8. It is best to build an adobe home on level ground.

_____ 9. Examine your space outdoors to see where a home can be built.

_____ 10. Before building, most people draw a plan of their home so they have an idea of what it will look like.

_____ 11. A basic plan for constructing the home is usually an outline that shows where each room will be and how big it will be.

_____ 12. The adobe will be made with a few simple materials.

_____ 13. One of the ingredients in an adobe brick is straw.

_____ 14. An adobe brick measures about half a foot long.

_____ 15. The completion of an adobe home is often cause for celebration.

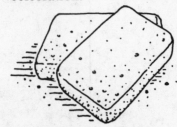

 Notes for Home: Your child identified the vowel sounds of words with *au (sauce), aw (saw), ew (few),* and *ou (out).* **Home Activity:** Read a story with your child. Try to find other words with these vowel sounds and spelling patterns. Make a list of these words together.

© Scott Foresman 6

Research Process

The **research process** involves locating information and organizing findings from that information. First, choose a research topic. Then list questions about the topic that you want to answer through your research. Next, locate and collect information from different sources. Take careful notes as you read the information you've collected. Use your notes to interpret, summarize, and organize information for your audience, revising your questions and answers as you proceed in the research process.

Directions: Use the description of the research process above and the resources pictured below to answer the questions that follow.

1. Why is it important to choose your topic as the first step in the research process?

_____

_____

2. How can forming questions about your topic help you begin your research?

_____

_____

© Scott Foresman 6

Name _____

3. Name several print and electronic media resources you might use to do research for a report.

_____

_____

_____

4. You can use outlines, time lines, tables, diagrams, and graphs to organize information. Choose one of these and explain why it is helpful for organizing information.

_____

_____

5. Why is it important to think about who your audience will be as you decide how to present your research?

_____

_____

6. Which of the resources shown would give a detailed history of the movement of settlers to the West?

_____

7. When they were children, both Laura Ingalls Wilder and Willa Cather moved west with their families and later wrote about the struggles of pioneers. What value might Laura Ingalls Wilder's and Willa Cather's novels have for a report about pioneers?

_____

_____

8. Why might old letters by a female pioneer be a useful resource for a report on pioneers?

_____

_____

9. Use the book titles shown to help you write a research question about pioneers.

_____

10. In "April's Mud," April and her family move to the Southwest and learn many new things. Choose a topic related to life in the Southwest and write a research question about it.

_____

_____

Notes for Home: Your child learned about the research process. *Home Activity:* Together with your child, brainstorm a list of research topics. Discuss questions you could ask about each topic and possible sources of information for each topic.

© Scott Foresman 6

Generalizing

- **A generalization** is a broad statement about what several people or things have in common.

- Clue words such as *most, many, all, sometimes, generally, always,* and *never* can help you identify generalizations in what you read

Directions: Reread "The Key." Then complete the table. Tell whether each of the statements is a generalization. Explain your answers.

Statement	Generalization?	How do you know?
Lek was a collector.	1. Yes No	2.
Many children in rural Thailand are collectors.	3. Yes No	4.
Collecting made sense to Nong.	5. Yes No	6.
Collectors sometimes collect items of great value.	7. Yes No	8.
Nong kept hunting for things to collect.	9. Yes No	10.

Notes for Home: Your child identified generalizations—statements that tell what several people or things have in common *Home Activity:* Ask your child to look around a room in your house and make a generalization about it, such as *All the walls are painted white.*

© Scott Foresman 6

Vocabulary

Directions: Draw a line to connect each word on the left with its definition on the right.

Check the Words You Know

__ anguish
__ correspondence
__ exotic
__ foreigner
__ gratitude
__ homeland
__ traditional
__ uprooted

1. anguish   your native land

2. correspondence   an exchange of letters

3. exotic   great pain or grief

4. gratitude   thankfulness

5. homeland   very different or unusual

Directions: Choose the word from the box that best completes each sentence. Write the word on the matching numbered line to the right.

The twins' first day at school was difficult. The other children thought the twins' clothes looked **6.** _____, although these were **7.** _____ clothes worn by many young girls in their culture. They felt **8.** _____ from their friends, and they missed their **9.** _____ very much. Each of the girls felt strange knowing that others saw her as a **10.** _____ living in a new country and culture.

6. _____

7. _____

8. _____

9. _____

10. _____

Write an E-mail Message

On a separate sheet of paper, write an e-mail message to a friend. Imagine you are traveling in some distant or exotic place. How does it feel to be a stranger in a new land? What new things might you see and do? Use as many vocabulary words as you can to describe what you see or how you feel.

Notes for Home: Your child identified and used vocabulary words from "Hot Dogs and Bamboo Shoots." **Home Activity:** Challenge your child to name objects that are ordinary to him or her but that might be exotic to someone from another place or culture.

© Scott Foresman 6

Generalizing

- A broad statement about what several people or things have in common is a **generalization.**

- Clue words such as *most, many, all, sometimes, generally, always,* and *never* can help you identify generalizations in what you read.

- Valid generalizations are supported by facts and agree with what you already know. Faulty generalizations are not.

Directions: Reread the part of "Hot Dogs and Bamboo Shoots" that tells about Obah San. Then answer the questions below. Look for generalizations that show actions that happen many times the same way.

We all went to the Japanese Union Church on Sundays, and Obah San was always the first one ready. Dressed in her best clothes, wearing her hat and gloves, she would sit on the sofa, patiently waiting for the rest of us to get ready.

She did the same thing if we invited her to go with us to see a movie. Obah San loved going out, and was always ready to have a good time with her grandchildren.

Because she'd never had much in life, she was always frugal and careful. She never let any food go to waste, and any fruit that was beginning to spoil had to be eaten before we could touch the good fruit.

Reprinted with the permission of Simon & Schuster Books for Young Readers, an imprint of Simon & Schuster Children's Publishing Division from THE INVISIBLE THREAD by Yoshiko Uchida. Copyright © 1991 by Yoshiko Uchida.

1. Is "We all went to the Japanese Union Church on Sundays" a generalization?

_____

_____

2. What generalization can you make about Obah San and her grandchildren?

_____

3. How is this generalization supported?

_____

4. List all the clue words you can find in the passage that signal generalizations.

_____

5. What generalization can you make about the importance of family among the Uchidas? Explain your thinking on a separate sheet of paper.

Notes for Home: Your child used story details to recognize and form generalizations. *Home Activity:* Challenge your child to state a generalization that shows what several people have in common. Encourage him or her to use clue words such as *always* or *most.*

© Scott Foresman 6

1.	Ⓐ	Ⓑ	Ⓒ	Ⓓ
2.	Ⓕ	Ⓖ	Ⓗ	Ⓙ
3.	Ⓐ	Ⓑ	Ⓒ	Ⓓ
4.	Ⓕ	Ⓖ	Ⓗ	Ⓙ
5.	Ⓐ	Ⓑ	Ⓒ	Ⓓ
6.	Ⓕ	Ⓖ	Ⓗ	Ⓙ
7.	Ⓐ	Ⓑ	Ⓒ	Ⓓ
8.	Ⓕ	Ⓖ	Ⓗ	Ⓙ
9.	Ⓐ	Ⓑ	Ⓒ	Ⓓ
10.	Ⓕ	Ⓖ	Ⓗ	Ⓙ
11.	Ⓐ	Ⓑ	Ⓒ	Ⓓ
12.	Ⓕ	Ⓖ	Ⓗ	Ⓙ
13.	Ⓐ	Ⓑ	Ⓒ	Ⓓ
14.	Ⓕ	Ⓖ	Ⓗ	Ⓙ
15.	Ⓐ	Ⓑ	Ⓒ	Ⓓ

© Scott Foresman 6

Selection Test

Directions: Choose the best answer to each item. Mark the letter for the answer you have chosen.

Part 1: Vocabulary

Find the answer choice that means about the same as the underlined word in each sentence.

1. Lester felt like a person who was <u>uprooted</u>.
   A. old and slow
   B. removed from a place
   C. smart and clever
   D. hard-working

2. Her neighbors thought of Liz as a <u>foreigner</u>.
   F. baby
   G. one who leads a group
   H. person from another country
   J. troublemaker

3. I would like to try those <u>exotic</u> foods.
   A. strange and unusual
   B. hot and spicy
   C. expensive
   D. tasty

4. Dad and Granddad keep up their <u>correspondence</u>.
   F. bitter disagreement
   G. garden or small farm
   H. contest against each other
   J. exchange of letters

5. Mom expressed her <u>gratitude</u>.
   A. thankfulness
   B. hopes
   C. plans
   D. beliefs

6. Alana wore a <u>traditional</u> dress.
   F. reddish blue
   G. long and white with lace
   H. very expensive; costly
   J. reflecting old beliefs or customs

7. Mr. Pearson planned a visit to his <u>homeland</u>.
   A. any gift of property
   B. place where people share a language
   C. subdivision
   D. original or native land

8. The old man cried in <u>anguish</u>.
   F. surprise
   G. great pain or grief
   H. joy or gladness
   J. excitement

Part 2: Comprehension

Use what you know about the selection to answer each item.

9. At the time of this selection, most young Japanese Americans did not know their grandparents because—
   A. their families were separated by war.
   B. their grandparents had died.
   C. their grandparents lived in Japan.
   D. they could not speak Japanese.

10. The first time Yoshiko Uchida understood that her mother was also a daughter was when—
    F. her mother saw Grandmother Umegaki on the pier in Japan.
    G. her family's ship left San Francisco.
    H. she saw her uncle and cousins in Union Station.
    J. her family gathered for the New Year's feast.

© Scott Foresman 6

GO ON

11. Why was Yoshiko Uchida in such awe of her cousins?
    A. She had never been to Los Angeles before.
    B. They were more sophisticated and worldly.
    C. She had never been to the movies before.
    D. They traveled more than she did.

12. Which generalization based on this selection is most likely valid?
    F. Children cannot have fun during a Japanese New Year's feast.
    G. Everyone likes all the dishes served at a Japanese New Year's feast.
    H. The Japanese New Year's feast is a very serious and quiet time.
    J. It usually takes several days to prepare a Japanese New Year's feast.

13. From the information in the selection, you can tell that most people in Japan—
    A. greet one another by bowing.
    B. forget about family who have moved away.
    C. have American names.
    D. cannot read Japanese.

14. Why did the author feel like an outsider when she was in Japan?
    F. She blended in with the other people in Japan.
    G. She did not like to eat the Japanese foods.
    H. She looked Japanese but did not know the language and culture.
    J. She did not like wearing Japanese clothes.

15. Yoshiko Uchida concludes that she is both American and Japanese because she—
    A. reads and writes both Japanese and English.
    B. wears Japanese clothes in America.
    C. speaks English in Japan.
    D. grew up in America, but with many Japanese customs.

STOP

© Scott Foresman 6

Sequence

Directions: Read the story. Then read each question about the story. Choose the best answer to each question. Mark the letter for the answer you have chosen.

A Day-Long Celebration

Connie and Joe arrived at the annual Fourth of July parade as the flag bearer and the drummers came into view. Then came the high school marching band. The musicians looked handsome in their navy uniforms and tall plumed hats.

The parade's highlight was next. The mayor, dressed in colonial costume, read the Declaration of Independence aloud. Afterwards, a boy rang a model of the Liberty Bell. People waved small American flags. Everyone cheered and clapped when a large, colorful float came into view.

After the parade, Connie and Joe went to a picnic. While everyone was eating, the Glee Club sang.

Later that evening, the mayor made a speech about America, giving thanks for the freedoms Americans enjoy. After dark, the day's celebration ended with a thrilling fireworks display. Connie and Joe went home, tired but excited and happy.

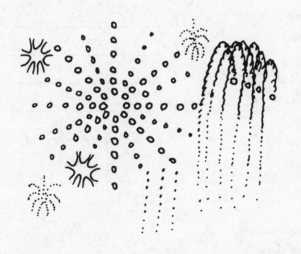

1. Directly after the flag bearer and drummers marched by, Connie and Joe saw—
   A. the Liberty Bell float.
   B. the mayor.
   C. the Glee Club.
   D. the marching band.

2. When a large, colorful float passed by—
   F. people cheered.
   G. the Glee Club sang.
   H. fireworks went off.
   J. the mayor gave a speech.

3. While people picnicked, they—
   A. heard speeches.
   B. watched fireworks.
   C. heard the Glee Club.
   D. listened to the mayor.

4. The mayor gave a speech—
   F. to start the day's celebration.
   G. just before the band came by.
   H. before the fireworks.
   J. while striking the model Liberty Bell.

5. The final event of the day's celebration was—
   A. a picnic.
   B. the mayor's speech.
   C. a fireworks display.
   D. the Glee Club performance.

© Scott Foresman 6

 Notes for Home: Your child recalled the order of events in a short story. *Home Activity:* Talk with your child about the events of a family tradition or preparations for the start of the school year. Challenge your child to list the events in order.

Phonics: *r*-Controlled Vowels

Directions: The letters **or** can have two different sounds. The **or** in **work** sounds different than the **or** in **for.** Read the words in the box. Say the words to yourself. Listen to the different sounds that the letters **or** represent. Sort the words by their sounds. Write each word in the correct column.

according	worry	boring	worse	world
porthole	sorts	worthy	morning	worship

work

1. _____
2. _____
3. _____
4. _____
5. _____

for

6. _____
7. _____
8. _____
9. _____
10. _____

Directions: Read each sentence. Read the words in ( ). Both words fit the sentence, but only one has the vowel sound you hear in **work.** Circle the word that has the vowel sound you hear in **work.** Write the word on the matching numbered line. Underline the letters that represent the **r-controlled vowel** sound.

Some people feel an **11.** (urgent/immediate) need to travel. Their curiosity about the world is **12.** (bubbling/bursting) within them. They are so excited, they never know what to look at **13.** (first/fully). A ruined castle? An old fortress? A famous **14.** (cathedral/church)? Someone should tell them there is no need to be in such **15.** (distress/turmoil).These buildings aren't going anywhere!

11. _____
12. _____
13. _____
14. _____
15. _____

 Notes for Home: Your child sorted and wrote words with *r*-controlled vowels, such as *for, world, first,* and *church.* **Home Activity:** Read a story with your child. As you find words spelled with *or, ir,* and *ur,* cover the words. Have your child tell you the correct spelling.

© Scott Foresman 6

Parts of a Book

The main **parts of a book** include its cover, title page, copyright page, table of contents, chapter titles, section heads, captions, footnotes, index, bibliography, and appendix.

Directions: Use the table of contents from a book of folk tales to answer the questions below and on the next page.

1. How are the folk tales organized in this book? How do you know?

_____

_____

2. From what country is the folk tale *The Five Sparrows?* _____

3. On which page does the first of the Indian folk tales begin? _____

4. Name two folk tales that are from India. _____

_____

5. Which part of the book would you look at to find information about other folk tales to read?

_____

6. Suppose you wanted to compare the fairy tale *Cinderella* with a similar folk tale from another country. Would this book be helpful? Explain.

_____

_____

_____

7. Suppose you wanted to see if any of these folk tales included a story about a tiger. Which section of the book would help you figure this out? Explain.

_____

_____

_____

8. Suppose you were writing a research report on jackals to tell facts about this animal. Would *The Blue Jackal* on page 66 be useful for your report? Explain.

_____

_____

_____

9. Can you judge a book by its cover? What information will you find on a book cover?

_____

_____

_____

_____

10. A copyright page tells when a book was published. Why might this information be important when you are doing research?

_____

_____

Notes for Home: Your child answered questions about different parts of a book. *Home Activity:* Examine some fiction and nonfiction books with your child. Have your child point out different parts of each book and explain what information it shows.

© Scott Foresman 6

Character

- **Characters** are the people or animals who take part in the events of a short story, novel, play, or other form of fiction.
- You can learn about characters from their thoughts, words, and actions.
- You can also learn about characters by paying attention to how other characters in the story treat them and what other characters say about them.

Directions: Reread "Granny's Chair." Then complete the table. Provide the missing phrases or sentences to tell what Rachel is like, how she is feeling, and how you know.

What is Rachel like? How is she feeling?	How do you know?
Rachel feels uncertain.	1.
Rachel's thoughts are wandering.	2.
3.	She remembers Granny's hands in detail.
4.	She stays inside with the grownups. She smiles at her uncle. She doesn't complain, and she tries to imitate the rhythm of their hands.
Rachel feels left out.	5.

 Notes for Home: Your child used details from a story to describe a character. *Home Activity:* Choose a character from a book or television show. Have your child describe what the character is like and provide details to support his or her description.

© Scott Foresman 6

Vocabulary

Directions: Choose the word from the box that best replaces the underlined word or words. Write the word on the line.

_____ 1. Sandy can <u>handle difficult situations</u> well.

_____ 2. She takes an <u>open, unprejudiced</u> approach when conflicts arise.

_____ 3. When people get angry, Sandy is <u>polite</u>, saying and doing just the right thing.

_____ 4. When she is in a state of <u>confusion</u>, she looks for facts that will help her solve the problem.

_____ 5. Her common sense and kindness were just what the <u>parentless child</u> needed.

Check the Words You Know
__ bewilderment
__ cope
__ objective
__ orphan
__ tactful

Directions: Choose the word from the box that best matches each clue. Write the letters of the word on the blanks. The boxed letters spell a synonym for *crisis*.

6. not influenced by emotion

7. great confusion

8. a child who has no living parents

9. to deal or struggle with

10. able to say and do the right thing

A synonym for *crisis:* _____

6. ___ ___ ___ [ ] ___ ___ ___
[m]

7. ___ ___ ___ ___ [ ] ___ ___
[ ]

8. ___ [ ] ___
[g]

9. ___ ___ [ ] ___
[n]

10. ___ ___ [ ] ___ ___ ___ ___
[y]

Write a Narrative

On a separate sheet of paper, write about an event or time in your life that was funny, sad, exciting, or interesting. Describe what happened in the order that it happened. Make sure your narrative has a beginning, middle and end. Use as many vocabulary words as you can.

Notes for Home: Your child identified and used vocabulary words from "The Telephone Call." *Home Activity:* With your child, explore different ways to describe feelings, using as many of the listed vocabulary words as you can.

© Scott Foresman 6

Character

- **Characters** are the people or animals who take part in the events of a short story, novel, play, or other form of fiction.

- You can learn about characters through their thoughts, words, and actions.

- You can also learn about characters by paying attention to how other characters in the story treat them and what others say about them.

Directions: Reread what happens in "The Telephone Call" when Uncle Douglas explains empathy. Then answer the questions below. Use the information in the passage to tell about the characters.

"But why does John know what to say, and how to say it, and all I can do is act stupid, as though it didn't matter?"

"Just because it matters too much. Have you ever heard of *empathy?*"

I shook my head.

"John can show Aunt Elena how sorry he is because he has a scientific mind and he can see what has happened from the outside. All good scientists have to know how to be observers. He can be deeply upset about Uncle Hal and deeply sorry for Aunt Elena, but he can be objective about it. You can't."

"Why?"

"Because you have an artistic temperament, Vicky, and I've never seen you be objective about anything yet. When you think about Aunt Elena and how she must be feeling right now, it is for the moment as though you *were* Aunt Elena; you get right inside her suffering, and it becomes your suffering, too. That's empathy. . . ."

Excerpt from "The Telephone Call" from MEET THE AUSTINS by Madeleine L'Engle. Copyright © 1997 by Crosswicks, Ltd. Reprinted by permission of Farrar, Straus & Giroux, Inc.

1. How does Vicky think she handles the situation?

_____

2. What does Uncle Douglas think of Vicky?

_____

3. What does Uncle Douglas think of John?

_____

4. Based on what he has said, what do you think of Uncle Douglas?

_____

5. Later in the story, Mother takes John and Vicky to watch the night sky. What does this action tell you about Mother? Explain your thinking on a separate sheet of paper.

Notes for Home: Your child read a short story and learned about the characters. *Home Activity:* Read a story together or watch a TV program together. Then encourage your child to explain what he or she has learned about each character.

© Scott Foresman 6

Name _____

1.	Ⓐ	Ⓑ	Ⓒ	Ⓓ
2.	Ⓕ	Ⓖ	Ⓗ	Ⓙ
3.	Ⓐ	Ⓑ	Ⓒ	Ⓓ
4.	Ⓕ	Ⓖ	Ⓗ	Ⓙ
5.	Ⓐ	Ⓑ	Ⓒ	Ⓓ
6.	Ⓕ	Ⓖ	Ⓗ	Ⓙ
7.	Ⓐ	Ⓑ	Ⓒ	Ⓓ
8.	Ⓕ	Ⓖ	Ⓗ	Ⓙ
9.	Ⓐ	Ⓑ	Ⓒ	Ⓓ
10.	Ⓕ	Ⓖ	Ⓗ	Ⓙ
11.	Ⓐ	Ⓑ	Ⓒ	Ⓓ
12.	Ⓕ	Ⓖ	Ⓗ	Ⓙ
13.	Ⓐ	Ⓑ	Ⓒ	Ⓓ
14.	Ⓕ	Ⓖ	Ⓗ	Ⓙ
15.	Ⓐ	Ⓑ	Ⓒ	Ⓓ

© Scott Foresman 6

Selection Test

Directions: Choose the best answer to each item. Mark the letter for the answer you have chosen.

Part 1: Vocabulary

Find the answer choice that means about the same as the underlined word in each sentence.

1. Grandma tries to cope with her illness.
   A.   heal
   B.   rest
   C.   deal with
   D.   fight against

2. Aunt Margaret is the most tactful person I have ever known.
   F.   warm and loving
   G.   skilled at saying the right thing in difficult situations
   H.   graceful and beautiful
   J.   direct and to the point

3. Elsie tried to write an objective letter.
   A.   long and detailed
   B.   clear and easy to understand
   C.   personal or friendly
   D.   not affected by personal feelings

4. Alexa looked at us in bewilderment.
   F.   great confusion
   G.   fear
   H.   eager excitement
   J.   wonder

5. Marie is an orphan.
   A.   a child whose parents are dead
   B.   an infant
   C.   a person who is married
   D.   a woman

Part 2: Comprehension

Use what you know about the story to answer each item.

6. What made the Saturday evening at the beginning of the story unusual?
   F.   Suzy was playing doctor with her dolls.
   G.   The house was filled with noise.
   H.   Aunt Elena called about an accident.
   J.   Daddy had to see a sick patient.

7. Maggy came to live with the Austins because she—
   A.   no longer had a family of her own.
   B.   was Suzy's best friend.
   C.   wanted to spend more time with other children.
   D.   did not like Aunt Elena.

8. How did Vicky feel when she first learned that Maggy would be staying with them?
   F.   excited about having a new friend
   G.   upset because she did not like Maggy
   H.   confused about how the changes would affect her
   J.   sorry that she could not help Maggy feel better

© Scott Foresman 6

GO ON

9. What happened just after Vicky found Aunt Elena trying to make coffee in the kitchen?
   A. John came in and hugged Aunt Elena.
   B. Uncle Douglas drove up to the house.
   C. Suzy and Maggy set the table.
   D. The telephone rang.

10. You can tell from the story that Vicky preferred people around her to be—
    F. misleading.
    G. secretive.
    H. loud.
    J. calm.

11. Compared with John, Vicky had a harder time trying to—
    A. feel sorry for other people.
    B. understand how Aunt Elena felt.
    C. feel her mother's pain.
    D. say the right things to people.

12. What was one way Aunt Elena dealt with losing Uncle Hal?
    F. She prayed that Hal would come back to her.
    G. She cried hard and felt no hope.
    H. She remembered the good times they had together.
    J. She kept busy so she could forget him.

13. The author's main purpose in this selection is to—
    A. describe how to make other people feel better.
    B. tell a story about how a family deals with a crisis.
    C. persuade people not to fly planes.
    D. explain why change is necessary.

14. Why did Vicky feel more sympathy for Aunt Elena than for Maggy?
    F. Vicky had known Maggy longer.
    G. Vicky liked and understood Aunt Elena.
    H. Vicky did not feel sorry for Aunt Elena.
    J. Vicky was closer to Maggy in age.

15. Why was Mother more patient with Maggy when she knocked over chairs than she would have been with her own children or their friends?
    A. Maggy was having a hard time and did not yet know what was expected of her.
    B. Maggy was too young to know any better.
    C. Maggy was always so well behaved that Mother assumed it was an accident.
    D. Maggy could not control the movements of her body.

© Scott Foresman 6

STOP

Cause and Effect

Directions: Read the story. Then read each question about the story. Choose the best answer to each question. Mark the letter for the answer you have chosen.

The Lucky Return

Steve couldn't wait to grow old enough to take care of his cousin's dog! Steve's cousin Sandy had a beautiful dog named Rex. Steve often visited Sandy because he enjoyed caring for and playing with her dog.

Imagine Steve's joy when Sandy asked him to care for Rex for an entire weekend. The first day that Steve was caring for Rex it was raining lightly, but Steve decided to take Rex outside to play.

Steve walked several blocks to a nearby park. Suddenly, the rain shower turned into a heavy rain and the wind began to blow.

As Steve was leaving the park with Rex, another dog ran in front of them. Rex surprised Steve by lunging after the large dog. Steve's hand was so wet from the rain that he couldn't hold the leash. Rex bolted after the other dog and the two animals ran swiftly through the park. Steve ran as fast as he could, but the dogs got farther and farther away.

When he realized that he couldn't catch Rex, Steve sat down, right in a puddle of rain, and began to cry. He was afraid that he had lost Sandy's beautiful dog forever.

As he was crying, Steve heard a familiar bark and looked up to see Rex running toward him. Steve gave Rex a big hug as Rex licked his face. "Please forgive me, Rex. I'll never take you out in bad weather again."

As the rain began to stop, Steve started to walk Rex home. This time he held the leash firmly with both hands.

1. Steve often visited Sandy because—
   A. she is his cousin.
   B. his parents were away a lot.
   C. he enjoyed caring for her cat.
   D. he enjoyed playing with her dog.

2. Steve was unable to hold the leash because—
   F. the wind was blowing.
   G. he was scared.
   H. his hand was wet and slippery.
   J. he couldn't see in the rain.

3. Steve begins to cry because—
   A. he didn't want to care for Rex.
   B. he sat in a rain puddle.
   C. he was afraid that he had lost Rex for good.
   D. he was afraid of the other dog.

4. Which of the following is **not** an effect of losing Rex?
   F. Steve promises not to take Rex out in bad weather again.
   G. The rainstorm makes it difficult for Steve to hold the leash.
   H. Steve cries.
   J. Steve sits in a rain puddle.

5. Steve might not have lost Rex if—
   A. the weather had been nice.
   B. the park wasn't so far away.
   C. he had not sat in the puddle.
   D. he had not cried.

Notes for Home: Your child used details to identify causes and effects in a story. *Home Activity:* Help your child identify some of the things she or he does to get good results, such as practicing for sports, setting aside enough time for homework, or studying for a test.

© Scott Foresman 6

Phonics: Complex Spelling Patterns

Directions: Read the words in the box. They may look alike, but they have very
different vowel sounds. Read the words to the left. Match each word to the left
with a word from the box that has the same vowel sound. Write the word on
the line.

through	thought	though

1. taught _____

2. throw _____

3. threw _____

Directions: Read the words in the box. Match them with the words below that
have the same vowel sound. Write the words on the lines.

bought	dough	sought	soup	soul	coupon

4. thought _____   _____

5. though _____   _____

6. through _____   _____

Directions: Read each sentence. Say the underlined word to yourself. Circle the
word in ( ) that has the same vowel sound as the underlined word.

7. Although it was getting late, they didn't want to leave Marcie alone. (bought/boulder)

8. She thought everyone was kind for trying to make her feel better. (caught/count)

9. After the death of her uncle, her emotions went through many changes. (though/rule)

10. No one thought she was insensitive for not being able to express her feelings. (foul/fought)

11. Everyone tried to be a little cheerful, even though the occasion was a somber one.
(bowl/brought)

12. It helps to have friends around to get you through the good times and the bad times.
(know/knew)

Directions: Write a sentence for each of these words: **through, thought, though.**

13. _____

14. _____

15. _____

Notes for Home: Your child identified the different vowel sounds for words with *ough,* such
as *through, thought,* and *though.* **Home Activity:** Write several *ough* words on separate slips
of paper. Have your child read each word and use it in a sentence.

© Scott Foresman 6

Telephone Directory

A **telephone directory** is a book with entries listed alphabetically by last name of a person or by the name of a business. The **white pages** lists telephone numbers and addresses of individuals and businesses. The **yellow pages** lists phone numbers, addresses, and advertisements of businesses. It is arranged alphabetically by category of business.

Directions: Use the following section of the yellow pages to answer the questions on the next page.

---

145   Movers—Newspapers

Movers

Great Bear Moving and Storage
   30 Morocco St 555-5645
Jack and Jill Movers
   315 3rd St 555-9080
Moonstone Movers Inc
   82 College Ave 555-1309
Two Guys Movers
   200 4th St 555-9008
Where or When Movers Inc
   3 College Ave 555-5536

Music Instruction

Arbor Music School
   321 7th St 555-6710

Music—Sheet

Napoleon's Guitars
   67 7th St 555-8971
Phantom Music Inc
   333 7th St 555-4439
Scores and More
   352 2nd St 555-1130

Musical Instruments—Repairs

Napoleon's Guitars
   67 7th St 555-7322
Poliuto's Pianos
   69 7th St 555-1083

Musical Instruments—Sales

Napoleon's Guitars
   67 7th St 555-4445
Poliuto's Pianos
   69 7th St 555-0102

We've Got Rhythm

No one has a larger selection of rhythm and percussion instruments than we do!

Monday–Friday, 10 A.M. to 6 P.M.
Saturday, 1:00 P.M. to 8 P.M.

Free drum lesson, Saturdays at 1 P.M.

**208 Garfield Place
(near Westwood Mall)
555-1782**

Newspapers

The Daily Yell
   74 College Avenue 555-6543
The Mirror
   85 College Avenue 555-3548
     Advertisements 555-0762
     Arts Desk 555-9398
     City Desk 555-8285
     Copy Chief 555-5301
     Sports Desk 555-5324
The Tribune
   99 College Avenue 555-9021

© Scott Foresman 6

Name _____

1. What business categories are listed?

_____

_____

2. Are these entries near the beginning, middle, or end of the yellow pages? Explain.

_____

3. Which of the newspapers listed is probably the largest? Why do you think so?

_____

4. Would you turn ahead or back in the directory to find a plumber? Why?

_____

5. Can you purchase a guitar and have one repaired at the same shop? Explain.

_____

6. Which business uses an advertisement? What information does the advertisement give that the other listings do not give?

_____

_____

7. Would Vicky Austin's phone number be in the white pages or the yellow pages? Explain.

_____

8. Would you look in the white pages or the yellow pages if you needed the phone number for a locksmith? Explain.

_____

_____

9. If you lived on Third Street, where would you go to buy sheet music? Why?

_____

10. Many directories will list emergency numbers at the front of the directory in a separate section. Why do you think this information is listed this way?

_____

_____

 Notes for Home: Your child answered questions about a telephone directory. *Home Activity:* Take turns saying a person's name or a name or type of business. Use the white pages or yellow pages to find each listing.

© Scott Foresman 6

Making Judgments

- **Making a judgment** means forming an opinion about someone or something.
- When you make a judgment, you think about your own experiences and beliefs, as well as the information the author provides.
- When an author expresses a judgment about someone or something, test the author's judgment by looking for evidence to support it.

Directions: Reread "The Truth About Wolves." Then complete the table. Tell what judgments the author expresses about lions and wolves and the evidence he provides to support each judgment. Then answer the question below.

The Author's Judgment About . . .	Supporting Evidence
Dogs: Dogs are humans' best friends.	Dogs are friendly, loyal, intelligent, and playful.
Lions: 1.	**2.**
Wolves: 3.	**4.**

5. Do you agree with the author's judgment about wolves? Does the author support his judgment well?

_____

_____

_____

Notes for Home: Your child identified judgments made by an author, and then made his or her own judgments about the author's ideas. ***Home Activity:*** Help your child identify the judgments expressed in a newspaper editorial. Check whether the judgments are supported.

© Scott Foresman 6

Vocabulary

Directions: Choose the word from the box that best matches each definition. Write the word on the line.

_____ 1. refused to stop

_____ 2. very active; not passive

_____ 3. revenge

_____ 4. qualities or characteristics

_____ 5. not open; having secrets

Directions: Choose the word from the box that best completes each sentence. Write the word on the line to the left. Then find and circle the words in the puzzle below. Words may appear across, down, or diagonally.

_____ 6. Tom Cat knew that the package on the counter contained fish. An experienced cat burgular like himself knew well the delicious _____ of fresh fish.

_____ 7. He did not want Teeter, the kitten, in on the heist, so he was very _____.

_____ 8. Tom planned to _____ the kitten and get the fish all for himself.

_____ 9. He wasn't afraid of Teeter's _____.

_____ 10. He was patient and _____ Teeter, but he didn't think the kitten was very smart.

Q	U	J	A	L	F	P	F	S	R	E	A	B	B	M
A	T	T	R	I	B	U	T	E	S	V	Z	T	J	U
I	D	E	B	T	V	F	I	C	A	T	I	O	N	W
L	U	I	A	X	Y	J	E	R	R	O	I	L	H	N
P	Z	H	I	Q	J	T	C	E	G	V	I	E	B	Z
B	K	E	O	U	T	W	I	T	F	L	A	R	X	E
I	W	H	J	D	T	U	I	I	X	S	S	A	H	K
N	Y	I	R	B	E	A	L	V	H	Z	E	T	T	O
T	I	J	Z	V	E	N	G	E	A	N	C	E	E	Q
A	J	U	W	I	M	L	Y	Z	G	F	D	D	L	D

Check the Words You Know

___ aggressive

___ attributes

___ outwit

___ persisted

___ secretive

___ tolerated

___ vengeance

Write a Story

On a separate sheet of paper, write a story about a character (an animal or imaginary person) who wants something so badly that he or she is willing to trick others to get it. Use as many vocabulary words as you can.

Notes for Home: Your child identified and used vocabulary words from "A Trouble-Making Crow." *Home Activity:* Think of fictional characters from a book or a movie that you or your child can describe using the vocabulary words.

© Scott Foresman 6

Name _____

Making Judgments

- **Making a judgment** means forming an opinion about someone or something.

- When you make a judgment, you think about your own experiences and beliefs, as well as the information the author provides.

- As you read, look for evidence to support your judgments or the author's judgments.

Directions: Reread what happens in "A Trouble-Making Crow" after Craig's mother tells him that the crow New York has to go. Then answer the questions below. Think about what happens in the story to help you make judgments.

"People come first," I said. "How would you feel if Hilde was blinded by our crow?"

His eyes widened as he understood the seriousness of New York's vengeance.

"I don't want to kill him," I said. "I want to take him far away and let him go—far from Hilde."

"Will he dive at anyone else's eyes?"

"No. Hilde must have kicked him or hurt him somehow, and he's taking it out on her. He won't forget. Crows are like that."

Craig ran into the yard to find New York, and I went to the cellar for an animal carrying case.

Copyright © 1996 by Julie Productions, Inc. Used by permission of HarperCollins Publishers.

1. Do you think it would make sense to kill New York? Explain your answer.

_____

2. Do you think that the mother's decision to let New York go free is fair? Explain.

_____

_____

3. Do you think Craig's mother understands animal behavior? Why?

_____

_____

4. Does Craig understand his mother's decision? How do you know?

_____

_____

_____

5. Think about the story of Dr. Kalmbach's crow at the end of "A Trouble-Making Crow." On a separate sheet of paper, explain how the story affected your opinion of what Craig's mother did about New York.

Notes for Home: Your child used story details to make judgments about characters and actions. *Home Activity:* With your child, make judgments about characters or actions in a movie you've seen or a book you've read together.

© Scott Foresman 6

Name _____

1.	Ⓐ	Ⓑ	Ⓒ	Ⓓ
2.	Ⓕ	Ⓖ	Ⓗ	Ⓙ
3.	Ⓐ	Ⓑ	Ⓒ	Ⓓ
4.	Ⓕ	Ⓖ	Ⓗ	Ⓙ
5.	Ⓐ	Ⓑ	Ⓒ	Ⓓ
6.	Ⓕ	Ⓖ	Ⓗ	Ⓙ
7.	Ⓐ	Ⓑ	Ⓒ	Ⓓ
8.	Ⓕ	Ⓖ	Ⓗ	Ⓙ
9.	Ⓐ	Ⓑ	Ⓒ	Ⓓ
10.	Ⓕ	Ⓖ	Ⓗ	Ⓙ
11.	Ⓐ	Ⓑ	Ⓒ	Ⓓ
12.	Ⓕ	Ⓖ	Ⓗ	Ⓙ
13.	Ⓐ	Ⓑ	Ⓒ	Ⓓ
14.	Ⓕ	Ⓖ	Ⓗ	Ⓙ
15.	Ⓐ	Ⓑ	Ⓒ	Ⓓ

© Scott Foresman 6

Selection Test

Directions: Choose the best answer to each item. Mark the letter for the answer you have chosen.

Part 1: Vocabulary

Find the answer choice that means about the same as the underlined word in each sentence.

1. The old dog <u>tolerated</u> the puppy.
   A.   chased after
   B.   looked for
   C.   played with
   D.   put up with

2. Sharon <u>persisted</u> for five days.
   F.   got better
   G.   refused to stop
   H.   went away
   J.   studied hard

3. Margo has many good <u>attributes</u>.
   A.   faults
   B.   feelings or emotions
   C.   qualities or characteristics
   D.   ways to help others

4. Sam cannot <u>outwit</u> his brother.
   F.   be more clever than
   G.   act friendly toward
   H.   catch by surprise
   J.   run faster than

5. Members of the club are very <u>secretive</u>.
   A.   talking for a long time
   B.   special in a certain way
   C.   not open; keeping things hidden from others
   D.   proud of themselves

6. The dog seemed to want <u>vengeance</u>.
   F.   revenge
   G.   comfort
   H.   warmth
   J.   safety

7. The tennis player made an <u>aggressive</u> move toward his opponent.
   A.   friendly
   B.   ready to attack
   C.   brief
   D.   quiet or shy

Part 2: Comprehension

Use what you know about the selection to answer each item.

8. New York got into trouble because he—
   F.   stole some food.
   G.   took money from children.
   H.   tore cabbage leaves.
   J.   dived at a child's eyes.

9. According to this selection, crows know how to—
   A.   sing songs with words.
   B.   polish shoes.
   C.   avoid danger.
   D.   give directions.

10. The George family began to teach Crowbar to talk just after—
    F.   Crowbar said hello at a picnic.
    G.   they read about how crows are like parrots.
    H.   the man delivering milk heard him say hello.
    J.   a police officer tried to scare him away.

11. Who is Hilde?
    A.   a pet crow
    B.   one of the author's children
    C.   one of the author's pet salamanders
    D.   a girl who lives in the neighborhood

© Scott Foresman 6

GO ON

12. Which example offers the best proof that crows are intelligent?
- F.   A crow that caws three times is identifying itself.
- G.   Crowbar ate a piece of cold cheeseburger.
- H.   New York flew into Baird Park and did not return.
- J.   Crowbar used a lid to slide with the children.

13. Crows do not make good pets because they—
- A.   seek revenge against those who hurt them.
- B.   can pick out one person in a crowd.
- C.   can learn to talk.
- D.   are able to count.

14. Most of the time, the author describes and reacts to the pets in her house as if they were—
- F.   wild animals.
- G.   friends.
- H.   scientific experiments.
- J.   celebrities.

15. At the end of the story, the author feels sad because she—
- A.   is afraid of the large flock of crows.
- B.   is happy that Crowbar will not bother her anymore.
- C.   will miss Crowbar.
- D.   worries that the wild crows will hurt Crowbar.

STOP

© Scott Foresman 6

Paraphrasing

Directions: Read the passage. Then read each question about the passage. Choose the best answer to each question. Mark the letter for the answer you have chosen.

The Crow Family

The crow family is a group of large black birds. Crows, jays, jackdaws, magpies, ravens, and rooks are all members of this family.

The common crow has glossy black feathers and a strong bill with a sharp point. Crows have strong feet that are good for walking. Male and female crows look very much alike, but the female is a little bit smaller.

Crows are highly intelligent. A crow can be a good pet if the owner obtains the crow when the crow is young. Most people recognize a crow's harsh cry, *"Caw! Caw!"* The crow can make many other noises. Sometimes people can teach crows to speak a few words.

Crows are attracted by shiny objects. They pick up stray coins, lost earrings, and any other small shiny things they find. Crows will keep these small treasures forever. They always have places where they hide their growing collections. They are famous for their habit of hoarding things.

Crows are found all over the world, except in New Zealand. The common crow is seen in many parts of North America. In recent years, crows have even become more common in big cities like New York City.

1. Which of the following statements accurately paraphrases information in the passage?
   A. There is only one kind of crow.
   B. Magpies, ravens, rooks are the only kinds of crows.
   C. There are many kinds of crows.
   D. No crows make good pets.

2. Which of the following statements accurately paraphrases information in the passage?
   F. Crows can't walk.
   G. Male and female crows are the same size.
   H. The common crow has black feathers.
   J. The crow's bill isn't pointed.

3. A crow—
   A. can't be a good pet.
   B. can make a good pet if disciplined.
   C. can be trained to be a pet at any age.
   D. can be a good pet if you get it when it is young.

4. A crow—
   F. can sometimes have a large vocabulary.
   G. can sometimes learn to say a few words.
   H. cannot imitate sounds.
   J. makes one noise.

5. The common crow—
   A. lives everywhere but New Zealand.
   B. lives everywhere but North America.
   C. lives only in New Zealand.
   D. lives only in North America.

 Notes for Home: Your child chose statements that paraphrased information in a nonfiction article. *Home Activity:* With your child, read a few paragraphs of a newspaper or magazine article. Have your child restate each paragraph in his or her own words.

© Scott Foresman 6

Phonics: Consonant Sounds for *c* and *g*

Directions: Read the sentences below. Two words in each sentence have the letter **c**. Circle the word with the **hard-c** sound as in **cold.** Underline the word with the **soft-c** sound as in **place.**

1. We were certain the country would be a great spot for our day off.
2. We saw a large bird sitting on the fence while we had our picnic.
3. Seeing a wild crow was a new experience for our family.
4. The bird eventually escaped our stares by flying to a nearby spruce tree.
5. No matter how we coaxed, the bird would not leave its place up high.

Directions: Read the sentences below. Two words in each sentence have the letter **g**. One has a **hard-g** sound as in **go.** The other word has a **soft-g** sound as in **gentle.** Circle the words with the **hard-g** sound. Underline the words with the **soft-g** sound.

6. Sometimes several crows would hide in the garden among the cabbages.
7. The crows gathered around looking for food like scavengers.
8. The birds seemed to beg urgently with their loud squawks.
9. It appeared as if the huge crow was the leader of the group.
10. Large crows can be very aggressive sometimes.

Directions: Read the sentences below. Each underlined word has both a **c** and a **g**. Circle the two words in each group that have the same consonant sounds as the **c** and **g** in the underlined word.

11. I did not <u>recognize</u> the calls of the little crow when I first heard it.

    cat   trance   goat   giant

12. The baby bird had fallen between the <u>cabbage</u> leaves and was calling for help.

    fence   frantic   good   giant

13. We <u>encouraged</u> the crow to fly off on its own.

    cellar   complex   forgive   page

14. It took a few hops, then it <u>gracefully</u> flew to a tree branch.

    gate   gem   corn   stance

15. Although some people may not like crows, it's hard to imagine that the gentle bird we saw would ever seek <u>vengeance</u>.

    frog   stage   certain   picnic

Notes for Home: Your child identified the sounds that the letters *c* and *g* can represent, such as *go, cabbage* (hard *g*, soft *g*), *crow, fence* (hard *c*, soft *c*). **Home Activity:** Read a book about animals with your child. Find words with these letters and have your child say them aloud.

© Scott Foresman 6

Questions for Inquiry

Formulating and revising **questions for inquiry** about a topic can help you set a purpose for your reading and help you focus your research. Before you begin your research, think about the questions you want answered about the topic. As you read, you may need to revise your questions to focus more specifically on the topic.

Directions: Before you read the encyclopedia entry below, answer the first two questions on the next page. Then read the entry and use it to answer the rest of the questions.

Common Crow

Family: *Corvidae* (includes jays, ravens, magpies, rooks, and jackdaws)

Scientific name: *Corvus brachyrhynchos*

Size: 17–21 inches long (43 to 53 centimeters)

Color: black

Diet: corn, wheat, insects, spiders, small birds, eggs, rodents, dead flesh

Common crow, also called the American crow, or *corvus brachyrhynchos,* is probably, with the robin and the pigeon, one of the three most easily-recognized birds in the United States. Crows are medium-sized, coal-black birds, much larger than robins and other songbirds, but much smaller than eagles, gulls, or hawks. This bird can be found in many parts of the world, although there are no crows in New Zealand, the Antarctic, or South America.

Crows use more than 23 different calls to communicate with one another. They cooperate with one another much more than other birds do. Both parents look after the nestling crows, and crows in the same flock will take turns keeping watch for enemies, gathering food, and attacking intruders. Flocks of crows can number in the thousands.

© Scott Foresman 6

Name _____

1. List information that you already know about crows. _____

_____

_____

_____

2. Write two questions of inquiry that you want answered about crows. _____

_____

_____

_____

3. Did the encyclopedia entry help answer your questions? If so, what answers did you find? If not, how might you revise your questions?

_____

_____

_____

_____

4. After reading the encyclopedia entry, what other questions of inquiry might you have about crows?

_____

_____

_____

_____

5. In what kinds of sources could you research to answer your questions of inquiry?

_____

_____

_____

_____

 Notes for Home: Your child formulated questions for inquiry about crows. *Home Activity:* Have your child write a list of questions about an interesting animal. Work together to answer these questions using a nature program, an encyclopedia, a nonfiction book, or the Internet.

© Scott Foresman 6

Predicting

- To **predict** means to state what might happen next in a story or article. To make a prediction, think about what you know and what has already happened.

- After making a prediction, continue reading to check its accuracy. Revise your prediction if it does not agree with new information.

Directions: Reread "At the Water's Edge." Then complete each box. Read each question and tell what logical prediction can be made based on what you have read up to that point in the story. Give a reason for each prediction.

Question: What do you predict Alec might see from the high rock?
1. Prediction:
2. Reason:

Question: What do you predict Alec might do after he first tastes the moss?
3. Prediction:
4. Reason:

Question: What might Alec do next? Why do you think so?
5. Prediction:
6. Reason:

© Scott Foresman 6

Notes for Home: Your child read a story and made predictions about what would happen next. *Home Activity:* Tell your child a story about a real-life experience. Pause throughout the story to have your child make and/or revise predictions about what will happen next.

Vocabulary

Directions: Choose the word from the box that best completes each sentence.
Write the word on the line to the left.

_____ 1. In winter, a person's _____ depends on
having a source of heat.

_____ 2. A _____ is a handy tool to cut small
pieces of dry wood for the fire.

_____ 3. Dry matches are needed to _____ a
campfire.

_____ 4. Without matches, it is a _____ job to get
a fire started.

_____ 5. Safety rules are very important with fires.
Many forest fires have begun from an untended
campfire that _____ and then burst into flames.

Check the Words You Know
__ hatchet
__ ignite
__ painstaking
__ smoldered
__ survival

Directions: Choose the word from the box that best matches each clue.
Write the word in the puzzle.

Down

6. small ax with a short handle

8. to set on fire

Across

7. requiring careful effort or attention

9. the act of staying alive

10. burned and smoked without flames

Write an Essay

On a separate sheet of paper, write
one or two paragraphs explaining the
uses of fire in everyday life. Do you
think fire is as imporant to our lives
today as to people in the past? Explain
your thinking using as many vocabulary
words as you can.

Notes for Home: Your child identified and used vocabulary words from "From a Spark."
Home Activity: With your child, make up a story of having to survive in the woods. Use as
many of the vocabulary words as you can.

© Scott Foresman 6

Predicting

- To **predict** means to state what you think might happen next in a story or article.

- To make a prediction, think about what you already know and what has already happened.

- Check and change your prediction as you encounter new information.

Directions: Reread what happens in "From a Spark" after Brian wakes up from the dream about his father and Terry. Then answer the questions below. Think about the predictions you made as you were reading the story.

Fire. The hatchet was the key to it all. When he threw the hatchet at the porcupine in the cave and missed and hit the stone wall it had showered sparks, a golden shower of sparks in the dark, as golden with fire as the sun was now.

The hatchet was the answer. That's what his father and Terry had been trying to tell him.

Somehow he could get fire from the hatchet. The sparks would make fire.

Brian went back into the shelter and studied the wall. . . . It only took him a moment to find where the hatchet had struck. The steel had nicked into the edge of one of the darker stone pieces.

Reprinted with the permission of Simon & Schuster Books for Young Readers, an imprint of Simon & Schuster Children's Publishing Division from HATCHET by Gary Paulsen. Copyright © 1987 by Gary Paulsen.

1. What do you think Brian will do with the hatchet?

_____

2. Which clues helped you make this prediction?

_____

_____

3. How will Brian use the wall to help him make fire?

_____

4. Which clues helped you make this prediction?

_____

_____

5. Do you think Brian will survive? Explain your thinking on a separate sheet of paper.

Notes for Home: Your child used story details to predict what would happen next in a story. *Home Activity:* With your child, read the first paragraph of an article or a story. Work together to predict what will happen next or what the article or story will be about.

© Scott Foresman 6

1.	Ⓐ	Ⓑ	Ⓒ	Ⓓ
2.	Ⓕ	Ⓖ	Ⓗ	Ⓙ
3.	Ⓐ	Ⓑ	Ⓒ	Ⓓ
4.	Ⓕ	Ⓖ	Ⓗ	Ⓙ
5.	Ⓐ	Ⓑ	Ⓒ	Ⓓ
6.	Ⓕ	Ⓖ	Ⓗ	Ⓙ
7.	Ⓐ	Ⓑ	Ⓒ	Ⓓ
8.	Ⓕ	Ⓖ	Ⓗ	Ⓙ
9.	Ⓐ	Ⓑ	Ⓒ	Ⓓ
10.	Ⓕ	Ⓖ	Ⓗ	Ⓙ
11.	Ⓐ	Ⓑ	Ⓒ	Ⓓ
12.	Ⓕ	Ⓖ	Ⓗ	Ⓙ
13.	Ⓐ	Ⓑ	Ⓒ	Ⓓ
14.	Ⓕ	Ⓖ	Ⓗ	Ⓙ
15.	Ⓐ	Ⓑ	Ⓒ	Ⓓ

© Scott Foresman 6

Selection Test

Directions: Choose the best answer to each item. Mark the letter for the answer you have chosen.

Part 1: Vocabulary

Find the answer choice that means about the same as the underlined word in each sentence.

1. Restoring an old house is painstaking work.
   A. fast
   B. very successful
   C. uncomfortable
   D. requiring careful attention

2. He made a list of what he needed for survival.
   F. staying alive
   G. happiness
   H. success in business
   J. homework

3. The ranger made kindling with a hatchet.
   A. small ax
   B. sharp knife
   C. large boot
   D. kind of saw

4. The trash pile smoldered behind the barn.
   F. spread to the trees
   G. grew out of control
   H. burned without flames
   J. made an awful smell

5. Mr. Dennison was afraid to ignite the wood.
   A. blow on
   B. set on fire
   C. break up
   D. cut into pieces

Part 2: Comprehension

Use what you know about the story to answer each item.

6. At the beginning of the story, Brian wakes up to the smell of—
   F. pine trees.
   G. an animal.
   H. smoke.
   J. raspberries.

7. A porcupine slapped Brian with its tail because Brian—
   A. had a hatchet.
   B. thought it was a bear.
   C. kicked it.
   D. was asleep in the cave.

8. After removing the quills from his leg, Brian feels—
   F. relieved.
   G. sick to his stomach.
   H. very discouraged.
   J. sure that someone will come to help him.

9. When Brian dreams of Terry lighting the charcoal, a reader is most likely to predict that—
   A. the porcupine will return.
   B. Brian will soon have a fever.
   C. Brian will die in the cave.
   D. Brian will make a fire.

10. Why does Brian think of the fire as "hungry"?
    F. It needs air.
    G. He is starving.
    H. He must keep feeding it with fuel.
    J. It reminds him of the barbecue in his dreams.

11. Based on what he has learned, if Brian's fire goes out he is most likely to—
    A. give up on having a fire.
    B. make a new fire.
    C. look for matches.
    D. cry in self-pity.

© Scott Foresman 6

GO ON

12. Brian's experience in getting the fire going shows that—

   F.   Brian is able to remember and use things he has learned.

   G.   most fires don't need oxygen.

   H.   Brian should have taken a survival course.

   J.   most animals will approach a fire if they need to get warm.

13. What is Brian most concerned about in this story?

   A.   controlling the fire

   B.   finding Terry

   C.   saving his money

   D.   staying alive

14. Brian threw the hatchet because he thought that—

   F.   a porcupine would be scared by a shower of sparks.

   G.   he had to protect himself from a large animal.

   H.   a snake would not be moving around at night.

   J.   a bad dream was coming true.

15. Which statement best describes Brian?

   A.   He has not had much experience living outdoors.

   B.   He does not like his family.

   C.   He does not have much patience.

   D.   He cannot think clearly because of his injury.

STOP

© Scott Foresman 6

Setting and Steps in a Process

Directions: Read the passage. Then read each question about the passage. Choose the best answer to each question. Mark the letter for the answer you have chosen.

A Cold Journey

Roald Amundsen left Norway secretly. He wanted to beat the British explorer Robert Scott to the South Pole. No explorer had traveled so far.

Amundsen and his team reached the edge of Antarctica in January. They took a few trips inland to set up supplies of food and fuel. Then they waited for spring to arrive so they could travel.

In October, spring arrived. Amundsen's team began its trip through Antarctica to the South Pole. The trip was painstaking. They ran out of the food they had brought. In order to survive, they had to kill and eat the weaker sled dogs. But on December 14, 1911, Amundsen and his team became the first people to reach the South Pole. Soon Amundsen was famous throughout the world.

1. Most of this story is set—
   A. in Norway.
   B. in Britain.
   C. in Antarctica.
   D. all over the world.

2. How would this story be different if Robert Scott had already reached the South Pole?
   F. Amundsen would not have left secretly.
   G. Amundsen could have traveled in January.
   H. Amundsen could have gotten food from Scott.
   J. Amundsen would have been as famous as Scott.

3. What did Amundsen do first?
   A. He set up camp at the edge of Antarctica.
   B. He left Norway secretly.
   C. He set up supplies.
   D. He began his trip through the Antarctic.

4. Before Amundsen left the edge of the Antarctic, he—
   F. killed weaker sled dogs.
   G. set up supplies of food and fuel.
   H. met with Robert Scott.
   J. traveled to the South Pole.

5. How does the Antarctic setting affect Amundsen's actions?
   A. Dogs have to be killed and eaten when food runs out.
   B. He has to get more dogs to keep traveling.
   C. He has to send far away for help.
   D. He has to travel alone.

Notes for Home: Your child identified the time and place in which a story takes place, and the order in which story events happened. *Home Activity:* Have your child choose a favorite story. With your child, identify the time and place in which the story takes place.

© Scott Foresman 6

Phonics: Silent Consonants

Directions: Some words have consonants that you don't hear. Say each word to yourself. Circle the word in each group that has the **silent consonant.** Underline the consonant that is silent.

1. liken
   list
   liter
   listening

2. not
   knee
   kept
   kite

3. bury
   raspberries
   raisin
   laundry

4. drop
   distance
   dumb
   disturb

5. signal
   sign
   signature
   sister

6. complete
   compound
   combine
   comb

7. wrist
   win
   work
   waist

8. fasten
   faster
   finally
   frantic

9. design
   desert
   dusty
   duplicate

Directions: Read the travel guide. Find seven words with **silent consonants.** Write each word on the lines, and circle the consonant that is silent.

Glenview Park

Located just a half hour from downtown, Glenview Park is a place known to hikers as the best park in town. You won't find any loud radios there. Bring a knapsack with a nice treat and a good book. Climb the old gnarled trees to get a better view. If you listen very closely, you can hear the quiet of the outdoors. Deer come at dusk to the side of a clearing, so bring your binoculars!

10. _____
11. _____
12. _____
13. _____
14. _____
15. _____
16. _____

Notes for Home: Your child reviewed silent consonants, such as the *w* in *write.* **Home Activity:** Read a travel guide with your child. Help your child identify words with silent consonants. Have your child write the words and circle the silent letters.

© Scott Foresman 6

Thesaurus

A **thesaurus** is a kind of dictionary that lists synonyms (words with the same or similar meanings), antonyms (words with opposite meanings), and other related words. Parts of speech are listed to show how a word is used. If a word has multiple meanings, synonyms for each type of meaning are given.

You can use a thesaurus to help you find new and interesting words so you don't repeat the same words too often in your writing. An index lists all the entry words in alphabetical order so you can look them up quickly.

Directions: Use these thesaurus entries to answer the questions that follow.

soundless (adj) still, mute, quiet. See SILENT.

spark (n) **1. flash:** flicker, flare, sparkle, glow, glint, glimmer; **2. stimulus:** goad, spur, motivation, inspiration.

spark (v) **1. flash:** flicker, flare, sparkle, glint; **2. stimulate:** goad, spur, motivate, inspire, ignite, start, activate. (ant) extinguish, douse.

sparkle (v) **1. with light:** glitter, shine, flicker, glint, glimmer, glow, dazzle, shimmer: *The silver ornaments sparkle in the firelight.* **2. with intelligence:** be lively, be vivacious, be the life of the party, shine, dazzle: *Her stories sparkle with clever humor.*

sparse (adj) scanty, meager, slight, scarce, thin, poor, spare, skimpy, few and far between. (ant) thick, abundant, plentiful.

1. What part of speech is *soundless?* How do you know? _____

_____

2. What are the synonyms for *soundless?* _____

© Scott Foresman 6

3. Why do you think the entry for *soundless* includes the cross-reference for *silent?*

_____

_____

_____

4. Why does this thesaurus show two entries for *spark?* _____

_____

5. Rewrite the following sentence using a synonym for *spark.*
   He saw a brief spark of light when the hatchet hit the rock.

_____

_____

6. Which meaning of *sparkle* is used in the following sentence? Which synonyms would you use to replace the word *sparkled?* Pick the synonyms that would make the most sense in the sentence.
   The stars sparkled like tiny diamonds scattered across the night sky.

_____

_____

_____

7. Write a sentence using any of the antonyms listed. Hint: You can use the list of synonyms to help you figure out the meaning of an antonym.

_____

_____

8. How is a thesaurus like a dictionary? How is it different? _____

_____

_____

_____

9. How can you find the synonyms for a word in a thesaurus? Describe the steps.

_____

_____

10. Why is a thesaurus a useful reference source when you are writing something?

_____

_____

Notes for Home: Your child used entries from a thesaurus to answer questions. ***Home Activity:*** Make a list of ten common words. Take turns with your child listing as many synonyms as you can for each word. Use the thesaurus, if one is available, to help you.

© Scott Foresman 6

Setting

- The **setting** of a story is the place and time in which the story occurs.

- Sometimes the author tells you the setting. Other times, the author reveals the setting through details.

- The setting can influence what happens to a character or how a character behaves. It can also contribute to the overall feeling, or mood.

Directions: Reread "The Glittering Cloud." Then complete the tables. Identify the place in which the story occurs. Then list story details that describe the setting and tell how the setting influences the characters and mood.

Story Setting	
Time: the 1800s	**Place: 1.**

Story Details About Setting	Influence on Characters and Mood
2. The prairie	The mood is one of discomfort caused by such strong heat.
3. The schoolhouse	**4.** The school children
5. The wheat	**6.** Pa
7. A cloud	**8.** The dog
9. Large brown grasshoppers	**10.** The mood

Notes for Home: Your child identified the details that reveal the setting of a story and described its effects on the characters. **Home Activity:** Choose a favorite story that has an interesting setting. Use details from the story to help your child draw a picture illustrating the setting.

© Scott Foresman 6

Vocabulary

Directions: Choose the word from the box that has the same or nearly the same meaning as each word below. Write the word on the line.

_____ **1.** odd; strange; unusual

_____ **2.** having bits of sand and dust

_____ **3.** scary; weird

_____ **4.** very long and slender

_____ **5.** unclear; murky

Check the Words You Know
___ eerie
___ grasslands
___ gritty
___ hazy
___ peculiar
___ spindly

Directions: Choose the word from the box that best completes each sentence. Write the word on the matching numbered line below.

The dry **6.** ____ stretched for miles and miles. The dusty air made the setting sun look **7.** ____ and unclear. In the dust storm, the air was **8.** ____ with sand. Tall, **9.** ____ stalks of grass bowed and waved. In the light of the rising moon, the moving grass seemed to come alive. The whole scene was very spooky and **10.** ____. I was glad when the sun rose bright and clear the next day.

6. _____   **9.** _____

7. _____   **10.** _____

8. _____

Write a Weather Report

On a separate sheet of paper, write a weather report describing a dust storm or some other kind of extreme weather. Use as many of the vocabulary words as you can.

Notes for Home: Your child identified and used vocabulary words from "Storm-a-Dust." *Home Activity:* With your child, name as many weather words that have similar meaning as you can, such as *hazy, murky, unclear,* and *misty.*

© Scott Foresman 6

Setting

- The **setting** is the place and time in which a story occurs. It may be directly identified or only suggested through story details.

- The setting of a story can influence what happens to a character and how a character behaves.

Directions: Reread what happens at the beginning of "Storm-a-Dust," when Lindy is wiping the red dust off. Then answer the questions below. Think about the story details to help you identify the setting.

> She must wipe each plant and flower clean. For red dust covered everything. Dust spotted her cheeks reddish brown. It covered her hands in red dust mittens. She took a last swipe at a stunted sunflower. "How are you this morning, yellow fella?" she asked the sunflower.
>
> "Oh, but I need some water," Lindy answered in a sunflower-high voice.
>
> "I'll water you at sundown, yellow fella," she told the flower.
>
> She tied her wiper around her waist. Her tank top and jeans were dusty. Lindy climbed up on the old wood fence and shook her head at their pie-shaped field. "Don't think the corn will make it," she called over to her dad.
>
> Excerpt from DRYSLONGO, copyright © 1992 by Virginia Hamilton, reprinted by permission of Harcourt Brace & Company.

1. Where do you think the story takes place? What details suggest this?

_____

_____

2. What is the weather like where Lindy lives? How do you know?

_____

_____

3. Why is the weather important where Lindy lives?

_____

4. What season of the year is it? How do you know?

_____

5. How does the setting affect Lindy and her parents? How might their lives be different in a different setting? Explain your thinking on a separate sheet of paper.

Notes for Home: Your child identified the setting of the story and explained why the setting is important to the story. *Home Activity:* Work with your child to describe your home as though it is the setting for a story. Discuss how each room is the setting for different activities.

© Scott Foresman 6

Name _____

1.	(A)	(B)	(C)	(D)
2.	(F)	(G)	(H)	(J)
3.	(A)	(B)	(C)	(D)
4.	(F)	(G)	(H)	(J)
5.	(A)	(B)	(C)	(D)
6.	(F)	(G)	(H)	(J)
7.	(A)	(B)	(C)	(D)
8.	(F)	(G)	(H)	(J)
9.	(A)	(B)	(C)	(D)
10.	(F)	(G)	(H)	(J)
11.	(A)	(B)	(C)	(D)
12.	(F)	(G)	(H)	(J)
13.	(A)	(B)	(C)	(D)
14.	(F)	(G)	(H)	(J)
15.	(A)	(B)	(C)	(D)

© Scott Foresman 6

Selection Test

Directions: Choose the best answer to each item. Mark the letter for the answer you have chosen.

Part 1: Vocabulary

Find the answer choice that means about the same as the underlined word in each sentence.

1. Mom did not want to use the gritty rag on the windshield.
   A. covered with oil or grease
   B. old; worn out
   C. containing small bits of dirt or sand
   D. having many holes

2. The sky was hazy.
   F. bright blue
   G. sparkling
   H. filled with black clouds
   J. not clear

3. The gardener watered the spindly bush.
   A. covered with flowers
   B. very long and slender
   C. huge
   D. young or newly planted

4. An eerie quiet filled the house.
   F. scary in a strange way
   G. happy and exciting
   H. complete; total
   J. cozy and comforting

5. The air had a peculiar odor.
   A. odd
   B. terrible
   C. lovely
   D. fruity

6. Alfonse hiked across the grasslands.
   F. low hills at the base of mountains
   G. lands covered with grass
   H. narrow strips of rocky pathways
   J. lands that rise up high

Part 2: Comprehension

Use what you know about the story to answer each item.

7. The "wall" that Lindy sees is actually a—
   A. dust storm.
   B. big flock of birds.
   C. snowstorm.
   D. line of thunderstorms.

8. Lindy's father watches the sky because he hopes he will see—
   F. a rainbow.
   G. rain clouds.
   H. flocks of birds.
   J. grasshoppers.

9. Throughout the story, Lindy sneezes and coughs because she is—
   A. getting sick.
   B. having a reaction to the plants.
   C. breathing dusty air.
   D. allergic to cats.

10. This story begins at what time of day?
    F. late afternoon
    G. morning
    H. sundown
    J. night

11. Which detail about the setting best conveys the mood of the story?
    A. "They stayed in the house with Drylongso."
    B. "This is 1975; we know more."
    C. "They all stared out at an eerie blue world."
    D. "Every window had little drifts in the corners."

© Scott Foresman 6

GO ON

12. When Drylongso arrives, the family—
- F.   is afraid of him.
- G.   cleans his face and gives him water.
- H.   asks him to tell them stories.
- J.   has him clean up their house.

13. From this story you can conclude that—
- A.   farmers should never use plows.
- B.   young seedlings cannot be saved with water during a drought.
- C.   overusing grasslands can cause dust storms.
- D.   dust storms do very little damage.

14. Lindy's family invites Drylongso to stay with them because—
- F.   they want Lindy to have a brother.
- G.   he has been separated from his family and has nowhere to go.
- H.   they need his help on the farm.
- J.   he is the only one who can make them laugh during hard times.

15. Drylongso tells Lindy some dust-storm stories in order to—
- A.   teach her lessons about farming.
- B.   convince her that he is her brother.
- C.   make her stay in the house.
- D.   keep her spirits up.

STOP

© Scott Foresman 6

Sequence

Directions: Read the story. Then read each question about the story. Choose the best answer to each question. Mark the letter for the answer you have chosen.

On the Map

When Tom and Stephanie looked at the map, they thought they had an easy hike. But they soon found out that a map doesn't show everything.

On the second day of the hike, Tom wanted to change the route they had planned. He and Stephanie looked at the map and found a shortcut. The trees were beautiful, and they saw several animals. But the shortcut was so hilly that their packs began to feel heavy. They got rid of everything they didn't want to carry. Unfortunately, this included one of their water bottles.

By the third day, they had drunk all the water from the bottle they had kept. Looking at the map, Stephanie found a detour that would take her and Tom past a stream, where they could refill their bottle. When they got there, they made a terrible discovery—the stream was dry! In the end, they had to radio the rangers for help.

"I'm sorry, Stephanie," said Tom. "If I hadn't wanted to change the hike, we would have followed a flat path near a strong stream."

"We both made mistakes," said Stephanie. "I'll never get rid of a heavy water bottle again!"

1. What was the first mistake Tom and Stephanie made?
   A. They took a shortcut that they were unfamiliar with.
   B. They decided to go on a hike.
   C. They went to a stream.
   D. They got lost.

2. Which of these events happened first?
   F. Tom took a detour to go to a stream.
   G. Tom and Stephanie got rid of everything they didn't want to carry.
   H. They went to a dry stream.
   J. They radioed for help.

3. If Stephanie had not thrown out her water bottle, they might have—
   A. avoided the first shortcut.
   B. been unable to radio for help.
   C. been able to climb the hills.
   D. avoided the detour to the dry stream.

4. The last thing that Tom and Stephanie did was to—
   F. talk about how they might have avoided their mistakes.
   G. go to a dry stream.
   H. radio for help.
   J. get rid of a water bottle.

5. If they had stayed on their original course, they probably would not have—
   A. needed help.
   B. needed a map.
   C. gotten tired.
   D. argued.

Notes for Home: Your child read a story and answered questions about the order of events.
Home Activity: Have your child think of a favorite story and list a few important events. Ask your child to explain how the story would have been different if one event had not happened.

© Scott Foresman 6

Word Study: Compound Words

Directions: Compound words are words formed by combining two other words. Compound words can be **closed** *(sunburn)*, **open** *(ice cream)*, or **hyphenated** *(half-time)*. Combine a word from the left box with a word from the right box to form a compound word that makes sense. Write both words and the resulting compound word on the lines below.

pan	bare	footed	cloth
snow	table	cakes	post
fence	sun	flake	out
beach	dead	end	umbrella
baby	through	sit	burn

1. _____ + _____ = _____

2. _____ + _____ = _____

3. _____ + _____ = _____

4. _____ + _____ = _____

5. _____ + _____ = _____

6. _____ + _____ = _____

7. _____ + _____ = _____

8. _____ + _____ = _____

9. _____ + _____ = _____

10. _____ + _____ = _____

Directions: Read the paragraph. Find five compound words. Write each compound word on the line.

The storm came up out of nowhere. Dresses and shirts on the clothesline flapped in the wind. The scarecrow looked like a stick-fella dancing in the field. A cloudburst of rain came pouring down. Then, as quickly as it had begun, the storm was over.

11. _____

12. _____

13. _____

14. _____

15. _____

Notes for Home: Your child wrote compound words, such as *sunburn, ice cream,* and *half-time. Home Activity:* Play a game with your child. Say one part of a compound word. Challenge your child to complete the compound word.

© Scott Foresman 6

Locate/Collect Information

You can **locate and collect information** about a topic using a variety of sources. Sources of information include print (textbooks, reference books, trade books, magazines/periodicals, newspapers, photographs), electronic media (computer: CD-ROMs, Internet websites; non-computer: audiotapes, videotapes, films, microfilms), and people (librarians, teachers, experts, eyewitnesses).

Directions: Suppose you are writing a report about volcanic eruptions. Use the sources of information below to answer the questions that follow.

1. Why might the encyclopedia be a good place to start your research? _____
   _____
   _____

2. Which key words might you look up in an encyclopedia to find the information you need?
   _____
   _____

© Scott Foresman 6

3. Which kind of sources would be best if you were looking for information about a volcano that erupted yesterday? Why?

_____

_____

4. What information can you find using *Readers' Guide to Periodical Literature?*

_____

_____

5. If you wanted to include pictures in your research report, which sources might include visual material that you could use?

_____

_____

6. What are some sources other than the ones shown that you might use to locate information for your research report?

_____

_____

7. Suppose you wanted to show information about famous volcanic disasters over a long period of time. Which of the sources shown might be the most helpful? Why?

_____

_____

8. What would be the best way to keep track of information if you interviewed an expert on volcanoes? Why?

_____

_____

9. An almanac often gives charts and tables listing facts about specific events. What kind of information might an almanac provide on volcanic eruptions?

_____

10. Write your own question of inquiry about volcanoes. Then tell which source of information you might use to try to find the answer for your question. Explain why this source of information would be helpful.

_____

_____

© Scott Foresman 6

Notes for Home: Your child learned to locate and collect information on a research topic. *Home Activity:* Give your child a topic for research. Have him or her suggest a number of sources that might contain useful information about that topic.

Visualizing

- To **visualize** is to create a mental image as you read.

- An author may help you visualize by using imagery, words that produce strong images, or sensory details, words that describe how something looks, sounds, smells, tastes, or feels.

Directions: Reread "The Wexford Doe." Then complete each box. List the words from the story that help you visualize what Deirdre experiences.

The Woods	The Stone Wall	The Doe
at the end of Scarlet Oak	low	7.
damp air	4.	8.
1.	5.	9.
2.	one web cradled a sleeping spider	scampered away
3.	6.	10.

Notes for Home: Your child identified words that appeal to the sense and that create strong mental images. *Home Activity:* Challenge your child to visualize a familiar place and then describe it to you by using imagery and sensory details.

© Scott Foresman 6

Vocabulary

Directions: Choose the word from the box that best completes each sentence.
Write the word on the line to the left.

_____ 1. While we were sailing, we saw a large
_____ floating past, just under the surface
of the water.

_____ 2. Swimmers need to be _____ of jellyfish.

_____ 3. Touching a single jellyfish _____ can be
very painful and even dangerous.

_____ 4. We set anchor near a beach, furled the sail,
and fastened it to the _____.

_____ 5. We gathered _____ for a small fire and
watched the sun set.

Check the Words You Know
__ driftwood
__ jellyfish
__ spar
__ tentacle
__ wary

Directions: Choose the word from the box that best matches each clue.
Write the word in the puzzle.

Down

  6. a sea animal made of jellylike tissue

  7. cautious; careful

Across

  8. a long, slender growth of a jellyfish

  9. wood that has been washed up on
the shore

  10. a wooden pole used as part of a
ship's sail

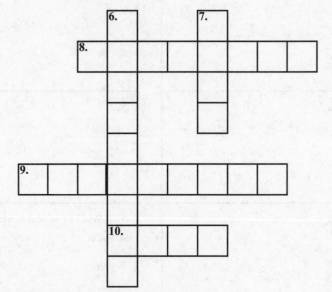

Write a Description

On a separate sheet of paper, write a description of an imaginary sea creature.
Is it friendly or dangerous? What does it look like? How does it move? Use vivid
details and your vocabulary words to make your writing interesting.

Notes for Home: Your child identified and used vocabulary words from "The Day of the
Turtle." *Home Activity:* Work together to create a sea story, using the listed vocabulary words.
Share your story with other family members.

© Scott Foresman 6

Visualizing

- To **visualize** is to create a mental image as you read.
- Imagery and sensory details help you visualize scenes from stories.

Directions: Reread what happens in "The Day of the Turtle" when Granny May tries to feed shrimp to the turtle. Then answer the questions below. Use imagery and sensory details from the story to help you visualize.

> She told me to dig a bowl in the sand right under the turtle's chin, and then she shook out her net. He looked mildly interested for a moment and then looked away. It was no good. Granny May was looking out to sea, shielding her eyes against the glare of the sun.
> "I wonder," she murmured. "I wonder. I won't be long." And she was gone down to the sea. She was wading out up to her ankles, then up to her knees, with her shrimping net scooping through the water around her. I stayed behind with the turtle and threw more stones at the gulls. When she came back, her net was bulging with jellyfish, blue jellyfish. She emptied them into the turtle's sandy bowl. At once he was at them like a vulture, snapping, crunching, swallowing, until there wasn't a tentacle left.
>
> From THE WRECK OF THE ZANZIBAR by Michael Morpurgo. Copyright © 1995 by Michael Morpurgo. Used by permission of Viking Penguin, a division of Penguin Putnam Inc.

1. Picture the day in your mind. Is it sunny, cloudy, hot, or cold? How do you know?

_____

_____

2. Describe how you think Granny May looks as she wades into the sea.

_____

_____

3. What details does the author use to help you picture the net with jellyfish?

_____

_____

4. Visualize the turtle as he eats the jellyfish. How does eating the jellyfish change his behavior?

_____

_____

5. Select another scene from the story, such as the turtle trudging toward the water. On a separate sheet of paper, describe the mental image you create from the story details.

Notes for Home: Your child used imagery and sensory details from the story to create a mental image of a scene. ***Home Activity:*** Have your child choose a favorite story. Work with your child to visualize and describe characters and places from the story using story details.

© Scott Foresman 6

Name _____

1.	Ⓐ	Ⓑ	Ⓒ	Ⓓ
2.	Ⓕ	Ⓖ	Ⓗ	Ⓙ
3.	Ⓐ	Ⓑ	Ⓒ	Ⓓ
4.	Ⓕ	Ⓖ	Ⓗ	Ⓙ
5.	Ⓐ	Ⓑ	Ⓒ	Ⓓ
6.	Ⓕ	Ⓖ	Ⓗ	Ⓙ
7.	Ⓐ	Ⓑ	Ⓒ	Ⓓ
8.	Ⓕ	Ⓖ	Ⓗ	Ⓙ
9.	Ⓐ	Ⓑ	Ⓒ	Ⓓ
10.	Ⓕ	Ⓖ	Ⓗ	Ⓙ
11.	Ⓐ	Ⓑ	Ⓒ	Ⓓ
12.	Ⓕ	Ⓖ	Ⓗ	Ⓙ
13.	Ⓐ	Ⓑ	Ⓒ	Ⓓ
14.	Ⓕ	Ⓖ	Ⓗ	Ⓙ
15.	Ⓐ	Ⓑ	Ⓒ	Ⓓ

© Scott Foresman 6

Selection Test

Directions: Choose the best answer to each item. Mark the letter for the answer you have chosen.

Part 1: Vocabulary

Find the answer choice that means about the same as the underlined word in each sentence.

1. Alfred filled a pail with <u>jellyfish</u>.
   - A. fish eggs
   - B. sea animals with soft, often clear, tissue
   - C. sea animals with shells
   - D. sea animals that look like horses

2. Jenny would not touch the <u>tentacle</u>.
   - F. part of the body by which an animal sees
   - G. organ in which digestion occurs
   - H. the outer surface of an animal
   - J. long, slender growth on an animal; feeler

3. When she saw the large dog, Liz felt <u>wary</u>.
   - A. cautious; careful
   - B. surprised
   - C. interested; curious
   - D. friendly

4. The crew returned with a new <u>spar</u>.
   - F. floor of a ship
   - G. door on a ship
   - H. wooden pole used to support a sail on a ship
   - J. a platform used by a lookout on a ship

5. Mr. Hong had a pile of <u>driftwood</u>.
   - A. wood washed up on the shore
   - B. highly polished wood
   - C. wood found under trees in an orchard
   - D. expensive wood

Part 2: Comprehension

Use what you know about the story to answer each item.

6. Why does Laura have such a hard time getting the turtle to the water?
   - F. It struggles against her.
   - G. It has lost its shell.
   - H. It likes lying in the sun.
   - J. It is very big and heavy.

7. What does Laura do first?
   - A. tries to turn the turtle over
   - B. digs a hole beside the turtle
   - C. digs a channel to the sea
   - D. piles seaweed on top of the turtle

8. What has happened to Granny May's house?
   - F. It is filled with water.
   - G. The roof has blown off.
   - H. It has burned down.
   - J. The doors and windows are broken.

9. On the beach, the gulls are waiting for—
   - A. a ship to appear.
   - B. the tide to come in.
   - C. a chance to eat the turtle.
   - D. the tide to go out.

10. Laura digs a channel to the sea to—
    - F. help the turtle return to the water.
    - G. hide the turtle.
    - H. keep the gulls away from the turtle.
    - J. collect food for the turtle.

11. Why doesn't the turtle return to the sea the first day?
    - A. It cannot breathe.
    - B. It is very young.
    - C. It is too weak.
    - D. It cannot walk on land.

© Scott Foresman 6

GO ON ▶

12. Laura thinks that the turtle—
    F.   wants to be her pet.
    G.   will always remember her.
    H.   is afraid of Granny May.
    J.   understands what she says.

13. Which sentence from the story best helps you visualize what the turtle looks like lying in the sand?
    A.   "I think it's called a leatherback turtle."
    B.   "After a while I gave up and sat down beside him on the sand."
    C.   "His flippers were quite still and held out to the clouds above as if he was worshiping them."
    D.   "That turtle would just be food to him, and to anyone else who finds him."

14. Granny May most likely helps Laura with the turtle because she—
    F.   understands why Laura wants to save it.
    G.   does not like turtle soup.
    H.   can always catch plenty of shrimp.
    J.   likes having secrets from Laura's father.

15. Based on what Laura says about her father, how will he probably react when he finds out that Laura and Granny May helped the turtle go back to the sea?
    A.   He will go down to the beach to look for it.
    B.   He will be angry because they need the food.
    C.   He will understand their concern for the turtle.
    D.   He will tell them to go catch another turtle.

STOP

© Scott Foresman 6

Making Judgments

Directions: Read the passage. Then read each question about the passage. Choose the best answer to each question. Mark the letter for the answer you have chosen.

Letters to the Editor

The Problem of Palmer's Pond

To the Editor,

The issue about what to do with Palmer's Pond has arisen once more. Some people think we should allow motorboats on Palmer's Pond. But independent studies have shown that oil from the boats would put fish in danger. So we should keep motorboats *out* of the pond.

We should also be wary of the plan to build a hotel near the pond. A hotel would destroy the quiet that we love. For the same reason, we should not build a new beach. No matter what the mayor's study says, we don't need a new beach yet.

My family has lived on Palmer's Pond for 120 years. I know what the pond needs. To save the pond, we need to keep it the same.

Sincerely,

Gillian Boswell

1. When the author says that motorboats should be kept off the pond, she—
   A. does not support her opinion.
   B. uses an independent study to support her opinion.
   C. is only stating facts.
   D. is ignoring facts.

2. The author's opinion about a new hotel is—
   F. supported by a study.
   G. supported by facts.
   H. not supported.
   J. contradicted by other statements in the article.

3. When the author says that a new beach should not be built, she—
   A. uses a study to support her opinion.
   B. seems free of bias.
   C. lists facts.
   D. ignores a study.

4. Which statement shows that the author might **not** be a fair judge of plans for the pond?
   F. She ignores the mayor's study.
   G. She ignores an independent study.
   H. She doesn't want motorboats.
   J. Her family has lived on the pond for 120 years.

5. Because the author wants the pond to stay the same, she probably—
   A. will not consider anything that might change it.
   B. considers all opposing opinions carefully.
   C. gives a balanced account of the situation.
   D. supports all of her opinions.

Notes for Home: Your child made judgments about the statements in a letter and how well the arguments are supported. *Home Activity:* With your child, read an editorial column. Discuss how well the author presents and supports his or her opinions.

© Scott Foresman 6

Word Study: Base Words

Directions: Many words are formed by adding letters to the beginning or end of a word. The word you start with is called the **base word.** Read each sentence. Find the base word in the underlined word. Write the base word on the line.

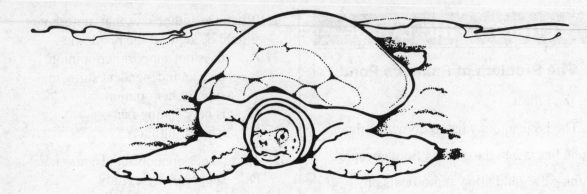

_____ 1. The turtle lay <u>gasping</u> for air.

_____ 2. It <u>seemed</u> as if it could not move an inch.

_____ 3. The turtle kept <u>shutting</u> its mouth.

_____ 4. I <u>shouted</u> at the turtle to get into the water.

_____ 5. But the creature was too <u>exhausted</u> to move.

_____ 6. The turtle lay <u>uncovered</u> and exposed.

_____ 7. It looked at me with <u>unblinking</u> eyes.

_____ 8. The turtle's <u>wrinkled</u> skin was becoming dry.

_____ 9. The birds made a <u>threatening</u> noise.

_____ 10. I <u>honestly</u> didn't know how to help the turtle.

Directions: Combine each base word and ending to make a new word. You might need to add, drop, or change letters to spell the word correctly. Write the new word on the line.

11. nudge   +   -ing   =   _____

12. drag   +   -ing   =   _____

13. noisy   +   -ly   =   _____

14. hungry   +   -er   =   _____

15. jump   +   -ing   =   _____

Notes for Home: Your child identified base words in longer words, such as *think* in *unthinking,* and used base words to write longer words. **Home Activity:** Read a news article with your child. Look for words that are formed from base words.

© Scott Foresman 6

Technology: Study Strategies

CD-ROM resources can help you gather information on a particular topic. You might use a CD-ROM dictionary, encyclopedia, or a topic-related CD-ROM. You can use search CD-ROMs to find specific information or click on underlined links to find related information.

Directions: Use the three CD-ROM sample screens to answer the questions that follow.

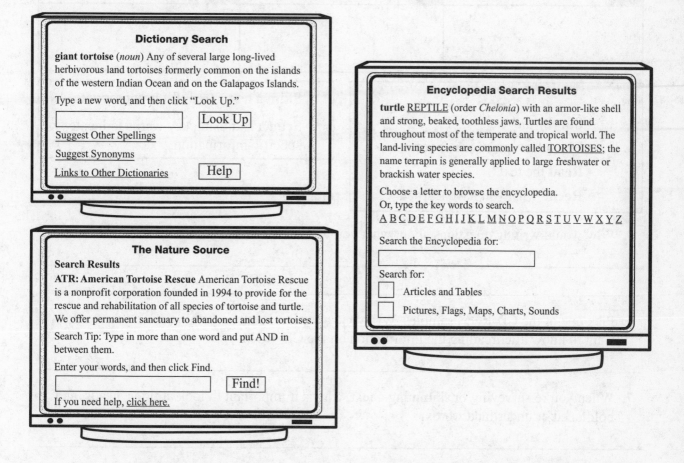

Dictionary Search

giant tortoise (*noun*) Any of several large long-lived herbivorous land tortoises formerly common on the islands of the western Indian Ocean and on the Galapagos Islands.

Type a new word, and then click "Look Up."

[Look Up]

Suggest Other Spellings

Suggest Synonyms

Links to Other Dictionaries   [Help]

Encyclopedia Search Results

turtle REPTILE (order *Chelonia*) with an armor-like shell and strong, beaked, toothless jaws. Turtles are found throughout most of the temperate and tropical world. The land-living species are commonly called TORTOISES; the name terrapin is generally applied to large freshwater or brackish water species.

Choose a letter to browse the encyclopedia.
Or, type the key words to search.
A B C D E F G H I J K L M N O P Q R S T U V W X Y Z

Search the Encyclopedia for:

Search for:
☐ Articles and Tables
☐ Pictures, Flags, Maps, Charts, Sounds

The Nature Source

Search Results
ATR: American Tortoise Rescue American Tortoise Rescue is a nonprofit corporation founded in 1994 to provide for the rescue and rehabilitation of all species of tortoise and turtle. We offer permanent sanctuary to abandoned and lost tortoises.

Search Tip: Type in more than one word and put AND in between them.

Enter your words, and then click Find.

[Find!]

If you need help, click here.

1. How would you find the meaning of "herbivorous" using the CD-ROM dictionary?

_____

2. How would you find examples of the sounds turtles make in the CD-ROM encyclopedia?

_____

3. How could you use the CD-ROM encyclopedia to find related information about tortoises?

_____

4. What key words could you use to find information about a turtle's diet in "The Nature Source" CD-ROM? Hint: Use AND between key words.

_____

© Scott Foresman 6

Use **study strategies** to help you save time and avoid reading irrelevant information. You can make a **K-W-L table,** follow the steps of **SQ2R,** or **skim and scan** text to focus your research.

Directions: Use the study strategies below and the three CD-ROM samples to answer the questions that follow.

K What I Know	**W** What I Want to Know	**L** What I Learned

SQ2R
- **Survey** the text
- Formulate **questions** about it.
- **Read** the text.
- **Recite** what you have learned.

Skim a text to see if it is appropriate.

Scan a text using key words to locate specific information.

5. Why would writing questions about what you want to know help you save research time?

_____

_____

6. Pick one of the CD-ROM samples. Write one question about something more you would want to know after reading the information on the CD-ROM.

_____

7. When you're surveying or skimming a text, why is it important to look at titles, heads, and boldfaced or underlined words?

_____

8. Why are the underlined words in the CD-ROM encyclopedia entry important?

_____

9. Scan the information in "The Nature Source" CD-ROM to find out what ATR stands for and when this group was formed.

_____

10. Which of the three study strategies would you be most likely to use? Why?

_____

_____

Notes for Home: Your child used CD-ROM resources to practice using different study strategies. *Home Activity:* With your child, pick one of the three study strategies described above. Help your child use one of these strategies to prepare for an upcoming test or research report.

© Scott Foresman 6

Persuasive Devices

- **Persuasive devices** are the special techniques an author uses to influence the way you think or feel.

- One type of persuasive device is the use of *loaded words*. Authors use *loaded words* to bring out an emotional response in readers and to convince readers of their ideas and views.

Directions: Reread "Why Care?" Then read the following paraphrases of the article. Complete the table by underlining the loaded word or words in each paraphrase. Then describe the response that readers are likely to have to the loaded words.

Paraphrase	Emotional Response
Humankind <u>dominates</u> the environment.	Readers feel sympathy for the weak and vulnerable environment.
We affect plants and animals <u>negatively</u>.	Readers feel ashamed of the way humans have affected plants and animals.
We shouldn't be bullying the rest of Earth's creatures.	1.
Plants and animals are important sources of beauty and fun.	2.
Many species enrich our lives just by existing.	3.
Our actions may force species into extinction.	4.
We are violating other living things' right to exist.	5.

Notes for Home: Your child identified loaded words, a persuasuve device used by writers to persuade readers of their point of view. *Home Activity:* Help your child identify loaded words in a newspaper editorial or letter to the editor.

© Scott Foresman 6

Vocabulary

Directions: Draw a line to connect each word on the left with its definition on the right.

1. contaminated   the air, water, soil, and so on

2. toll   polluted

3. environment   delicate; easily damaged

4. muck   filth

5. fragile   something paid, lost, or suffered

Check the Words You Know

__ cleanup
__ contaminated
__ environment
__ fragile
__ muck
__ toll
__ widespread

Directions: Choose the word from the box that best completes each sentence. Write the letters of the word on the blanks. The boxed letters spell a problem that humans have created.

6. Some problems with our air are so _____ that they extend for miles.

6. __ __ __ __ __ [o] __ __ __ __

7. Chemicals released into our air and water take a _____ on all of Earth's life forms.

7. __ __ __ [l]

8. Harmful waste from factories mixes with soil and water and creates a _____ that no one wants to touch!

8. __ [t] __ __

9. Businesses that dump this type of waste can cause great damage to Earth's _____ ecosystems.

9. __ __ __ __ __ [o] __ __

10. If we all work together, can we do a complete _____ of our environment?

10. __ __ __ __ __ __

A problem humans have created: _____

Write an Editorial

On a separate sheet of paper, write an editorial in which you state your opinion on an environmental issue or a law, such as recycling or noise pollution. Talk about how the issue affects your neighbors and your community. Use as many vocabulary words as you can.

Notes for Home: Your child identified and used vocabulary words from the selection "Saving the Sound." *Home Activity:* With your child, discuss the environment and how it could be made better. Encourage your child to use the listed vocabulary words as you talk.

© Scott Foresman 6

Persuasive Devices

- **Persuasive devices** are the special techniques an author uses to influence the way you think or feel.

- One type of persuasive device is the use of loaded words. Authors use loaded words to bring out an an emotional response in readers and to convince readers of their ideas and views.

Directions: Reread the section of "Saving the Sound" in which the author describes the coming of spring to Prince William Sound. Then answer the questions below. Look for loaded words that the author uses to influence your thinking.

> In the springtime, the Sound is waking from winter. Ice and snow are melting. Bears emerge from their hibernation dens. Fish and birds that winter elsewhere begin to return. Prince William Sound is coming to life.
>
> The wreck of the *Exxon Valdez,* however, changed all that. The oil spill turned a time of awakening and beauty into a time of nightmare and death. The Sound awoke on March 24, 1989, to find itself the victim of a disaster unlike anything that had occurred before in the United States.

From SPILL! THE STORY OF THE EXXON VALDEZ by Terry Carr. Text copyright © 1991 by Terry Carr. Reprinted by permission. All rights reserved.

1. Which sentences are statements of simple facts? Underline these facts.

2. Write some loaded words from the selection that are positive. Explain what the author's purpose is in using these words.

   _____

   _____

3. Write some loaded words from the selection that are strongly negative. Explain what the author's purpose is in using these words.

   _____

   _____

4. The author writes "The Sound awoke. . ." as if the place were a person. Why do you think the author makes this suggestion?

   _____

   _____

5. On a separate sheet of paper, describe the author's main purpose of "Saving the Sound" and explain whether or not you think the author influenced your thinking.

 Notes for Home: Your child read a work of nonfiction and looked at ways the author might try to influence readers. *Home Activity:* With your child, look at an advertisement. Discuss ways in which it tries to persuade you to make a decision.

© Scott Foresman 6

1.	Ⓐ	Ⓑ	Ⓒ	Ⓓ
2.	Ⓕ	Ⓖ	Ⓗ	Ⓙ
3.	Ⓐ	Ⓑ	Ⓒ	Ⓓ
4.	Ⓕ	Ⓖ	Ⓗ	Ⓙ
5.	Ⓐ	Ⓑ	Ⓒ	Ⓓ
6.	Ⓕ	Ⓖ	Ⓗ	Ⓙ
7.	Ⓐ	Ⓑ	Ⓒ	Ⓓ
8.	Ⓕ	Ⓖ	Ⓗ	Ⓙ
9.	Ⓐ	Ⓑ	Ⓒ	Ⓓ
10.	Ⓕ	Ⓖ	Ⓗ	Ⓙ
11.	Ⓐ	Ⓑ	Ⓒ	Ⓓ
12.	Ⓕ	Ⓖ	Ⓗ	Ⓙ
13.	Ⓐ	Ⓑ	Ⓒ	Ⓓ
14.	Ⓕ	Ⓖ	Ⓗ	Ⓙ
15.	Ⓐ	Ⓑ	Ⓒ	Ⓓ

© Scott Foresman 6

Selection Test

Directions: Choose the best answer to each item. Mark the letter for the answer you have chosen.

Part 1: Vocabulary

Find the answer choice that means about the same as the underlined word in each sentence.

1. Cleanup began right away.
   A. act of removing dirt and filth
   B. use of bright lights
   C. act of building something
   D. the burning of oil

2. Karen works hard to save the environment.
   F. bird's nest
   G. large trees
   H. body shape
   J. natural surroundings

3. There is a fragile balance among living things in the sea.
   A. delicate; easily damaged
   B. lasting forever
   C. new; invented recently
   D. changing quickly

4. That red barrel holds contaminated water.
   F. clear
   G. polluted
   H. used for drinking
   J. nearly frozen

5. Alison scooped muck into the pail.
   A. clear water
   B. dirt; filth
   C. sea animals
   D. white sand

6. The accident took a heavy toll on the local economy.
   F. benefits resulting from an event
   G. warning sign
   H. something lost, paid, or suffered
   J. cause

7. The storm had widespread effects.
   A. local
   B. felt immediately
   C. minor; not very large
   D. distributed over a large area

Part 2: Comprehension

Use what you know about the selection to answer each item.

8. Where did the *Exxon Valdez* spill its oil?
   F. Anchorage
   G. Kodiak Island
   H. Cook Inlet
   J. Prince William Sound

9. The first step in the cleanup was to—
   A. try to contain the spill.
   B. rescue birds and animals.
   C. scoop up oil and take it to shore.
   D. build walls to protect fishing grounds.

10. In the first few days after the spill, why did nice weather hamper the cleanup efforts?
    F. Oil washed over the containment booms.
    G. Chemicals used to break up the oil require rough seas.
    H. It made the oil slick spread faster.
    J. Workers were slow to respond to the disaster.

11. In this selection, the author is trying to persuade readers to—
    A. support the fishing industry.
    B. visit Alaska to see the effects of the spill.
    C. help protect the natural environment.
    D. send money to organizations that rescue wildlife.

© Scott Foresman 6

GO ON

12. The author of this selection makes the effects of the oil spill seem terrible by—
  - F. noting that other spills have occurred since then.
  - G. comparing the size of the Sound with New Jersey.
  - H. naming the company that spilled the oil.
  - J. using words that bring out an emotional response in the reader.

13. "Loaded words" are used as a persuasive device in which of the following sentences from the selection?
  - A. "The wreck of the *Exxon Valdez*, however, changed all that."
  - B. "The oil spill turned a time of awakening and beauty into a time of nightmare and death."
  - C. "One of the worst parts of the first few hours of the spill is that no one was prepared for it."
  - D. "The oil-spill response plan calls for spill-fighting equipment to be on hand five hours after a spill occurs."

14. To make this selection more balanced, the writer could have included the point of view of—
  - F. commercial fishermen.
  - G. wildlife biologists.
  - H. oil-company employees.
  - J. local residents.

15. Which sentence states an opinion?
  - A. "The Sound's most appealing sea creature is the playful sea otter."
  - B. "Much smaller than sea lions, they [sea otters] usually weigh less than 250 pounds (113 kg)."
  - C. "Otters live in the region year-round."
  - D. "Bears wander the forests and mountains, searching for food."

STOP

© Scott Foresman 6

Fact and Opinion and Graphic Sources

Directions: Look at the table and read the caption. Then read each question about the table and caption. Choose the best answer to each question. Mark the letter for the answer you have chosen.

Air Quality of U.S. Cities, 1991–1994				
	1991	**1992**	**1993**	**1994**
Chicago	8	7	1	8
Dallas	1	3	5	1
Los Angeles	182	185	146	136
New York	22	4	6	8
San Francisco	0	0	0	0

This table shows the number of days in a year that the air in five American cities failed to meet acceptable air-quality standards. The source of the data is the U.S. Environmental Protection Agency.

1. Which of the following is a statement of opinion?
   A. Los Angeles had 185 days with unacceptable air quality in 1992.
   B. The source of the data is the U.S. Environmental Protection Agency.
   C. Los Angeles is the worst place to live in the U.S.
   D. San Francisco had the fewest days of unacceptable air quality.

2. Which is an incorrect statement of fact?
   F. San Francisco has better air quality than any other city in the table.
   G. Los Angeles has the most polluted air of the five cities.
   H. The air quality in New York improved greatly after 1991.
   J. 1994 had more days of unacceptable air quality than 1992.

3. Which statement of opinion is supported by data in the table?
   A. Air quality in the U.S. is improving.
   B. No one likes poor air quality.
   C. The author is the best authority on air quality.
   D. The U.S. Environmental Protection Agency is working hard to improve air quality.

4. Which statement of opinion is supported by data in the table.
   F. San Francisco is a very pretty city.
   G. The trend shown in the table is encouraging.
   H. The air will improve because we need to make a difference.
   J. Air pollution is still a problem because of corrupt city governments.

5. If the trend continues, 2004 will have—
   A. no days with bad air.
   B. the same number of days with bad air as 1994.
   C. more days with bad air than 1994.
   D. fewer days with bad air than 1994.

© Scott Foresman 6

Notes for Home: Your child read a table and a caption and used it to identify related statements of fact and opinion. **Home Activity:** With your child, look through a newspaper for a graphic source, such as a graph or a table. Identify statements of fact and opinion in it.

Phonics: Complex Spelling Patterns

Directions: The vowels **ou** can have several different sounds. Match each **ou** word on the left with a word from the box that has the same vowel sound. Write the matching word on the line.

storm	power	bubble	secure

_____ 1. trouble   _____ 2. hour   _____ 3. pour   _____ 4. tourist

Directions: Read each sentence below. Circle the word that has the same vowel sound as the underlined word.

5. Prince William Sound in Alaska is a great <u>source</u> of fish.

   sound   sour   sir   sore

6. <u>Mountains</u> rim the edge of the Sound.

   mounds   mold   months   mute

7. But disaster struck in 1989 when a large <u>amount</u> of oil was spilled into the water.

   about   almost   above   absorb

8. People in <u>countries</u> around the world were shocked by the oil spill.

   count   cook   cup   cool

9. Many <u>tourists</u> used to visit before the spill.

   shout   sure   sour   some

10. <u>Four</u> hundred workers were flown to the site.

    north   fought   naught   found

11. The oil kept pouring <u>out</u> of the ship.

    odd   ox   pout   punt

12. <u>Southern</u> shores were also affected.

    court   cousin   count   sour

13. Volunteers worked <u>around</u> the clock to try to save the wildlife.

    sought   road   rot   sound

14. <u>Thousands</u> of birds died as a result of the spill.

    hound   though   through   thought

15. Many sea otters were also <u>found</u> dead on the shores.

    first   frog   pound   pond

Notes for Home: Your child matched the different *ou* vowel sounds, such as *sound, southern, source,* and *tourist* to words with similar vowel sounds. *Home Activity:* Ask your child to read a chapter of a book to you. Help your child look for words with *ou* vowels.

© Scott Foresman 6

Graphs

Graphs display data in visual form. They can quickly show how one piece of information compares to other pieces or how something changes over time. There are several types of graphs. **Bar graphs** use vertical and horizontal bars to show amounts that you can compare easily. **Circle graphs** have a pie shape. They show how a whole is divided into parts. **Line graphs** are named for the lines that connect a series of points on a graph. They show how things change over time.

Directions: Use the graphs to answer the questions that follow.

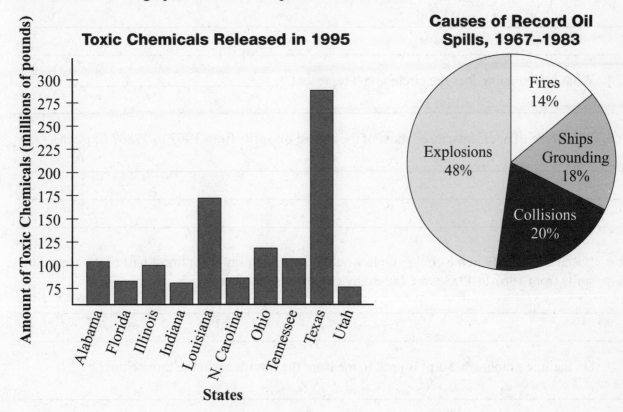

Toxic Chemicals Released in 1995

Causes of Record Oil Spills, 1967–1983

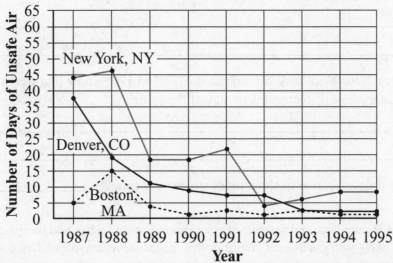

Air Quality of Three Cities, 1987–1995

1. According to the bar graph, which state released the greatest amount of toxic chemicals in 1995? How do you know?

_____

_____

2. What unit is used to measure the amount of toxic chemicals released? _____

_____

3. How does a bar graph help you compare the amounts of toxic chemicals released by different states?

_____

_____

4. What information does the circle graph represent? _____

_____

5. What type of accident caused most of the record oil spills from 1967 to 1983? Explain.

_____

_____

_____

6. Based on the data in the circle graph, would it be true to say that almost half of the record oil spills from 1967 to 1983 were caused by explosions? Explain.

_____

_____

7. On the line graph, what unit is used to measure the unsafe air in the three cities?

_____

8. For about how many days in 1988 was the air not safe in New York? For how many days in 1989 was the air not safe in New York?

_____

_____

9. Does the line graph for New York for the period 1988 to 1989 show that the number of days of unsafe air has increased, decreased, or stayed the same?

_____

_____

10. Which graph is most effective in showing changes over time? _____

Notes for Home: Your child answered questions about circle, bar, and line graphs. *Home Activity:* Show your child some graphs from a magazine or newspaper. Discuss with your child what information each graph shows. Take turns asking one another questions about the graphs.

© Scott Foresman 6

Drawing Conclusions

- To **draw a conclusion** means to make a decision or form an opinion about what you read.

- A conclusion should be sensible. It should make good sense based on the facts and details in the piece of writing and your own experience.

Directions: Reread "To the Rescue." Then complete the table. Write a conclusion for each piece of evidence. Write evidence that supports each conclusion.

Evidence (Story Details and What I Already Know)	Conclusions
1.	Clara Barton is risking her life by coming to Sharpsburg.
2.	The doctors at Sharpsburg do not have enough medical supplies.
Clara Barton has spent more than a year gathering medical supplies from friends and concerned citizens.	3.
4.	The doctors appreciate Clara Barton's help.
Clara Barton sees a bullet hole in her in sleeve. Undaunted, she keeps on working.	5.

Notes for Home: Your child read a passage and drew conclusions from its details. ***Home Activity:*** With your child, discuss a familiar book, movie, or television show. Work with your child to draw conclusions about what the characters did and why.

© Scott Foresman 6

Vocabulary

Directions: Choose the word from the box that best completes each sentence.
Write the word on the line to the left.

_____

1. After she graduated, she framed her ____ and hung it with her other certificates of study.

_____

2. It is hard for anyone to deal with ____ because everyone wants to be accepted.

_____

3. Anyone may go to a ____ for inexpensive medical treatment.

_____

4. The doctor cleaned the patient's wound carefully to avoid the risk of an ____ spreading.

_____

5. A ____ is a physician who performs surgical operations.

Check the Words You Know
__ application
__ clinic
__ diploma
__ independent
__ infection
__ qualified
__ rejection
__ surgeon

Directions: Choose the word from the box that best fits each definition. Write the word on the line. Then find and circle the words in the puzzle. Words may appear across, down, or diagonally.

_____ 6. having the necessary skills and abilities

_____ 7. a written request for something

_____ 8. able to act without help from others

_____ 9. a refusal of an attempt to gain acceptance

_____ 10. a place to get medical treatment

```
T G I V A H N A P W J O R
X F M E P S S U B N O K E
I N D E P E N D E N T D J
B I L Q L V I A C L T J E
H N A Z I T Y L X Z V B C
C S D I C L I N I C N A T
J G H O A W F V T A I N I
S B E O T X I I C D U V O
Q U A L I F I E D L L U N
M I X X O S V K A I B L A
Y T Z A N J N Q U A F I D
```

Write a Conversation

On a separate sheet of paper, write a conversation between a doctor and a patient. The doctor could be asking about a patient's health. The patient could be checking on the doctor's qualifications. Use as many vocabulary words as you can.

Notes for Home: Your child identified and used vocabulary words from "Elizabeth Blackwell: Medical Pioneer." ***Home Activity:*** Work with your child to write a definition for each of the listed vocabulary words. Use a dictionary as needed.

© Scott Foresman 6

Drawing Conclusions

- To **draw a conclusion** means to make a decision or form an opinion about what you read.

- A **conclusion** should make good sense based on the facts and details in the piece of writing.

Directions: Reread what happens in "Elizabeth Blackwell: Medical Pioneer,"
when Elizabeth tries to go to medical school. Then answer the questions below.
Use story details to think about the characters and to draw conclusions of your own.

DR. BARNES: No woman has ever gone to medical school!

ELIZABETH: You told me I had the ability.

DR. BARNES: You do! But it's 1847, Miss Blackwell. There isn't a college in the country that will accept you.

ELIZABETH: Times won't change unless we make them change!

DR. BARNES (Slowly.): There is one way.

ELIZABETH: What? What?

DR. BARNES: Disguise yourself as a man, and go study in Paris.

ELIZABETH (Shocked.): How can I help other women, if I'm in disguise?

From MS. COURAGEOUS by Joanna Halpert Kraus. Copyright 1997 by Joanna Halpert Kraus.
Reprinted by permission of New Plays Incorporated.

1. Why does Dr. Barnes think no college will accept Elizabeth?

_____

_____

2. Why does Elizabeth think it won't help other women if she disguises herself as a man to attend medical school?

_____

_____

3. Why do you think Elizabeth asks Dr. Barnes for help?

_____

4. How would you describe Elizabeth's character?

_____

5. On a separate sheet of paper, explain how Elizabeth helps to get women accepted as doctors. Use details from the story to support your answer.

Notes for Home: Your child has read part of a play and used details to draw conclusions.
Home Activity: Describe some of your recent actions. Challenge your child to draw logical conclusions about why you did what you did.

© Scott Foresman 6

Name _____

1.	Ⓐ	Ⓑ	Ⓒ	Ⓓ
2.	Ⓕ	Ⓖ	Ⓗ	Ⓙ
3.	Ⓐ	Ⓑ	Ⓒ	Ⓓ
4.	Ⓕ	Ⓖ	Ⓗ	Ⓙ
5.	Ⓐ	Ⓑ	Ⓒ	Ⓓ
6.	Ⓕ	Ⓖ	Ⓗ	Ⓙ
7.	Ⓐ	Ⓑ	Ⓒ	Ⓓ
8.	Ⓕ	Ⓖ	Ⓗ	Ⓙ
9.	Ⓐ	Ⓑ	Ⓒ	Ⓓ
10.	Ⓕ	Ⓖ	Ⓗ	Ⓙ
11.	Ⓐ	Ⓑ	Ⓒ	Ⓓ
12.	Ⓕ	Ⓖ	Ⓗ	Ⓙ
13.	Ⓐ	Ⓑ	Ⓒ	Ⓓ
14.	Ⓕ	Ⓖ	Ⓗ	Ⓙ
15.	Ⓐ	Ⓑ	Ⓒ	Ⓓ

© Scott Foresman 6

Selection Test

Directions: Choose the best answer to each item. Mark the letter for the answer
you have chosen.

Part 1: Vocabulary

Find the answer choice that means about the
same as the underlined word in each sentence.

1. Mrs. Ashland took her children to the
   clinic.
   A. school for nurses
   B. place where people receive medical
      care
   C. hospital for blind people
   D. shopping mall

2. The baby's infection was gone in several
   days.
   F. discomfort or pain
   G. sneezing caused by dust
   H. sadness or extreme loneliness
   J. condition caused by disease-
      producing germs

3. The surgeon checked her knee.
   A. business manager
   B. doctor who performs operations
   C. type of lawyer
   D. person who specializes in teeth

4. My sister framed her diploma.
   F. realistic image such as a photograph
   G. self-portrait
   H. certificate awarded for completing a
      course of study
   J. oil painting

5. She is an independent person.
   A. well-traveled
   B. wealthy
   C. self-employed
   D. able to act without help from others

6. The writer got a letter of rejection.
   F. praise
   G. act of giving thanks
   H. condition of not being accepted
   J. criticism

7. Brian sent in his application.
   A. written request for admission
   B. essay
   C. homework
   D. order to appear in court

8. He was certainly qualified for the job.
   F. having the necessary training or
      skills
   G. nervous; shaky
   H. receiving praise
   J. not prepared

Part 2: Comprehension

Use what you know about the play to answer
each item.

9. Why did Elizabeth Blackwell have
   difficulty getting into medical school?
   A. She was not very well prepared.
   B. No woman had ever gone to medical
      school.
   C. She was not very highly
      recommended.
   D. The medical schools did not need
      any new students.

10. Elizabeth Blackwell took a job as a student
    nurse because she—
    F. was not yet trained to be a doctor.
    G. needed to learn to work with poor
       eyesight.
    H. thought she could learn more from
       being a nurse than from being a
       doctor.
    J. could not find a hospital that would
       hire her as a doctor.

© Scott Foresman 6

GO ON ➡

11. You can conclude that Dr. Blackwell's eyesight improved because she—
   A. became a practicing doctor in New York.
   B. wanted to become a surgeon.
   C. was accepted to study at St. Bartholomew's.
   D. changed her dream.

12. Dr. Blackwell did not become a surgeon because—
   F. there had never been a female surgeon before.
   G. she could not get into a medical school.
   H. her eyesight was not good enough.
   J. she was more interested in practical medicine.

13. You can conclude that Sean confronted the mob outside Dr. Blackwell's clinic because he—
   A. did not want to pay medical bills.
   B. thought all doctors should be women.
   C. appreciated her work.
   D. had been saved by her.

14. Which of these goals became most important to Elizabeth Blackwell after she set up her clinic in New York?
   F. overcoming prejudice
   G. making a good living
   H. having a family
   J. becoming a surgeon

15. From the end of the play you can conclude that Elizabeth Blackwell—
   A. thought women were designed to help men.
   B. believed that very few doctors would ever be women.
   C. argued that women were better doctors than men.
   D. believed more women would become doctors.

STOP

© Scott Foresman 6

Compare and Contrast/ Text Structure

REVIEW

Directions: Read the story. Then read each question about the story. Choose the best answer to each question. Mark the letter for the answer you have chosen.

Two Peas in a Pod

Neil and Nancy are brother and sister, but you wouldn't know it to look at them. Neil's face is serious. His eyes seem to see all the way into your thoughts. He is not especially tall, but broad-shouldered and strongly built. In contrast, Nancy is very tall and slender, with long arms and legs. Her eyes always twinkle. When you hear her laugh, you have to laugh too!

Underneath the surface, though, they are as alike as identical twins. When they make up their minds to do something, nothing stops them. They have different talents and interests, but similar ways of doing things.

All through the fall and winter, Nancy practiced daily to break the school's sprint racing record. Rain or shine, Nancy was out on the track, working to run faster each week. She competed with herself as much as with other runners. When the spring track meet was held, Nancy was the fastest runner on her team.

Neil was in charge of designing and building the sets for the December class play. Even when his crew all came down with the flu and he was on his own, Neil didn't give up. He got some friends to help, and he worked late into the night for several days to finish the sets on time. When the play was performed, everyone praised his work.

In their different ways, Nancy and Neil show the value of staying focused. Brother and sister work hard to achieve their goals.

1. Nancy and Neil—
   A. are alike inside and out.
   B. look like brother and sister.
   C. don't act alike.
   D. don't look alike.

2. Neil and Nancy are both—
   F. hard-working.
   G. talkative.
   H. unfocused.
   J. solemn.

3. Neil and Nancy—
   A. never have setbacks.
   B. work hard to get what they want.
   C. change their goals when problems arise.
   D. focus only on their setbacks.

4. The title and the second paragraph tell that Nancy and Neil—
   F. are very similar, despite appearances.
   G. are identical twins.
   H. make up their minds easily.
   J. are more different than alike.

5. The passage is organized to show how Neil and Nancy are—
   A. related.
   B. different.
   C. alike.
   D. different in some ways and similar in other ways.

Notes for Home: Your child has read a story, compared and contrasted characters, and described the story's organization. *Home Activity:* Read a short story to your child. Challenge him or her to identify similarities and differences among the characters.

© Scott Foresman 6

Word Study: Regular Plurals

Directions: To make most nouns plural, add **-s.** For nouns that end in **x, s, ss, ch,** or **sh,** add **-es.** For nouns that end in a **consonant** and **y,** change the **y** to **i** and add **-es.** Read the paragraph below. Make each word in ( ) plural. Write the plural word on the line.

(Doctor) and (nurse) must attend school and complete special training before they are ready to help others. They listen to (lecture) presented by people who are important in the medical field. They must achieve excellent (grade) in most of their (class). They spend hours in (library) and (laboratory). With all these (experience), these highly-trained men and women are ready to handle most (emergency). Many of these dedicated professionals work to become the (leader) in their field.

1. _____
2. _____
3. _____
4. _____
5. _____
6. _____
7. _____
8. _____
9. _____
10. _____

Directions: Write the plural of each word. For some words, you will add **-s.** For others, you will add **-es.** You may need to change **y** to **i** before adding **-es.**

11. study _____
12. pioneer _____
13. canary _____
14. league _____
15. officer _____
16. beach _____
17. sympathy _____
18. circus _____
19. pickax _____
20. lady _____

21. narrator _____
22. eyelash _____
23. hobby _____
24. monkey _____
25. tax _____
26. dictionary _____
27. charlatan _____
28. messenger _____
29. mystery _____
30. eyeglass _____

© Scott Foresman 6

Notes for Home: Your child formed plural nouns by adding *-s,* or *-es.* **Home Activity:** Choose individual items from around your home. Have your child write the names of the items. Help your child to write the plural form of each item.

Technology: Card Catalog/Library Database

You can use a **card catalog** or **library database** to find books, magazines, audiotapes, videotapes, CD-ROMs, and other materials in the library. You can search for materials by author, title, or subject. If you don't know exactly what you are searching for in the library database, you can use key words. Be sure to type and spell words carefully. If you use more than one key word in your search, put the word "AND" between the key words.

Directions: Look at the starting search screen for a library database below. Tell which box and key words you would use to search for the book or books listed below.

Search Kempe High Library

☐ Title (exact search)

☐ Title (key words)

☐ Author (last name, first name)

☐ Author (key words)

☐ Subject (exact search)

☐ Subject (key words)

Check a box and type your key words in the box below. Press return.

[   ]

---

1. books about Elizabeth Blackwell _____

_____

2. books written by Joanna Halpert Kraus _____

_____

3. a book titled *Women in Nineteenth-Century America* _____

_____

4. books about famous women in medicine _____

_____

5. a book titled *Elizabeth Blackwell: First Woman Doctor* _____

_____

6. books about the history of medicine _____

_____

© Scott Foresman 6

If you search with a broad subject such as "medicine," the database may give you more choices. These might be arranged according to more specific topics.

Directions: Use the list of specific topics to answer the questions that follow.

> **Subject:** medicine
>
> | **Search Results** | **Number of Items** |
> | --- | --- |
> | 1 Medicine - history | (13) |
> | 2 Medicine - women | (4) |
> | 3 Medicine - drugs | (12) |
> | 4 Medicine - fiction | (8) |
> | 5 Medicine - hospitals | (13) |
> | 6 Medicine - preventative | (7) |
> | 7 Medicine - disease | (23) |
> | 8 Medicine - schools | (6) |
>
> Type a number or press return to enter a new search.

7. Which topics might be useful to find out more about women and medicine in the 1800s?

_____

8. Which number would you type to find a fictional story about medicine? _____

9. What are some ways to find information on Marie Curie, another medical pioneer?

_____

_____

_____

10. How is searching a library database like and unlike using a card catalog?

_____

_____

_____

Notes for Home: Your child answered questions about using a card catalog and a library database. ***Home Activity:*** Ask your child to name two topics to research. Together, make a list of subject key words for each topic that you could use to search the database at the library.

© Scott Foresman   6

Name _____

Compare and Contrast

- To **compare** means to tell how two or more things are alike. To **contrast** means to tell how two or more things are different.

- Some common clue words for likenesses are *like, similarly, as, in addition, likewise,* and *in the same way.* Some common clue words for differences are *but, however, differing, although, in spite of,* and *on the other hand.*

Directions: Reread "One for All." Then complete the table. Compare and contrast Julio to Lucas, Cricket, and Julio's brothers. Tell how Julio is like or unlike these other characters. One has been done for you.

Julio and Lucas	Julio and Cricket	Julio and His Brothers
1. Alike:	3. Alike:	5. Alike:
2. Different:	4. Different:	Different: Julio is younger than his brothers.

 Notes for Home: Your child compared and contrasted the characters in a story. *Home Activity:* With your child, discuss how three people you know are alike and different. Create a table similar to the one above.

Vocabulary

Directions: Choose the word from the box that best matches each definition. Write the word on the line.

_____ 1. deeply embedded surface dirt

_____ 2. a liquid mixture

_____ 3. a mindset; a way of thinking

_____ 4. to oversee others' activities

_____ 5. a worker performing manual labor

Check the Words You Know
__ accompanied
__ attitude
__ collapsed
__ grime
__ laborer
__ solution
__ supervise

Directions: Choose the word from the box that has the same or nearly the same meaning as each underlined word below. Write the word on the line.

_____ 6. The scientist prepared a <u>mixture</u> of three different liquids, including water.

_____ 7. The doctor explained that the young man had <u>fainted</u> because he had been working out in the hot sun without drinking enough water.

_____ 8. The movie star was <u>escorted</u> to the movie opening by her agent, her director, and her producer.

_____ 9. The foreman of the construction crew thought Tom was the best <u>worker</u> of the group.

_____ 10. The head of the sales department has to <u>oversee</u> the work of thirty customer service representatives.

Write a Thank-you Note

On a separate sheet of paper, write a note thanking someone for some work he or she has done that has made life easier for you. Use as many vocabulary words as you can.

Notes for Home: Your child learned new vocabulary words from "Born Worker." ***Home Activity:*** Play a game in which one of you describes a kind of work and the other names the worker, for example: *teaching/teacher.*

© Scott Foresman 6

Compare and Contrast

- To **compare** means to tell how two or more things are alike. To **contrast** means to tell how two or more things are different.

- Clue words such as *like* or *as* can signal comparisons. Clue words such as *but* or *unlike* can signal contrasts.

Directions: Reread what happens in "Born Worker" when José and Arnie agree to work together. Then answer the questions below. Think about the characters in the story to help you compare and contrast.

José agreed to a seventy-thirty split, with the condition that Arnie had to help out. Arnie hollered, arguing that some people were meant to work and others to come up with brilliant ideas. He was one of the latter. Still, he agreed after José said it was that or nothing.

In the next two weeks, Arnie found an array of jobs. José peeled off shingles from a rickety garage roof, carried rocks down a path to where a pond would go, and spray-painted lawn furniture. And while Arnie accompanied him, most of the time he did nothing.

Excerpt from PETTY CRIMES, copyright © 1998 by Gary Soto, reprinted by permission of Harcourt Brace & Company.

1. How are Arnie's and José's ambitions alike?

_____

_____

2. What does José do to get what he wants?

_____

_____

3. What does Arnie do to get what he wants?

_____

_____

4. How are their attitudes about work different?

_____

_____

5. On a separate sheet of paper, explain which boy you would hire and why. Give an example from the story.

Notes for Home: Your child read a short story and used details to compare and contrast its characters. *Home Activity:* Take turns comparing and contrasting the personalities and actions of people you and your child both know.

© Scott Foresman 6

1.	Ⓐ	Ⓑ	Ⓒ	Ⓓ
2.	Ⓕ	Ⓖ	Ⓗ	Ⓙ
3.	Ⓐ	Ⓑ	Ⓒ	Ⓓ
4.	Ⓕ	Ⓖ	Ⓗ	Ⓙ
5.	Ⓐ	Ⓑ	Ⓒ	Ⓓ
6.	Ⓕ	Ⓖ	Ⓗ	Ⓙ
7.	Ⓐ	Ⓑ	Ⓒ	Ⓓ
8.	Ⓕ	Ⓖ	Ⓗ	Ⓙ
9.	Ⓐ	Ⓑ	Ⓒ	Ⓓ
10.	Ⓕ	Ⓖ	Ⓗ	Ⓙ
11.	Ⓐ	Ⓑ	Ⓒ	Ⓓ
12.	Ⓕ	Ⓖ	Ⓗ	Ⓙ
13.	Ⓐ	Ⓑ	Ⓒ	Ⓓ
14.	Ⓕ	Ⓖ	Ⓗ	Ⓙ
15.	Ⓐ	Ⓑ	Ⓒ	Ⓓ

© Scott Foresman 6

Selection Test

Directions: Choose the best answer to each item. Mark the letter for the answer you have chosen.

Part 1: Vocabulary

Find the answer choice that means about the same as the underlined word in each sentence.

1. Please use that green <u>solution</u>.
   - A. type of hammer
   - B. type of sponge
   - C. liquid mixture
   - D. powder

2. Laurel is a good <u>laborer</u>.
   - F. follower
   - G. person who remembers everything he or she reads
   - H. leader
   - J. person who does work that requires strength rather than skill

3. Did Mrs. DiCamillo <u>supervise</u> the other teachers?
   - A. do the same job as
   - B. oversee the work of
   - C. greet in a friendly way
   - D. cooperate with

4. The walls were covered with <u>grime</u>.
   - F. dirt
   - G. paint
   - H. flakes of ash
   - J. thin coating of water

5. After the race, Jim's <u>attitude</u> changed.
   - A. height from the ground
   - B. appearance
   - C. way of thinking
   - D. goal

6. Mr. Daily <u>collapsed</u> on the sidewalk.
   - F. sat still
   - G. fell down suddenly
   - H. walked quickly
   - J. wandered slowly

7. Yuki <u>accompanied</u> us to the show.
   - A. followed
   - B. raced
   - C. led
   - D. went along with

Part 2: Comprehension

Use what you know about the story to answer each item.

8. Why doesn't José like Arnie?
   - F. Arnie does not earn what he gets.
   - G. José is jealous of how easily Arnie makes friends.
   - H. Arnie always works harder than José.
   - J. José cannot ask people for work as easily as Arnie does.

9. What did Mr. Clemens do while José was scrubbing the pool?
   - A. He ate loquats.
   - B. He took his poodle for a walk.
   - C. He got dressed.
   - D. He lay in the lounge chair.

10. José shows that he is different from Arnie when he—
    - F. leaves the scene of an accident.
    - G. takes care of Mr. Clemens.
    - H. rides a bike.
    - J. acts cheerful.

11. José's attitude toward work is most like—
    - A. Mr. Clemens's.
    - B. Arnie's.
    - C. his parents'.
    - D. Mr. Bechtel's.

© Scott Foresman 6

GO ON

12. Why does José agree to work with Arnie?
    F. He feels sorry for Arnie.
    G. He does not like asking for work.
    H. He wants to teach Arnie to be a good laborer.
    J. He wants to be rich.

13. Arnie is best described as—
    A. lazy and spoiled.
    B. sensitive and caring.
    C. talented and independent.
    D. hard-working and responsible.

14. José's opinion of Arnie is primarily based on—
    F. Mr. Clemens's reactions to him.
    G. comments neighbors have made.
    H. his parents' comments about Arnie's family.
    J. personal experience and direct observation.

15. The next time he decides to work with Arnie, José will most likely—
    A. provide transportation for Arnie.
    B. take charge of arranging the work.
    C. insist on receiving more of the pay.
    D. say he does not want to work in a backyard.

© Scott Foresman 6

Predicting and Plot

Directions: Read the story. Then read each question about the story. Choose the best answer to each question. Mark the letter for the answer you have chosen.

Different Directions

When we set off on our trip to Aunt Bess's that Thanksgiving, Mom teased Dad, "Are you planning to get lost again?" He never fails to lose the way. Dad has no sense of direction. Unfortunately, he doesn't know that! He is always sure he knows the way. Only as time passes does he begin a series of stops at gas stations for further directions. We are always so late that Aunt Bess has learned to tell Dad to arrive an hour earlier than she really wants us there. That way, she knows we will probably be on time.

This time, however, I was determined to get us there well before the turkey was overdone and the stuffing all gone. First, I called Aunt Bess and wrote down detailed directions. I knew it was in the final part of the trip that Dad made his worst mistakes. I read that part of the directions back to Aunt Bess to be sure I had it right. I also decided to take the road atlas.

The first time Dad got into the wrong lane, I told him I had directions, and he should go left instead of right. Dad was annoyed for a moment, but had to give in at Mom's heartfelt "Thank goodness you thought of that!" Dad swung back into the left lane.

Unfortunately, things did not go quite as I had planned. Somewhere between Lima and Elyria, my sister moaned, "I don't feel so well. Open the windows, quick!" As big gusts of air blew into the car, making Annie feel better, my careful notes blew out the window!

Mom and I stared at each other; then Mom began to laugh. All of us joined in, knowing that Aunt Bess would be as amused as we were. "I have the best solution," said Mom. "Next time, I'll drive!"

1. What conflict, or problem, do the characters in this story face?
   A. Dad is always getting lost.
   B. Aunt Bess cooks Thanksgiving dinner.
   C. Aunt Bess lives far away.
   D. The narrator gets directions from Aunt Bess.

2. What does the first paragraph lead you to expect next?
   F. Mom will tease Dad.
   G. Dad will not get lost this time.
   H. Aunt Bess will call.
   J. Dad will get lost.

3. After the instructions blow away, the narrator will probably—
   A. get lost.
   B. look at the road atlas.
   C. arrive early at Aunt Bess's.
   D. blame Dad for getting into the wrong lane.

4. The part of the story in which the instructions fly away is called the—
   F. plot.
   G. rising action.
   H. climax.
   J. conflict.

5. When Aunt Bess hears the story of the lost directions, she will probably—
   A. cry.
   B. laugh.
   C. never invite her relatives to dinner again.
   D. tell the narrator to be more careful in the future.

Notes for Home: Your child predicted events in a story and identified plot elements. *Home Activity:* Read a story aloud with your child. After every few paragraphs, ask your child to predict what will happen next.

© Scott Foresman 6

Word Study: Irregular Plurals

Directions: Most plural nouns are formed by adding **-s** and **-es**. Some plural nouns do not follow a regular spelling pattern. These are called **irregular plurals.** For some irregular plurals, you need to change the spelling of the singular noun, as in **man** and **men,** or **scarf** and **scarves.** Other irregular plurals have the same singular and plural form, such as **series.** Read each word below. Write the plural form for each word on the line.

1. tooth _____   6. goose _____   11. shelf _____

2. fireman _____   7. knife _____   12. fish _____

3. moose _____   8. sheep _____   13. ox _____

4. half _____   9. mouse _____   14. deer _____

5. foot _____   10. salmon _____   15. life _____

Directions: Find the plural nouns in the paragraph. Write each word in the correct column.

The park needed a lot of work if it was going to open soon. A gardener had been hired to clean it, and he quickly got to work. First he raked around the flower beds. It was springtime, and the flowers would need the sunlight. He knew that children would want to play near the pond and geese would come to rest on it, so he used a net to collect any floating pieces of trash. He cleared rocks from the bike path and picked up discarded cans. Lastly, he repainted the bench so men and women could picnic under the shady leaves of the old oak tree. The work had been hard, but at last the park was clean and ready.

Regular Plurals	**Irregular Plurals**
16. _____	21. _____
17. _____	22. _____
18. _____	23. _____
19. _____	24. _____
20. _____	25. _____

Notes for Home: Your child formed and identified irregular plurals, such as *mice* and *deer*. *Home Activity:* Read a newspaper article with your child. Help your child identify both regular and irregular plurals.

© Scott Foresman 6

Organize and Present Information

As you research and take notes, be sure to **organize information** in a logical manner that makes it easier to **present** your findings. If you have information that includes a lot of comparative quantities, you might consider using line graphs or bar graphs. Summaries, maps, time lines, illustrations, charts, and tables are other ways to organize and present information.

Thinking about text structure can also help you decide how to present your information. You may choose to organize it using chronological order, problem-solution, or cause-effect.

Directions: Read the article. Then answer the questions that follow.

In 1938, the Fair Labor Standards Act went into effect to assist people who were struggling financially because of the Great Depression. This period was a time of great poverty throughout the United States.

The most important law in the Fair Labor Standards Act was the minimum wage law. "Minimum" means "lowest," and the law made sure workers in most trades were paid no less than a set minimum amount of money per hour. In 1938, the amount was $0.25. (In 1938, a quarter was enough to buy a hearty meal at a restaurant.)

The minimum wage was reviewed in 1939 and raised to $0.30. In 1945, it went up another ten cents. In 1950, it was raised to $0.75. Six more years went by before it was raised again, this time to $1.00. Since then, the minimum wage has been raised 15 more times. The highest jump in the minimum wage took place in 1991, when it went from $3.50 to $4.25. It currently stands at $5.15.

Waiters and waitresses are not covered by the minimum wage law because they are paid "tips." Customers normally add 15% of the cost of a meal for the waiter or waitress. In addition to these tips, waiters or waitresses usually earn a certain amount of money per hour, but this wage does not have to be the minimum wage.

---

1. Underline or highlight the important ideas presented in this article.

2. Summarize the article briefly. _____

_____

_____

3. Why was a minimum wage law created? _____

_____

4. Why aren't employers required to pay waiters and waitresses a minimum wage?

_____

5. If you were giving a speech to a class about the minimum wage, what kind of graphic organizer might be a good visual aid? Why?

_____

_____

© Scott Foresman 6

Directions: Study the table. Then answer the questions below.

Percentage of Female Workers in Selected Jobs, 1975 to 1997 (as a percentage of total workers)				
Job	**1975**	**1985**	**1996**	**1997**
Auto Mechanic	0.5	0.6	1.2	1.5
Cab Driver/Chauffer	8.7	10.9	10.7	8.3
Carpenter	0.6	1.2	1.3	1.6
Dentist	1.8	6.4	13.7	17.3
Dental Assistant	100.0	99.0	79.8	96.7
Journalist	44.6	51.7	55.7	51.2
Professor	31.1	35.2	43.5	42.7
Waitress	91.1	84.0	77.9	77.8
Welder	4.4	4.8	5.0	5.6

6. Explain what the number 96.7 means in the column "1997." _____

_____

7. Which four types of jobs showed a steady increase in the percent of female workers from 1975 to 1997? Which job shows a steady decrease?

_____

_____

8. How else might you organize the data in this table? Why might this be a good way to organize this data?

_____

_____

9. Why is it important to organize information as you do research? _____

_____

_____

10. Why is it important to think about text structure when you are preparing to present the information you have collected?

_____

_____

Notes for Home: Your child read a passage, examined a table, and described ways to organize and present the information in them. *Home Activity:* Have your child read a newspaper or magazine article. Discuss ways your child could organize and present the information it contains.

© Scott Foresman 6

Cause and Effect

- An **effect** is something that happens. A **cause** is why something happens.
- To find an effect, ask yourself "What happened?" To find a cause, ask yourself "Why did it happen?"

Directions: Reread "Sunday Visitors." Then complete the table. Write the cause of each given effect. Write the effect of each given cause.

Cause (Why Did It Happen?)	Effect (What Happened?)
1.	Alice doesn't know what she wants from Peg's family.
Peg understands Alice and feels compassion for her.	2.
3.	The other girls are as excited about visiting day as Peg.
4.	Alice combs her hair.
5.	Dorothy blushes.

Notes for Home: Your child read a passage and linked events with their causes. *Home Activity:* Describe a simple event, such as a car stopping in the middle of a street. With your child, discuss possible causes of the event.

© Scott Foresman 6

Vocabulary

Directions: Choose the word from the box that best completes each sentence. Write the word on the line to the right.

The fall left her **1.** ____ and almost unable to move. She felt **2.** ____ grief that she would not be able to run ever again. She had always been very **3.** ____, but she knew that those days of playing sports were over. Then came a **4.** ____ day, one that she would never forget. She found that she could still enter a **5.** ____ and be an athlete.

1. _____

2. _____

3. _____

4. _____

5. _____

Check the Words You Know
__ athletic
__ competition
__ intense
__ memorable
__ paralyzed
__ unlimited

Directions: Choose the word from the box that best matches each clue. Write the word in the puzzle.

Down

6. a contest

7. free; not restricted

Across

8. not to be forgotten

9. something having to do with active games and sports

10. very much; extreme

Write an Awards Certificate

On a separate sheet of paper, write an awards certificate to someone who has overcome something very difficult. It can be someone you know or someone you imagine. Use as many vocabulary words as you can.

Notes for Home: Your child identified and used vocabulary words from *Wilma Unlimited*. *Home Activity:* Talk with your child about someone you know who has overcome an obstacle or difficult task. Make a list of words to describe that person.

© Scott Foresman 6

Cause and Effect

- An **effect** is something that happens. A **cause** is why it happens.

- To find an effect, ask yourself "What happened?" To find a cause, ask yourself "Why did this happen?"

Directions: Reread what happens in *Wilma Unlimited* after Wilma gets polio. Then answer the questions below. Ask yourself about what happens and why to help you identify causes and effects.

Doctors and nurses at the hospital helped Wilma do exercises to make her paralyzed leg stronger. At home, Wilma practiced them constantly, even when it hurt.

To Wilma, what hurt most was that the local school wouldn't let her attend because she couldn't walk. Tearful and lonely, she watched her brothers and sisters run off to school each day, leaving her behind. Finally, tired of crying all the time, she decided she had to fight back—somehow.

Wilma worked so hard at her exercises that the doctors decided she was ready for a heavy steel brace. With the brace supporting her leg, she didn't have to hop anymore. School was possible at last.

Excerpt from WILMA UNLIMITED: HOW WILMA RUDOLPH BECAME THE WORLD'S FASTEST WOMAN, copyright © 1996 by Kathleen Krull, reprinted by permission of Harcourt Brace & Company.

1. Why does Wilma keep exercising her paralyzed leg even when it hurts?

_____

_____

2. What upsets Wilma the most about not being able to walk?

_____

3. What makes Wilma stop crying and fight back?

_____

4. What are the results of Wilma's hard work?

_____

_____

5. On a separate sheet of paper, explain what you think is the major cause of Wilma's success. Give examples from the story to support your answer.

Notes for Home: Your child read a short story and identified causes and effects. ***Home Activity:*** With your child, read or listen to a local news story. Challenge him or her to identify the causes and effects of individual news events.

© Scott Foresman 6

Name _____

1.	Ⓐ	Ⓑ	Ⓒ	Ⓓ
2.	Ⓕ	Ⓖ	Ⓗ	Ⓙ
3.	Ⓐ	Ⓑ	Ⓒ	Ⓓ
4.	Ⓕ	Ⓖ	Ⓗ	Ⓙ
5.	Ⓐ	Ⓑ	Ⓒ	Ⓓ
6.	Ⓕ	Ⓖ	Ⓗ	Ⓙ
7.	Ⓐ	Ⓑ	Ⓒ	Ⓓ
8.	Ⓕ	Ⓖ	Ⓗ	Ⓙ
9.	Ⓐ	Ⓑ	Ⓒ	Ⓓ
10.	Ⓕ	Ⓖ	Ⓗ	Ⓙ
11.	Ⓐ	Ⓑ	Ⓒ	Ⓓ
12.	Ⓕ	Ⓖ	Ⓗ	Ⓙ
13.	Ⓐ	Ⓑ	Ⓒ	Ⓓ
14.	Ⓕ	Ⓖ	Ⓗ	Ⓙ
15.	Ⓐ	Ⓑ	Ⓒ	Ⓓ

© Scott Foresman 6

Selection Test

Directions: Choose the best answer to each item. Mark the letter for the answer you have chosen.

Part 1: Vocabulary

Find the answer choice that means about the same as the underlined word in each sentence.

1. The Scott family had a memorable vacation.
   A. lengthy
   B. dull or boring
   C. not to be forgotten
   D. involving the wilderness

2. The pass gives us unlimited use of Henderson Park.
   F. without restrictions; boundless
   G. paid in advance
   H. from morning to night
   J. cheap; inexpensive

3. Those girls entered the competition.
   A. show of affection
   B. contest
   C. friendly support
   D. equipment used in track and field

4. Alano worked in intense heat.
   F. occasional
   G. mild
   H. humid
   J. extreme

5. Shem looked at his paralyzed legs.
   A. small and thin
   B. unable to move
   C. spotted
   D. covered with hair

6. Carrie joined the athletic club.
   F. having to do with sports
   G. secret
   H. related to art
   J. for girls only

Part 2: Comprehension

Use what you know about the selection to answer each item.

7. Why did the people of Clarksville think that Wilma would never walk again?
   A. The doctor had her wear a brace.
   B. She had no one to take care of her.
   C. There was no cure for polio at that time.
   D. She had always been a small and sickly child.

8. Wilma was not allowed to go to school at first because—
   F. her mother needed her help.
   G. she might make others sick.
   H. her leg was supported by a brace.
   J. she could not walk.

9. Which word best describes Wilma Rudolph throughout her life?
   A. quiet
   B. sickly
   C. determined
   D. lonely

10. What is the main idea of this selection?
    F. Wilma Rudolph overcame polio and won three Olympic gold medals.
    G. Wilma Rudolph did leg exercises until she could walk without her leg brace.
    H. Wilma Rudolph was the first person in her family to go to college.
    J. Wilma Rudolph was the fastest woman in the world.

© Scott Foresman 6

GO ON

11. School was not as wonderful as Wilma had thought it would be because—
- A. the other kids made fun of her.
- B. she was a better basketball player than the others.
- C. there were no other African American children there.
- D. she had a hard time doing her schoolwork.

12. You can conclude that Wilma Rudolph felt supported by her community because she—
- F. did leg exercises at home.
- G. first tried to walk without her brace at church.
- H. ran in Olympic track-and-field events.
- J. went to Tennessee State University.

13. What effect did Wilma's experiences as a child overcoming polio have on her during the Olympics?
- A. She had stronger legs than the other athletes.
- B. She was well prepared to receive the baton.
- C. She was popular with the audience.
- D. She was able to really concentrate on her goal.

14. Which is a statement of opinion?
- F. It was the bravest thing she had ever done.
- G. She waited while other people filled the building.
- H. She took off her leg brace and set it by the door.
- J. She placed one foot in front of the other.

15. The biggest obstacle Wilma Rudolph had to overcome in order to become an Olympic runner was that—
- A. her mother had twenty-two children.
- B. she was African American.
- C. her leg had been paralyzed by polio.
- D. she weighed just four pounds at birth.

STOP

© Scott Foresman   6

Main Idea and Supporting Details/Context Clues

Directions: Read the passage. Then read each question about the passage. Choose the best answer to each question. Mark the letter for the answer you have chosen.

The Struggle for America

Large numbers of Chinese people came to California during the Gold Rush in the mid-1800s. They were not made welcome in their new country. They were often forced to pay special taxes and fees. Only a few jobs, such as laundry work and mining, were open to them. In some places, schools refused to accept Chinese children. No state let them argue in court against non-Chinese people, and they were not allowed to become citizens.

Prejudice against Chinese people in America was intense enough in 1882 for the U.S. to pass the Chinese Exclusion Act. This barred Chinese people from entering the country as immigrants for more than sixty years. During this time, many Chinese Americans tried to change the law by going to court.

During World War II, thousands of Chinese Americans joined the U.S. armed forces. Thousands of others went to work in defense factories. In 1943, the repeal of the Chinese Exclusion Act meant that Chinese immigrants were welcome again.

Since that time, Chinese immigration has grown rapidly. Chinese Americans have settled in many states besides California. Today, Chinese Americans have better opportunities for education and employment.

1. The main idea of this passage is that—
   A. Chinese people came to America after the Gold Rush.
   B. Chinese immigrants paid special taxes and fees.
   C. Chinese Americans are citizens today.
   D. Racial prejudice once denied opportunities to Chinese Americans.

2. The word <u>prejudice</u> in this passage means—
   F. exclusion.
   G. strong dislike.
   H. Chinese.
   J. immigrants.

3. Because of prejudice, Chinese people in America—
   A. had few rights.
   B. settled in California.
   C. became citizens.
   D. paid no taxes.

4. The Chinese Exclusion Act kept Chinese people from—
   F. going to court.
   G. going to school.
   H. entering the United States.
   J. becoming citizens.

5. Chinese immigration grew when—
   A. the Exclusion Act was overturned.
   B. Chinese Americans fought in court.
   C. World War II began.
   D. California became a state.

Notes for Home: Your child identified the main idea and supporting details of a passage and used context clues to understand new words. *Home Activity:* Have your child tell you the main idea of an article. Encourage him or her to use context clues to understand new words.

© Scott Foresman 6

Phonics: Schwa Sound (Within Word)

Directions: The **schwa sound** is a vowel sound heard in unstressed syllables. The **o** in **person** is an example of a schwa sound. This sound can be spelled with any vowel combination of vowels. Read each word below. Underline the vowel or vowels that stand for the schwa. Some words may contain more than one schwa sound.

1. remedies
2. television
3. several
4. celebrate

5. permanently
6. Tennessee
7. favorite
8. competition

9. against
10. stability
11. opponent
12. different

Directions: In each sentence, one of the underlined words contains the schwa sound. Write the word on the line. Underline the vowel or vowels that stand for the schwa sound.

_____ 13. The track competition was being held in the central field area.

_____ 14. People from dozens of states filled the stadium to watch the competitors.

_____ 15. The racers in the relay practiced passing the baton.

_____ 16. They were a bit nervous about the upcoming race.

_____ 17. One runner was able to regain her balance after her initial fall at the starting line.

_____ 18. Everyone was relieved that the athlete had not injured herself again.

_____ 19. The winner was honored for her amazing speed and stamina at the medal ceremony.

_____ 20. The spectators cheered all of the athletes for giving their best.

Notes for Home: Your child identified the schwa sound in words. *Home Activity:* Read a sports story with your child. Help your child find words with schwa sounds and check them in a dictionary. (The symbol for the schwa sound is ə.)

© Scott Foresman 6

Almanac

An **almanac** is a yearly book that contains calendars, weather information, and dates of holidays, as well as charts and tables of current information in many different subject areas.

Directions: Study the information from an almanac. Then answer the questions that follow.

Table of Contents

General Index

Olympic Games—Summer Medals Table

Berlin, 1936		Rome, 1960		Barcelona, 1992	
Country	**Medals Won**	**Country**	**Medals Won**	**Country**	**Medals Won**
Germany	89	USSR	99	Unified Team	111
USA	56	USA	71	USA	108
Hungary	16	Italy	36	Germany	82

Medalists, Women's 100-meter race

Berlin, 1936		Rome, 1960		Barcelona, 1992	
Athlete	**Time (sec.)**	**Athlete**	**Time (sec.)**	**Athlete**	**Time (sec.)**
H. Stephens, USA	11.5	W. Rudolph, USA	11.0	G. Devers, USA	10.82
S. Walasiewicz, POL	11.7	D. Hyman, GBR	11.3	J. Cuthbert, JAM	10.83
K. Krauß, GER	11.9	G. Leone, ITALY	11.3	I. Privalova, EUN	10.84

© Scott Foresman 6

1. Which subject area in the almanac might tell you how many miles equal one kilometer? On which page does this section of the almanac begin?

_____

_____

2. In which section would you look for information about the imports and exports of India?

_____

3. In which section might you find the birth date of Albert Einstein? _____

_____

4. On which page in the almanac does the section on the arts begin? _____

5. In which section of the almanac will you find information about the Olympics?

_____

6. If you were looking for specific information on the Special Olympics, would you use the table of contents or the index? Explain.

_____

_____

7. How much faster did Wilma Rudolph run the 100-meter race than Dorothy Hyman?

_____

8. How many medals did the United States win in the 1992 Summer Olympics? Where were these Olympic games held?

_____

_____

9. The winner of the Olympic 100-meter race is often referred to as the world's fastest runner. Suppose you were writing a report on the history of the world's fastest women. Would the data in the second table be useful? What other data might you need? Explain.

_____

_____

_____

10. If you were making a line graph of the local high weather temperatures for the past month, would an almanac be useful? If you were making a weather map to show the highest temperatures ever recorded, would an almanac be useful? Explain.

_____

_____

_____

Notes for Home: Your child studied an almanac and answered questions about its use. ***Home Activity:*** Look at the almanacs in a library's reference section with your child. Use the table of contents and index to find out and discuss what kinds of information can be found in almanacs.

© Scott Foresman 6

Summarizing

- To **summarize** means to give a brief statement of the main idea of an article or the most important events in a story.

- When you summarize an article, include the main idea or ideas and only the most important supporting details.

Directions: Reread "Winners Never Quit." Summarize the main idea of the article. Then summarize the important supporting details by completing each sentence in the web. One sentence has been completed for you.

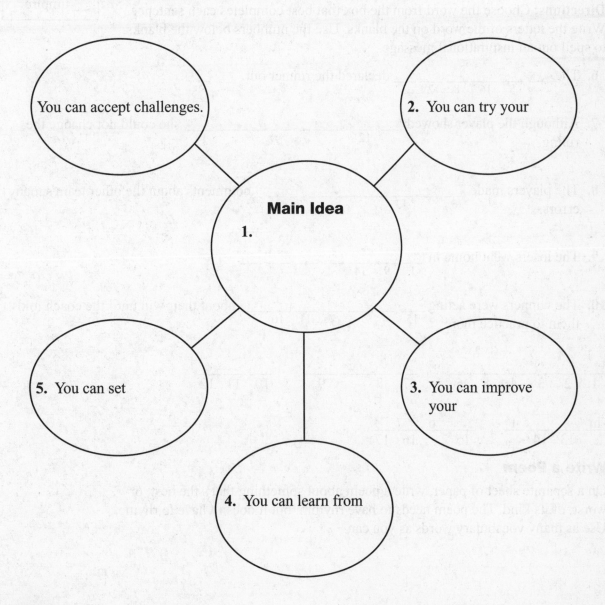

You can accept challenges.

2. You can try your

Main Idea

1.

5. You can set

3. You can improve your

4. You can learn from

Notes for Home: Your child summarized the main idea and most important supporting details of an article. *Home Activity:* With your child, summarize a newspaper or magazine article that you have both read. Create a web similar to the one above.

© Scott Foresman 6

Vocabulary

Directions: Choose the word from the box that is the most opposite in meaning from each word below. Write the word on the line.

Check the Words You Know

__ defiance
__ despair
__ grandeur
__ haughty
__ scornful
__ umpire

_____ 1. humble

_____ 2. compliance

_____ 3. admiring

_____ 4. hope

_____ 5. shabbiness

Directions: Choose the word from the box that best completes each sentence. Write the letters of the word on the blanks. Use the numbers below the blanks to spell out an inspirational message.

6. The ___ ___ ___ ___ ___ declared the runner out.
      5   16 8   2   3

7. Although the player showed ___ ___ ___ ___ ___ ___ ___ ___, she could not change the
                                    12   17
   ruling.

8. The players made ___ ___ ___ ___ ___ ___ ___ ___ comments about the other team's many
                      6   13
   errors.

9. The losers went home in ___ ___ ___ ___ ___ ___ ___.
                            1   9   14

10. The winners were acting ___ ___ ___ ___ ___ ___ ___ about their win until the coach told
                            15 4   7   11 10
    them to practice more!

___ ___ ___ ___ ___ ___   ___ ___ ᵛ ___ ___   ___ ___ ___
 1   2   3   4   5   6   7   8   9   10 11 12

m ___ ___ t   ___ o ___ ___.
  13 14   15   16 17

Write a Poem

On a separate sheet of paper, write a poem about something that's the best, or worst, of its kind. The poem needs to have rhythm, but it doesn't have to rhyme. Use as many vocabulary words as you can.

Notes for Home: Your child identified and used vocabulary words from the poem *Casey at the Bat*. **Home Activity:** Use the vocabulary words *defiance, scornful,* and *haughty* and challenge your child to act out each emotion. Then let your child give you similar words to act out.

© Scott Foresman 6

Summarizing

- **Summarizing** means giving a brief statement—no more than a few sentences—of the main idea of an article or the most important events in a story.

Directions: Reread the part of *Casey at the Bat* in which Casey waits for and swings at the last pitch. Then answer the questions below. Think about Casey's actions and their outcome to help you summarize.

> The sneer is gone from Casey's lip, his teeth are clenched in hate,
> He pounds with cruel violence his bat upon the plate;
> And now the pitcher holds the ball, and now he lets it go,
> And now the air is shattered by the force of Casey's blow.
>
> Oh, somewhere in this favored land the sun is shining bright,
> The band is playing somewhere, and somewhere hearts are light;
> And somewhere men are laughing, and somewhere children shout,
> But there is no joy in Mudville—mighty Casey has struck out.
>
> From *Casey at the Bat* by Ernest Lawrence, 1888.

1. Summarize what happens in the first group of lines.

_____

_____

2. What happens after the first group of lines that isn't stated in the second group of lines?

_____

_____

3. What is the most important phrase in the second group of lines? Why?

_____

_____

4. Summarize the action for this part of the poem (both groups of lines).

_____

_____

5. On a separate sheet of paper, summarize the action of the Mudville team during the game.

Notes for Home: Your child summarized events in a poem. *Home Activity:* Discuss a favorite story, movie, or television show. Read another poem. Encourage your child to summarize the most important events.

© Scott Foresman 6

1.	Ⓐ	Ⓑ	Ⓒ	Ⓓ
2.	Ⓕ	Ⓖ	Ⓗ	Ⓙ
3.	Ⓐ	Ⓑ	Ⓒ	Ⓓ
4.	Ⓕ	Ⓖ	Ⓗ	Ⓙ
5.	Ⓐ	Ⓑ	Ⓒ	Ⓓ
6.	Ⓕ	Ⓖ	Ⓗ	Ⓙ
7.	Ⓐ	Ⓑ	Ⓒ	Ⓓ
8.	Ⓕ	Ⓖ	Ⓗ	Ⓙ
9.	Ⓐ	Ⓑ	Ⓒ	Ⓓ
10.	Ⓕ	Ⓖ	Ⓗ	Ⓙ
11.	Ⓐ	Ⓑ	Ⓒ	Ⓓ
12.	Ⓕ	Ⓖ	Ⓗ	Ⓙ
13.	Ⓐ	Ⓑ	Ⓒ	Ⓓ
14.	Ⓕ	Ⓖ	Ⓗ	Ⓙ
15.	Ⓐ	Ⓑ	Ⓒ	Ⓓ

© Scott Foresman 6

Selection Test

Directions: Choose the best answer to each item. Mark the letter for the answer you have chosen.

Part 1: Vocabulary

Find the answer choice that means about the same as the underlined word in each sentence.

1. Everyone stared at the umpire.
   A. manager of a baseball team
   B. player on a professional sports team
   C. fan at a baseball game
   D. person who rules on the plays in the game

2. The fans watched in despair.
   F. state of looking forward to something
   G. state of hopelessness
   H. state of excitement
   J. state of nervousness

3. Sean had a scornful expression on his face.
   A. able to agree with others
   B. courteous; polite
   C. mocking
   D. full of teasing and fun

4. Aunt Mildred is a haughty woman.
   F. well-mannered
   G. very happy; always cheerful
   H. full of grace
   J. overly proud and self-confident

5. The house had a sense of grandeur.
   A. ability to last a long time
   B. originality; newness
   C. greatness; splendor
   D. simple style

6. Leon answered with defiance.
   F. resistance to power or authority
   G. uncontrolled energy
   H. lack of enthusiasm
   J. impatience

Part 2: Comprehension

Use what you know about the poem to answer each item.

7. The fans felt sure the Mudville team would win if—
   A. Flynn got on base.
   B. Casey got a chance to bat.
   C. Blake got a walk.
   D. the umpire was fair.

8. Why did the fans stop yelling at the umpire?
   F. They realized the calls were fair.
   G. Casey signaled for them to be quiet.
   H. Casey yelled at the umpire himself.
   J. The umpire yelled back.

9. How did Casey feel as he stepped up to the plate?
   A. confident
   B. nervous
   C. excited
   D. angry

10. Which is the best summary of the events before Casey's turn at bat?
    F. Two batters made outs.
    G. There were six points scored and two outs.
    H. The game was close until two Mudville players made outs.
    J. Mudville was losing four to two with two outs and two players on base.

© Scott Foresman 6

GO ON

11. Which is the best summary of the events after Casey stepped up to the plate?
    - A. Casey let two strikes go by, swung at and missed the third pitch, and struck out.
    - B. The umpire made sure that Casey would not hit the ball.
    - C. The pitcher changed the way he threw each ball, so Casey missed three pitches in a row and struck out.
    - D. The pitcher threw three balls, but Casey swung at them and struck out.

12. How can you tell which team won the game?
    - F. Mudville won, because Casey is a local hero.
    - G. The opposing team won, because its players were more talented.
    - H. Mudville won, because the narrator did not name the other team.
    - J. The opposing team won, because no one is laughing or shouting.

13. Which line from the poem suggests that Casey became determined after two strikes were called?
    - A. "With a smile of Christian charity great Casey's visage shone"
    - B. "They saw his face grow stern and cold, they saw his muscles strain"
    - C. "But Casey still ignored it, and the umpire said, 'Strike two.'"
    - D. "And now the air is shattered by the force of Casey's blow."

14. Calling Flynn a "lulu" suggests that he—
    - F. is a better fielder than hitter.
    - G. doesn't have much experience.
    - H. is a bit crazy.
    - J. doesn't get along with Casey.

15. The speaker's point of view in this poem is most like that of—
    - A. an umpire.
    - B. an angry fan.
    - C. a reporter.
    - D. a judge.

STOP

© Scott Foresman 6

Predicting

Directions: Read the story. Then read each question about the story. Choose the best answer to each question. Mark the letter for the answer you have chosen.

The Humble Princess

As the two knights entered the inn, they stopped short in the doorway. A ragged young woman was scrubbing the table. She looked up at the sight of the knights and spoke in a soft and sweet voice: "Please come and sit down. Come in and hear my story." The knights sat down. If this woman were in trouble, they were ready to help.

"Once I was a princess," began the woman. "I was beautiful to look at, but I wasn't nice. My parents spoiled me. They gave me everything I wanted, and it only made me greedy for more toys and more gowns. Soon I was famous for my rudeness and selfishness. I was very unkind to my servants. I never thought about their feelings at all.

"Hoping I could learn better manners, my parents went to my wise old uncle for advice. After some thought, he said, 'Make her wear old clothes and work for a living. That way, she will learn to put other people first and stop thinking so much about herself. Let her come back to you in two years. I think by then she will have learned her lesson.'

"They sent me away as he suggested. I have done all kinds of work and traveled many miles. I have learned my lesson! The two years are up and my parents expect me to return. May I ask you to take me back to the palace?"

The knights looked at one another, then the Red Knight spoke. "Your highness, we will! But we must first continue our search for the lost prince of our Kingdom. Will you help us?"

1. The princess used to be—
   A. humble.
   B. ugly.
   C. rude.
   D. a liar.

2. The princess's punishment is fitting because—
   F. she wants to be a servant.
   G. her parents are disappointed.
   H. her uncle hates her.
   J. she treated her servants badly.

3. Stories of this kind usually—
   A. are in rhyme.
   B. have lots of jokes.
   C. describe characters who get away with bad behavior.
   D. end happily.

4. How will the princess answer the Red Knight?
   F. She will help him.
   G. She will refuse to help him.
   H. She will remain a servant.
   J. She will lead him straight to the lost prince.

5. When the princess's parents see her again, they will be—
   A. pleased.
   B. disappointed.
   C. angry.
   D. upset.

© Scott Foresman 6

Notes for Home: Your child read a story and predicted what would happen next. *Home Activity:* Watch a TV show with your child. At a break, challenge her or him to predict what will happen next. Compare your child's prediction with what actually happens.

Phonics: Schwa Sound (Final Syllable)

Directions: The **schwa sound** is a vowel sound heard in unstressed syllables. In the word **even,** the last **e** has a schwa sound. It can be spelled with any vowel or combination of vowels. Read each word below. Listen for the schwa sound in the final syllable. Underline the vowel or vowels that stand for the schwa sound.

1. silence
2. humor
3. former
4. seven
5. instant

6. Simon
7. listen
8. audience
9. rehearsal
10. random

11. anxious
12. instant
13. pretzel
14. patience
15. unravel

Directions: Circle the word with a schwa sound in each sentence. Underline the vowel or vowels that stand for the schwa sound in the final syllable.

_____ 16. The next batter saw that the softball game was on the line.

_____ 17. She walked to the plate, feeling the pressure to win.

_____ 18. The players and fans yelled her name.

_____ 19. She tried not to hear the noise, but she was only human.

_____ 20. It was a good thing that she was the anchor of the team.

_____ 21. The pitcher threw the ball low and fast, and she swung hard.

_____ 22. She hit a grounder to the shortstop.

_____ 23. The shortstop threw the ball to the person at first base.

_____ 24. She got to first just a second before the baseman caught the throw.

_____ 25. Now she could focus on stealing the next base.

Notes for Home: Your child identified the schwa sound in unstressed syllables, such as the *e* in *even*. **Home Activity:** Help your child identify words with more than one syllable that have a schwa sound in the final syllable. Ask your child to say the words aloud.

© Scott Foresman 6

Announcement/Poster/Advertisement

An **announcement** is something that is made known. A **poster** is a type of announcement that gives specific facts about an event. It should answer the questions *Who?, What?, When?, Where?,* and *Why?* An **advertisement** is an announcement that tries to persuade readers, listeners, or viewers to do something, buy something, or feel a particular way.

Directions: Read the poster advertising a car wash. Use it to answer the questions that follow.

Get a Clean Car and Support Your Little League

The Rapid River Little League will be holding a car wash to raise money for much needed new uniforms and equipment.

Car Wash
Saturday, May 23rd
10:00 A.M. to 6:00 P.M.
State Fair Grounds, 2122 Lincoln Avenue
Single (wash only) $4.00
Double (wash + wax) $6.00
Grand Slam (wash, wax, windows, interior) $10.00

Rain Date:
Saturday, May 30th

You'll get a shine so bright, you'll need sunglasses!

---

1. What is the purpose of the poster/advertisement? _____
   _____
   _____

2. What event will take place? _____

3. At what time and on what day does the event take place? _____
   _____

4. Who organized this event? _____

5. What will the organizers of this event do with the money they raise? _____
   _____

© Scott Foresman 6

6. What will happen if it rains on May 23rd? _____

_____

7. What words does the poster/advertisement use to persuade readers? _____

_____

8. Why do you think the poster/advertisement uses different sizes and types of letters?

_____

_____

9. Why do you think the poster includes art? _____

_____

_____

10. Use the space below to make your own poster to advertise the opening Little League game between the Dairy Flo Dragons and the Supreme Taco Superstars. Be sure to answer the five "W" questions.

 Notes for Home: Your child answered questions about a poster advertising a fundraiser and created a poster to persuade people to attend a Little League game. ***Home Activity:*** Work with your child to create a poster about an upcoming family event.

© Scott Foresman 6

Theme

- The **theme** of a story is the underlying meaning or message.

- To determine the theme of a story, ask yourself, "What does the author want me to learn or know?" Your answer should be a "big idea" that can stand on its own away from the story.

- Many stories have more than one theme. To be valid, a statement of theme should be supported by evidence from the text.

Directions: Reread "A Winning Essay." Then complete the table. Write three pieces of evidence that support the first theme. Use the supporting evidence given to write a second theme and give another piece of evidence that supports it.

Theme	Evidence that Supports the Theme
Theme 1: People have different ways of expressing love.	1.
	2.
	3.
4. **Theme 2:**	4. Mattie has a hard time expressing her love for her mother.
	5.

Notes for Home: Your child identified the themes in a story and provided evidence to support those themes. *Home Activity:* Discuss a familiar book or movie with your child. Help your child identify one or more themes of the story.

© Scott Foresman 6

Vocabulary

Directions: Draw a line to connect each word on the left with its definition on the right.

1. constellation

2. marveled

3. orbit

4. solar

5. universe

a planet's elliptical path around another body in space

the whole of existing things, including all space and matter

a group of stars with a recognizable shape

wondered at

of the sun

Check the Words You Know

__ constellation
__ marveled
__ orbit
__ relative
__ solar
__ universe

Directions: Choose the word from the box that best completes each sentence. Write the word on the line to the left. Then find and circle the words in the puzzle below. Words may appear across, down, or diagonally.

_____ 6. Any body that goes around our Sun is part of our _____ system.

_____ 7. Jupiter is huge _____ to Earth.

_____ 8. The comet's _____ brought it near Earth.

_____ 9. The _____ contains everything there is, including all space and matter.

_____ 10. The Big Dipper is a _____ that got its name because the stars are in the shape of a dipper in the night sky.

Write a News Report

On a separate sheet of paper, write about the discovery of a new planet. Describe the planet's size, its stars, its sun(s), and so on. Use as many vocabulary words as you can.

```
E V B A C S O R B I T Z I N
G Y J U Q U C E X S S O S Y
F C O N S T E L L A T I O N
B W F I A C D A M I Z T L I
P Y A V J U A T I Y L L A Z
S N T E R R B I A T V X R E
R J H R V S O V H N X D O F
D N I S G M J E Z A J I H Y
N Q T E A H N Y S S H D E M
```

Notes for Home: Your child identified and used vocabulary words from "The Night of the Pomegranate." *Home Activity:* With your child, look for names and descriptions of parts of the universe. Together, make a picture dictionary of the words you find.

© Scott Foresman 6

Theme

- The **theme** of a story is the underlying meaning or message.
- Many stories have more than one theme.

Directions: Reread the part of "The Night of the Pomegranate" about Harriet 's and Clayton's models. Then answer the questions below. Ask yourself what the author wants you to learn by reading this story.

Mars was near the Earth this month. The nights had been November cold but clear as glass, and Harriet had been out to see Mars every night, which was why she hadn't gotten her solar system finished, why she was so tired, why Mom made Tom drive her to school. It was all Mars's fault.

She was using the tape on Ms. Krensky's desk when Clayton Beemer arrived with his dad. His solar system came from the hobby store. The planets were Styrofoam balls, all different sizes and painted the right colors. Saturn's rings were clear plastic painted over as delicately as insect wings.

Harriet looked down at her own Saturn. Her rings were drooping despite all the tape. They looked like a limp skirt on a . . . on a ball of scrunched-up newspaper.

From SOME OF THE KINDER PLANETS. Text copyright © 1993 by Tim Wynne-Jones. First published in Canada by Groundwood Books / Douglas McIntyre. Reprinted by their permission and Orchard Books, New York.

1. Why is it Mars's fault that Harriet has not completed her model?

_____

2. In your own words, what is Clayton's model like? Why is it like that?

_____

_____

3. In your own words, what is Harriet's model like? Why is it like that?

_____

_____

4. What is the difference between Clayton's and Harriet's approaches to learning about the solar system?

_____

_____

5. On a separate sheet of paper, explain what you think the theme of this story is.

Notes for Home: Your child identified a story's theme, or the underlying meaning or message. **Home Activity:** Read a favorite story together. Encourage your child to explain its theme. Discuss how this theme relates to real-life experiences.

© Scott Foresman 6

Name _____

1.	Ⓐ	Ⓑ	Ⓒ	Ⓓ
2.	Ⓕ	Ⓖ	Ⓗ	Ⓙ
3.	Ⓐ	Ⓑ	Ⓒ	Ⓓ
4.	Ⓕ	Ⓖ	Ⓗ	Ⓙ
5.	Ⓐ	Ⓑ	Ⓒ	Ⓓ
6.	Ⓕ	Ⓖ	Ⓗ	Ⓙ
7.	Ⓐ	Ⓑ	Ⓒ	Ⓓ
8.	Ⓕ	Ⓖ	Ⓗ	Ⓙ
9.	Ⓐ	Ⓑ	Ⓒ	Ⓓ
10.	Ⓕ	Ⓖ	Ⓗ	Ⓙ
11.	Ⓐ	Ⓑ	Ⓒ	Ⓓ
12.	Ⓕ	Ⓖ	Ⓗ	Ⓙ
13.	Ⓐ	Ⓑ	Ⓒ	Ⓓ
14.	Ⓕ	Ⓖ	Ⓗ	Ⓙ
15.	Ⓐ	Ⓑ	Ⓒ	Ⓓ

© Scott Foresman 6

Selection Test

Directions: Choose the best answer to each item. Mark the letter for the answer you have chosen.

Part 1: Vocabulary

Find the answer choice that means about the same as the underlined word in each sentence.

1. Imagine what it would be like to travel throughout the universe.
   A. solar system
   B. all that exists
   C. group of stars
   D. wide desert

2. Sandra drew a picture showing Pluto's orbit.
   F. color
   G. planet's path around the sun
   H. size
   J. what a planet is made of

3. That constellation is called Orion.
   A. ring around a planet
   B. spaceship
   C. large number of planets
   D. group of stars that form a shape

4. We marveled at the hummingbird.
   F. had great hopes
   G. set a value for
   H. were filled with wonder
   J. refused to believe

5. The relative strength of steel makes it a good choice for cars.
   A. as compared with others
   B. important
   C. of or related to metal
   D. unusual

6. Heather's house uses solar power.
   F. of or from the sun
   G. electrical
   H. modern
   J. without heat

Part 2: Comprehension

Use what you know about the story to answer each item.

7. Why did Harriet use grape gum to construct her model of Pluto?
   A. She ran out of tape and glue.
   B. Pluto is cold.
   C. She liked the purple color.
   D. Pluto is small.

8. How did Harriet recognize Mars in the night sky?
   F. It twinkled.
   G. It was red.
   H. Mrs. Pond pointed to it.
   J. She had a map of the constellations.

9. Clayton Beemer's solar-system model—
   A. was very similar to Harriet's.
   B. made many students ask him questions.
   C. was elaborate and neatly done.
   D. used marbles and pomegranate seeds.

10. With Earth represented by Kevin's marble, Harriet compared Mars to a pomegranate seed because it—
    F. was the only thing she had with her.
    G. reminded her of Mrs. Pond.
    H. had a surprising taste.
    J. was the right color and relative size.

© Scott Foresman 6

GO ON

11. What did Harriet learn about herself in this story?
    A.   She was glad her parents were not interested in helping her with school projects.
    B.   She did not know very much about any of the planets.
    C.   She did not care what her classmates though about her project.
    D.   She was more interested in observing Mars than in making a model.

12. What is a theme of this story?
    F.   Pomegranates are tart.
    G.   Sometimes Mars is visible in the sky.
    H.   Sometimes we learn more from direct experience than from a school project.
    J.   Work is easier if you have a partner.

13. Why did Harriet joke about her solar-system model and pull it apart?
    A.   She was embarrassed by it.
    B.   She was hungry.
    C.   She wanted to improve it.
    D.   She wanted to show off her strength.

14. Ms. Krensky's opinion of Harriet's work improved when she realized that Harriet—
    F.   had a better model before she took it apart.
    G.   was more interested in learning about pomegranates than planets.
    H.   knew a great deal about Mars.
    J.   had seen Mars in a movie.

15. Mrs. Pond tells Harriet about *The War of the Worlds* broadcast in order to—
    A.   scare Harriet.
    B.   share an interesting childhood memory with Harriet.
    C.   show how foolish people can be.
    D.   prove that Mars will someday collide with Earth.

STOP

© Scott Foresman 6

Name _____

Compare and Contrast

Directions: Read the story. Then read each question about the story. Choose the best answer to each question. Mark the letter for the answer you have chosen.

Wish You Were Here

Helen knew all about Rome from her aunt's picture postcards. Each week a new one arrived, and Helen added it to her album. Now, visiting her aunt for the first time, she felt as if the postcards had come to life!

The postcards had made Rome seem still and calm. But the living city was filled with movement and noise. Bus passengers stuck in traffic complained as much as the people back home. Here, though, most poked their heads out the window to see what was the matter and to offer advice. Cars and motorcycles roared by and seemed to park wherever they pleased, even on sidewalks.

Pictures hadn't told Helen how different eating in Rome would be. Unlike stores in America, shops were closed for a few hours for lunch. People took a long time over their meals. Helen liked that. Lunch was always such a rush back home! Helen loved the food. Her favorite was *gelato,* Italian ice cream. It was richer and much better than ice cream at home.

Helen could not get used to the age of the buildings. Rome had many new buildings, of course, but she knew that nothing in America was as old as most of what she saw in Rome. Helen felt that every café, every house, and every sidewalk was a piece of history. She was so overwhelmed by her experiences, that when she wrote to her friend Pablo all she could say was, "Wish you were here."

1. Helen feels that her postcards have come to life because—
   A. things are different in Rome.
   B. she can see things firsthand.
   C. she is a tourist.
   D. her aunt lives in Rome.

2. Compared to Americans, Helen finds Romans —
   F. openly curious.
   G. very stuffy.
   H. faster eaters.
   J. bus riders.

3. Helen observes that when stuck in traffic, both Romans and Americans—
   A. get involved.
   B. suffer in silence.
   C. complain.
   D. get out and walk.

4. Americans eat hastily at lunch while Romans—
   F. eat a lot.
   G. take their time.
   H. eat *gelato*.
   J. eat on the run.

5. Helen observes that most buildings in Rome are—
   A. newer than those in America.
   B. about the same age as those in America.
   C. in worse shape than those in America.
   D. much older than those in America.

© Scott Foresman 6

Notes for Home: Your child read a passage and made comparisons and contrasts. *Home Activity:* With your child, compare and contrast some popular ethnic foods. For instance, pizza and burritos are made of grains and vegetables, though they look and taste different.

Word Study: Contractions

Directions: A **contraction** is a word formed by joining two words with an **apostrophe.** The apostrophe takes the place of one or more letters. Read the journal entry below. Circle each contraction. Write the contraction on the line to the left. Then write the two words that the contraction combines on the right.

> I wasn't sure what I saw the other night. As I looked up at the night sky, gazing at the stars I know so well, I spotted bright bands of shimmering light. They didn't look like stars, and I realized I hadn't seen anything like them before. Waves of greenish light rippled in the sky. "They're moving!" I thought to myself. I couldn't believe my eyes when the whole sky seemed to come alive with these lights. "It's not possible!" I said. I later found out that these bands of light are called Northern Lights. I'll never forget that sight as long as I live!

Contraction

1. _____
3. _____
5. _____
7. _____
9. _____
11. _____
13. _____

Two Words It Combines

2. _____
4. _____
6. _____
8. _____
10. _____
12. _____
14. _____

Directions: Combine each word pair to form a contraction. Write the contraction on the line.

15. do not   _____
16. you would _____
17. let us   _____

18. will not   _____
19. should not _____
20. are not   _____

Notes for Home: Your child formed contractions, such as *that's* from the words *that* and *is.* *Home Activity:* Listen to a radio or television program, and work with your child to identify spoken contractions. Ask your child to tell you the two words that each contraction represents.

© Scott Foresman 6

Textbook/Trade Book/Magazine/Periodical

A **textbook** teaches about a particular subject matter, such as science, social studies, or math. A **trade book** is any book that is not a textbook, periodical, or reference book. A **magazine** or **periodical** is published at set intervals (weekly, monthly, quarterly, and so on). It contains news articles, opinion columns, advertisements, cartoons, reports, and other current information. To locate information in these sources, scan the table of contents, chapter titles, headings, subheadings, captions, and index. You can also locate specific magazine articles using *The Readers' Guide to Periodical Literature.*

Directions: Use the textbook, trade book, and magazine samples below to answer the questions that follow.

The Universe Around Us • Unit 2

Chapter 5
Lesson 2: The Planets

Vocabulary   solar, Sun, planet, moon

Study Questions: How many planets are in our solar system? What are they called? What is a moon? How many of our planets have moons?

Solar means "of the Sun." Our solar system has a sun at its center, and nine planets that orbit it. (See Fig. 1.)

The **Sun** is a giant, hot star. It gives off energy in the form of visible light, invisible light (ultraviolet and infrared light), and gamma rays.

The nine **planets** in our solar system are Mercury, Venus, Earth, Mars, Jupiter, Saturn, Uranus, Neptune, and Pluto.

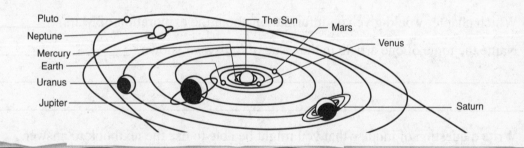

Space Exploration: Travels to the Moon and Beyond

Table of Contents

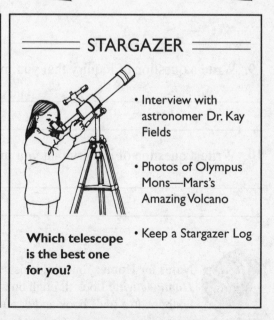

STARGAZER

- Interview with astronomer Dr. Kay Fields

- Photos of Olympus Mons—Mars's Amazing Volcano

- Keep a Stargazer Log

Which telescope is the best one for you?

© Scott Foresman 6

1. Would you most likely find the textbook page from *The Universe Around Us* in a science, social studies, or math class? Explain.

_____

2. Why does the textbook page include study questions near the beginning of the lesson? Read the first study question and answer it.

_____

_____

_____

3. Why do you think *solar, Sun,* and *planet* on the textbook page are set in **boldfaced** type?

_____

_____

4. Scan the table of contents in the trade book *Space Exploration*. What is this book about? What kinds of information would you expect to find in it?

_____

_____

5. What was the name of the spacecraft that flew to the moon? _____

6. Which chapter would give you information about the exploration of Mars? _____

7. Name the topic of one article in the issue of *Stargazer* shown. _____

_____

_____

8. Write a question of inquiry that you might be able to use the textbook to answer.

_____

_____

9. Write a question of inquiry that you might be able to use the trade book to answer.

_____

_____

10. Write a question of inquiry that you might be able to use the magazine to answer.

_____

_____

Notes for Home: Your child answered questions about a textbook, trade book, and a magazine. *Home Activity:* Look through one of your child's textbooks with your child. Compare the textbook to a trade book and/or a magazine. Discuss how to find information in each source.

© Scott Foresman 6

Drawing Conclusions

- When you **draw a conclusion,** you make a decision or form an opinion about what you read. Drawing conclusions is also known as *making inferences.*

- A conclusion should make sense and be based on facts and details in the writing, as well as your own experience.

Directions: Reread "Dumbfounded." Then complete the table. Read the three possible conclusions about Grandpa, choose the best conclusion, and then give evidence from the story to support your choice. Then do the same for the possible conclusions about Billy. Below the table, write your own conclusion about the relationship between Billy and Grandpa.

Possible Conclusions	Best Conclusion	Evidence (Story Details and What I Know)
Grandpa is allergic to dust. Grandpa is amazed at Billy's achievement. Grandpa always becomes emotional around Billy.	1.	2.
Billy thinks saving money is fun. Billy thinks spending money is fun. Billy is willing to work hard to get himself some dogs.	3.	4.

5. What conclusion can you draw about the relationship between Billy and Grandpa? Why?

_____

_____

Notes for Home: Your child drew conclusions about characters in a story. *Home Activity:* Discuss with your child the conclusions drawn by letter writers in the editorial section of the local newspaper. Check to see whether the writers provide supporting evidence for their conclusions.

© Scott Foresman 6

Vocabulary

Directions: Write the word from the box that best matches each definition.
Write the word on the line.

Check the Words You Know

__ ancestor

__ boundary

__ gnarled

__ reassuring

__ wigwam

_____ 1. knotted; twisted

_____ 2. a dome-shaped hut made of bark

_____ 3. a distant relative from whom one
is descended

_____ 4. restoring to confidence

_____ 5. limit; border

Directions: Choose the word from the box that best completes each sentence.
Write the word on the line to the left.

_____ 6. The _____ of our property is marked by a stone wall.

_____ 7. Next to the stone wall is a _____ tree with branches that twist
around each other.

_____ 8. When I look at that tree, I feel calm; it is very _____.

_____ 9. I can imagine an _____ of mine from a hundred years ago
sitting under that same tree.

_____ 10. I wonder if long ago, my family lived
in a _____ near this tree and had the
same view as I have now.

Write a Postcard

On a separate sheet of paper, write a postcard. Imagine you are visiting
the home of one of your ancestors. Describe what you see and what
you imagine life might have been like for your ancestor. Use as many
vocabulary words as you can.

 Notes for Home: Your child identified and used vocabulary words from "Spring Paint."
Home Activity: Talk about how life was the same or different for your ancestors. Try to
include the vocabulary words in your discussion.

© Scott Foresman 6

Drawing Conclusions

- **Drawing conclusions** means making sensible decisions or forming reasonable opinions about what you read.

- A **conclusion** should be based on facts and details in the writing, as well as your own experience.

Directions: Reread the scene in "Spring Paint" in which the young man enters the lodge. Then answer the questions below. Use story details to help you draw conclusions.

"Come in, then," said the old man. He smiled a hard smile, knowing that whoever came into his lodge would freeze.

Then a young man entered the wigwam. His face was painted with red lines and circles that looked like the sun. There was a warm smile on his face; and as he sat down on the other side of the fire, the old man felt the young man's warm breath. The old man began to sweat. He felt himself growing weaker.

"Go away," said the old man.

"No," said the young man, his voice as gentle as the sound of a summer breeze. "It is you who must leave now. Your season has ended."

"Spring Paint" from BOWMAN'S STORE by Joseph Bruchac. Copyright © 1997 by Joseph Bruchac. Used by permission of Dial Books for Young Readers, a division of Penguin Putnam Inc.

1. Which season of the year does the young man represent? How do you know?

_____

_____

2. Which season does the old man represent? How do you know?

_____

_____

3. Why do you think the old man tells the young man to go away?

_____

_____

4. The word *wigwam* suggests that the story originated in which culture or cultures?

_____

_____

5. On a separate sheet of paper, explain how this myth relates to the grandfather's search for bloodroot flowers.

Notes for Home: Your child formed conclusions based on story details. ***Home Activity:*** Discuss specific actions of real-life people. Challenge your child to draw conclusions about why these actions happened and what these actions reveal about each person.

© Scott Foresman 6

1.	Ⓐ	Ⓑ	Ⓒ	Ⓓ
2.	Ⓕ	Ⓖ	Ⓗ	Ⓙ
3.	Ⓐ	Ⓑ	Ⓒ	Ⓓ
4.	Ⓕ	Ⓖ	Ⓗ	Ⓙ
5.	Ⓐ	Ⓑ	Ⓒ	Ⓓ
6.	Ⓕ	Ⓖ	Ⓗ	Ⓙ
7.	Ⓐ	Ⓑ	Ⓒ	Ⓓ
8.	Ⓕ	Ⓖ	Ⓗ	Ⓙ
9.	Ⓐ	Ⓑ	Ⓒ	Ⓓ
10.	Ⓕ	Ⓖ	Ⓗ	Ⓙ
11.	Ⓐ	Ⓑ	Ⓒ	Ⓓ
12.	Ⓕ	Ⓖ	Ⓗ	Ⓙ
13.	Ⓐ	Ⓑ	Ⓒ	Ⓓ
14.	Ⓕ	Ⓖ	Ⓗ	Ⓙ
15.	Ⓐ	Ⓑ	Ⓒ	Ⓓ

© Scott Foresman 6

Selection Test

Directions: Choose the best answer to each item. Mark the letter for the answer you have chosen.

Part 1: Vocabulary

Find the answer choice that means about the same as the underlined word in each sentence.

1. Ali's <u>ancestor</u> built the house.
   A. offspring, such as a child or grandchild
   B. relative by marriage
   C. relative from whom one is descended, such as a grandparent
   D. person of the same generation or age group

2. They built a <u>wigwam</u>.
   F. dome-shaped hut
   G. light, narrow boat
   H. cone-shaped tent
   J. large rectangular dwelling

3. A river formed the <u>boundary</u>.
   A. pathway; trail
   B. landscape
   C. property
   D. border line; limit

4. The branches were <u>gnarled</u>.
   F. rough and twisted
   G. carved with a sharp object
   H. old and weak
   J. marked with dark blotches

5. Miguel was <u>reassuring</u> the new student.
   A. getting to know
   B. introducing
   C. giving confidence to
   D. preparing

Part 2: Comprehension

Use what you know about the selection to answer each item.

6. When the author was a boy, his special place was—
   F. Always Winter Land.
   G. the Woods.
   H. a tree house.
   J. the old man's lodge.

7. How did the author's grandfather make a living?
   A. He hunted and gathered.
   B. He owned a store.
   C. He bred wolves as pets.
   D. He worked for a neighbor.

8. What is special about the bloodroot flower?
   F. It looks like a paintbrush.
   G. It has an especially bright color.
   H. It has a wonderful smell.
   J. It is the first flower of spring.

9. The Abenaki and the Mohawks used the juice of bloodroot stems for—
   A. repelling insects.
   B. curing headaches.
   C. flavoring foods.
   D. healing wounds.

10. In the myth about Old Man Winter, what caused the bloodroot flowers to bloom?
    F. the Great White Bear
    G. Winter's cold fire
    H. the coming of spring
    J. the songs of birds

© Scott Foresman 6

GO ON

11. The myth explains why—
    A.   some animals sleep all winter.
    B.   the seasons change.
    C.   flowers bloom.
    D.   the sun rises and sets.

12. As a child, the author was—
    F.   a good storyteller.
    G.   a bit too reckless.
    H.   a skillful painter.
    J.   a careful observer.

13. One reason the author's grandfather painted the boy's face with bloodroot juice was to—
    A.   tell an old story in a new way.
    B.   make people laugh.
    C.   mark the boy as a warrior.
    D.   celebrate spring.

14. You can tell from this selection that the author's memories of his grandfather are closely linked with his memories of—
    F.   making up games.
    G.   learning about nature.
    H.   becoming a writer.
    J.   hunting for fossils.

15. Why did the author begin this story about his childhood by retelling a myth?
    A.   The myth connects in important ways with events in his own life.
    B.   The myth was one his grandfather loved to tell.
    C.   The myth gives the reader an entertaining mix of fact and fiction.
    D.   The myth helps the reader understand the author's family.

STOP

© Scott Foresman 6

Author's Viewpoint

REVIEW

Directions: Read the passage. Then read each question about the passage. Choose the best answer to each question. Mark the letter for the answer you have chosen.

Save That Green!!

Dear Editor,

What will be built on the last green area in the center of town? Will it be an unhealthy fast-food spot or another parking lot? We don't need those! There are two diners within a few blocks of the area, and people usually don't drive into the town center. Everyone knows there are always plenty of places to park on Mattingly Avenue and on Ruth Street.

What we need is a park to protect the gnarled old oak tree growing there. Everyone knows the tree I mean, the one with the trunk that's too big to put your arms around! That tree has been there for more than 100 years. Children climb it and use it as a lookout when they play pirates. Cows used to graze in its shade. Many a pair of sweethearts met underneath its leafy branches.

The old oak tree has its small place in history too. The great American writer Mark Twain once rested under it! He told the story in a letter. His train was late and he strolled into the town. Tired from his long day's journey, he stretched out in the shade of the oak and took a nap.

That old tree and this town both need a cool, peaceful park, not another parking lot. Let's save the green and tree!

         Signed,
         Theresa Ver

1. The main purpose of this article is to—
   A. entertain.
   B. persuade.
   C. explain.
   D. express.

2. Which of the following is a statement of fact that the author uses to support her argument?
   F. A parking lot will be built on the lot.
   G. The town does not need another park.
   H. Mark Twain once rested under the tree.
   J. Fast-food shops are unnecessary.

3. The author hopes readers will agree that—
   A. the oak tree must be saved.
   B. the town needs more parking.
   C. Mark Twain was a great writer.
   D. cows should be allowed to graze in the center of town again.

4. Words used to influence the reader include—
   F. pirates, cows
   G. trunk, branches
   H. train, nap
   J. unhealthy, peaceful

5. The author believes that—
   A. Mark Twain deserves a monument.
   B. a park would be the best use of the space around the tree.
   C. nothing more must be built in town.
   D. oak trees are the best trees.

Notes for Home: Your child identified the author's viewpoint in a letter to the editor. **Home Activity:** Discuss with your child an author's viewpoint for individual letters to editors from the local newspaper.

© Scott Foresman 6

Word Study: Inflected Endings: -ed, -ing

Directions: Two endings that are commonly added to verbs are **-ed** and **-ing**. Read the paragraph below. Circle the words with **-ed** and **-ing** endings. Then write the base word for each circled word.

Summers were a great time for harvesting fresh food from our grandparents' farm. Friends and family helped us gather the crops. Most of us worked in the fields and gardens, weeding and picking the fruits and vegetables until the sun went down. And every night—the food was delicious! We ate fresh corn, sweet green beans, and tomatoes plump with juice. I miss spending summers on the farm and being with my grandparents.

1. _____
2. _____
3. _____
4. _____
5. _____
6. _____
7. _____

Directions: Add **-ed** and **-ing** to each base word. Write the new word on the line.

Base Word	Add -ed	Add -ing
flicker	8. _____	9. _____
follow	10. _____	11. _____
search	12. _____	13. _____
watch	14. _____	15. _____
surround	16. _____	17. _____
return	18. _____	19. _____
invent	20. _____	21. _____
wander	22. _____	23. _____
stroll	24. _____	25. _____

Notes for Home: Your child identified and wrote words ending in *-ed* and *-ing*. **Home Activity:** Help your child think of other words with these endings. Make a table with two columns, one for *-ed* words and one for *-ing* words. Have your child write the words in the correct columns.

© Scott Foresman 6

The Readers' Guide to Periodical Literature

The *Readers' Guide to Periodical Literature* is a set of books that alphabetically lists, by author and subject, the articles that are published in periodicals.

Directions: Look at the set of *Readers' Guides*. Then answer the questions that follow.

1. How are the guides organized? How can you tell? _____

_____

2. Suppose you wanted to know more about a large Navaho Pow Wow that took place in the summer of 1997. Which volume would you use to see whether any articles had been written about this gathering? Explain.

_____

_____

3. Suppose you are writing about the lives and customs of Native Americans living on reservations today. Would it be more helpful to search recent volumes of the *Readers' Guide* or look in an encyclopedia? Explain.

_____

_____

4. Suppose you are writing about Native American stories by Joseph Bruchac. Why might you have to check several volumes to find an article about or by Joseph Bruchac?

_____

_____

5. Some libraries are now using computer databases to store information about articles published in periodicals. Why might a computer database be easier to use than the *Readers' Guide?* Explain.

_____

_____

© Scott Foresman 6

Name _____

Entries in the *Readers' Guide to Periodical Literature* are arranged alphabetically by subject or author. Each entry provides the title of the article, author of the article, title of the publication in which the article appears, volume number of the periodical, pages of the article, and other information. Information about abbreviations used in entries can be found at the front of each volume.

Directions: Scan these entries from the *Readers' Guide*. Then answer the questions that follow.

INDIANS OF NORTH AMERICA—
Art
Hidden art treasures of the Indian missions. S. Lowe. il *Arizona Highways* v72 p12-17 D '96
The impact of tradition on Native American art. B. Wright. il *Arizona Highways* v72 p12-19 O '96
Objects of power. A. Wardwell. il Natural History v106 p42-3 Mr '97
Representing Indians [treatment of Indian art in museums] R. White. il *The New Republic* v216 p28-34 Ap 21 '97
Collectors and collecting
Black Hawk's drawing of a vision. G. T. Vincent and J. C. Berlo.il *The Magazine Antiques* v151 p200-1 Ja '97
Exhibitions
American expressions [Native American jewelry and metalwork: contemporary expressions at the Institute of

American Indian Arts Museum, Santa Fe] L. Coulter. *American Craft* v57 p72-7 O/N '97
American Indian art [Gifts of the spirit: works by the nineteenth century and contemporary Native American artists at the Peabody Essex Museum] A. E. Ledes. il *The Magazine Antiques* v150 p760 D '96
Nineteenth-century Plains Indian drawings. J. C. Berlo. bibl f il *The Magazine Antiques* v150 p686-95 N '96
Arts and crafts
Buying Indian arts and crafts. B. Wright. il *Arizona Highways* v72 p18-21 N '96
Last of the old-time traders [trading posts in Arizona] S. Negri. il *Arizona Highways* v73 p4-9 Ja '97
The legend of Hubbell Trading Post. L. E. Jacka. il *Arizona Highways* v73 p10-15 Ja '97

From READERS' GUIDE TO PERIODICAL LITERATURE. Edited by Jean M. Marra.
Copyright © 1998 by the H. W. Wilson Company. All rights reserved.

---

6. What main subject and two subtopics are shown? _____

_____

7. Name the magazine, volume, page numbers, and year that you could find an article about the impact, or effect, of tradition on Native American art.

_____

8. In which article would you find drawings by the Plains Indians of the nineteenth century?

_____

9. Which magazine would give you more information about buying Native American arts and crafts? Name the magazine title, volume, month, and year.

_____

10. How is using the *Readers' Guide to Periodical Literature* similar to using an index at the back of a textbook or trade book? How is it different?

_____

_____

_____

Notes for Home: Your child answered questions about using the *Readers' Guide to Periodical Literature.* **Home Activity:** With your child, look through some magazines. Ask your child to find information such as the volume number, date of publication, and the titles and authors of articles.

© Scott Foresman 6

Name _____

Plot

> - The **plot** of a story is the series of important events from the story's beginning, middle, and end. The plot revolves around a central problem, or **conflict.**
>
> - In most stories, the conflict is introduced in the beginning. As the story progresses, the conflict leads to other problems. Gradually, the **rising action** builds to a high point, or climax. The **climax** is the highest point of interest in the story. Following the climax, there is **resolution** of the conflict and the action winds down.

Directions: Reread "The Sailor and the Fly." Then complete the plot structure map by identifying each element of the plot. One has been done for you.

Climax (High-Interest Point)

4. _____

_____

Rising Action (Other Problems)

2. _____

_____

3. _____

_____

The fisherman nearly crashes into the sailor.

Resolution (Outcome)

5. _____

_____

Conflict (Central Problem)

1. _____

_____

_____

Notes for Home: Your child identified the elements of plot in a short story. *Home Activity:* Use a plot structure map like the one shown to help you and your child make up a short story that features a character with a big problem.

© Scott Foresman 6

Vocabulary

Directions: Choose the word from the box that best completes each sentence. Write the word on the line to the left.

_____ 1. The Statue of Liberty is _____; it is more than 300 feet tall.

_____ 2. The statue _____ freedom.

_____ 3. Many _____ people help maintain national monuments.

_____ 4. The Statue of Liberty stands on a large _____.

_____ 5. Many people contributed to a _____ that was used to pay for the pedestal.

Check the Words You Know
___ contribution
___ fund
___ gigantic
___ patriotic
___ pedestal
___ spyglass
___ symbolizes

Directions: Choose the word from the box that best matches each clue. Write the word in the puzzle.

Down

6. a mounting platform

8. demonstrating a love for one's country

Across

7. a small telescope

9. what one gives

10. of huge proportions

Write an Advertisement

On a separate sheet of paper, write an advertisement for a tourist attraction that a patriotic person might wish to visit. For example, you might write about Mount Rushmore or the Statue of Liberty. Use as many vocabulary words as you can.

Notes for Home: Your child identified and used vocabulary words from "A Brother's Promise." *Home Activity:* Work with your child to write a paragraph about celebrating a national holiday. Encourage your child to use as many of the listed vocabulary words as possible.

© Scott Foresman 6

Plot

- A story's **plot** is the series of important events from the story's beginning, middle, and end.

- A plot revolves around a central problem, or conflict. Other elements of plot include the background, the rising action, the climax, and the resolution, or outcome.

Directions: Reread Joseph Pulitzer's speech about Annie from "A Brother's Promise." Then answer the questions below. Think about which story details are important to the plot.

> "You see," he said, turning back to his audience, "she lost her brother last year, a brother who loved the Statue of Liberty. He'd actually seen it in Paris, and Annie sold his special spyglass and sent the money to the Pedestal Fund in his memory. And that led many others to do the same thing."
>
> A few people clapped, and Annie looked down at their faces.
>
> "Annie, I have a surprise for you." He turned around, and someone handed him a long, thin wooden box.

"A Brother's Promise" copyright © 1993 by Pam Conrad. WITHIN REACH: TEN STORIES copyright © 1993 by Donald R. Gallo. Used by permission of HarperCollins Publishers.

1. List the events that brought Annie and Pulitzer together.

_____

_____

_____

2. How did Annie's sale of the spyglass lead to other story events?

_____

3. What does the last line suggest will happen next?

_____

4. Why is Pulitzer's surprise important to the story?

_____

_____

5. On a separate sheet of paper, identify the climax of "A Brother's Promise." Remember, the climax is the "high point" of the story where the story's problem is directly confronted.

Notes for Home: Your child read a passage and identified various parts of its plot. ***Home Activity:*** Encourage your child to draw a diagram that shows the basic plot of an episode of a recent television show.

© Scott Foresman 6

1.	Ⓐ	Ⓑ	Ⓒ	Ⓓ
2.	Ⓕ	Ⓖ	Ⓗ	Ⓙ
3.	Ⓐ	Ⓑ	Ⓒ	Ⓓ
4.	Ⓕ	Ⓖ	Ⓗ	Ⓙ
5.	Ⓐ	Ⓑ	Ⓒ	Ⓓ
6.	Ⓕ	Ⓖ	Ⓗ	Ⓙ
7.	Ⓐ	Ⓑ	Ⓒ	Ⓓ
8.	Ⓕ	Ⓖ	Ⓗ	Ⓙ
9.	Ⓐ	Ⓑ	Ⓒ	Ⓓ
10.	Ⓕ	Ⓖ	Ⓗ	Ⓙ
11.	Ⓐ	Ⓑ	Ⓒ	Ⓓ
12.	Ⓕ	Ⓖ	Ⓗ	Ⓙ
13.	Ⓐ	Ⓑ	Ⓒ	Ⓓ
14.	Ⓕ	Ⓖ	Ⓗ	Ⓙ
15.	Ⓐ	Ⓑ	Ⓒ	Ⓓ

© Scott Foresman 6

Selection Test

Directions: Choose the best answer to each item. Mark the letter for the answer you have chosen.

Part 1: Vocabulary

Find the answer choice that means about the same as the underlined word in each sentence.

1. He placed it on a <u>pedestal</u>.
   A. wide post
   B. table with hinged sides
   C. mound of earth
   D. base on which something stands

2. She looked into the <u>spyglass</u>.
   F. magnifying glass
   G. small telescope
   H. round window
   J. small mirror

3. The statue is <u>gigantic</u>.
   A. huge
   B. strange
   C. expensive
   D. lovely

4. He made a <u>contribution</u>.
   F. statement against something
   G. loud noise or disturbance
   H. description of something
   J. gift of money or help

5. They decided to set up a <u>fund</u>.
   A. work done for the common good
   B. community organization
   C. money set aside for a special purpose
   D. small company

6. We sang <u>patriotic</u> songs.
   F. showing love of one's country
   G. expressing strong emotion
   H. of or about soldiers
   J. originating and handed down among the common people

7. Do you know what the statue <u>symbolizes</u>?
   A. celebrates
   B. attracts
   C. stands for
   D. includes

Part 2: Comprehension

Use what you know about the story to answer each item.

8. Where did Geoffrey see the Statue of Liberty?
   F. Madison Square
   G. Paris
   H. New York Harbor
   J. Philadelphia

9. Why was there a problem in bringing the Statue of Liberty to America?
   A. It was too heavy to move.
   B. The body was not finished.
   C. The statue was a hoax.
   D. There was no base to put it on.

10. After Geoffrey died, Annie's main goal was to—
    F. take Geoffrey's spyglass into the Statue of Liberty.
    G. make sure the Statue of Liberty was placed in New York Harbor.
    H. help others appreciate how wonderful the Statue of Liberty was.
    J. go to France to see where the Statue of Liberty was made.

© Scott Foresman 6

GO ON

11. Why did Annie pawn the spyglass?
    A. She hoped someone just like Geoffrey would buy it.
    B. She did not like it.
    C. She wanted to give money to the pedestal fund.
    D. It brought back sad memories.

12. Mr. Pulitzer helped persuade many people to give money for the pedestal by—
    F. buying Geoffrey's spyglass.
    G. printing Annie's letter in the *New York World*.
    H. proving that the statue was real.
    J. giving a speech on Bedloe's Island.

13. The climax of the story occurs when—
    A. Annie writes to Mr. Pulitzer.
    B. Geoffrey and Annie climb up into the torch together.
    C. Geoffrey is killed in an accident.
    D. Annie climbs to the top of the statue with Geoffrey's spyglass.

14. When Annie speaks to Geoffrey from the top of the Statue of Liberty, it—
    F. helps the reader know what Annie sees and feels.
    G. makes the reader wonder whether Geoffrey is really dead.
    H. gives the story the spooky feeling of a ghost story.
    J. ties up loose ends and solves the riddle of the plot.

15. In historical fiction, some parts of the story are based on facts. Which of these statements can you be quite sure is true?
    A. Annie is ten years younger than Geoffrey.
    B. The Statue of Liberty was erected on Bedloe's Island in 1886.
    C. Joseph Pulitzer bought Geoffrey's spyglass from a pawnshop.
    D. Geoffrey was an art student in France.

STOP

© Scott Foresman   6

Visualizing and Theme

Directions: Read the passage. Then read each question about the passage. Choose the best answer to each question. Mark the letter for the answer you have chosen.

A Floating Monument

First the boat dock grew smaller until only a gigantic flag could be seen, waving like an unruly child. Then the traffic jam noises of sirens and horns grew fainter as tugboats guided the *USS Constitution* to the open ocean. Salty winds cooled the excited guests and crew.

Once this old ship had proudly served her country. She was launched in 1797, and took part in many naval battles. During the War of 1812, a sailor gave her the nickname "Old Ironsides." He claimed to have seen British cannonballs bouncing off the sides of the *Constitution!*

By 1830, Old Ironsides' proud career seemed to be over. The navy declared that she was too old and no longer safe to sail. The navy planned to destroy her. But when the poet Oliver Wendell Holmes wrote a farewell poem to the great ship, people remembered her glory and wrote to the navy. They wanted to save Old Ironsides. The navy, surprised, agreed to the people's wishes. In 1833, the *Constitution* was afloat again.

Now, 200 years after her launching, she was about to travel under sail power again. A signal pierced the air. It was time. High above the deck, sailors worked lines and unfurled sails. At first nothing happened. Then sail after sail caught the wind. The ship came alive like a bird carried across the water by huge white wings. As the ship proudly sailed forth, people were once more reminded that the *USS Constitution* symbolizes the courage of a nation.

1. The flag is compared to—
   - **A.** a huge white bird.
   - **B.** the open ocean.
   - **C.** an unruly child.
   - **D.** the bravery of a nation.

2. The words <u>traffic jam</u> are used to describe—
   - **F.** the confusing jumble of sounds.
   - **G.** why the ship sails slowly.
   - **H.** decks aboard the ship.
   - **J.** crowds of boats in the harbor.

3. The nickname "Ironsides" suggests—
   - **A.** age.
   - **B.** strength.
   - **C.** beauty.
   - **D.** grace.

4. As the ship sets sail, it is compared to—
   - **F.** a bird.
   - **G.** the wind.
   - **H.** a flag.
   - **J.** a child.

5. One theme the passage expresses is the—
   - **A.** courage of sailors.
   - **B.** importance of sail power.
   - **C.** unusual demands placed on naval vessels.
   - **D.** power of patriotic symbols to inspire people.

© Scott Foresman 6

Notes for Home: Your child identified the descriptive details and the underlying meaning of a passage. ***Home Activity:*** Encourage your child to use a variety of descriptive words that convey the sights, sounds, smells, and mood of a specific place.

Word Study: Inflected Endings -er, -est

Directions: The ending **-er** is added to words to compare two things. The ending **-est** is added to words to compare two or more things. Add **-er** and **-est** to each base word below. Write the new word on the line.

Base Word	Add -er	Add -est
old	1. _____	6. _____
short	2. _____	7. _____
near	3. _____	8. _____
grand	4. _____	9. _____
small	5. _____	10. _____

Directions: Read each sentence. Add **-er** to the word in ( ). Write the new word on the line.

_____ 11. It had taken much (long) to finish the building than we thought.

_____ 12. Now that the building was complete, it reached (high) than ever before.

_____ 13. The stars never looked (bright) as I stood on the new rooftop.

_____ 14. Even though I was (young) than the others, I could still appreciate the moment.

_____ 15. Looking down, the cars below seemed (small) than ants.

Directions: Read each sentence. Add the ending **-est** to the word in ( ). Write the new word on the line.

_____ 16. The new building was now the (tall) in the city.

_____ 17. The architect expressed his (deep) gratitude when he was presented with the award.

_____ 18. The observation tower was the (great) I had ever seen.

_____ 19. The elevator ride to the top was the (fast) ride I had ever taken.

_____ 20. After stepping off the elevator, I realized I was looking down from the (high) point of the city.

Notes for Home: Your child formed new words by adding *-er* and *-est* to base words. **Home Activity:** Listen to radio advertisements or watch television commercials with your child to find words that end in *-er* and *-est*. Make a list of these words and the products they compare.

© Scott Foresman 6

Technology: Encyclopedia

An **encyclopedia** gives general information about many different subjects. If you are using a CD-ROM or online encyclopedia, you can search the entire encyclopedia for your topic. You can usually search by letter or by typing key words. The welcome screen for an on-line encyclopedia might look like this:

Welcome to the Encyclopedia

Choose a letter to browse the encyclopedia.

Or, type the key words to search. Use AND between key words.

A B C D E F G H I J K L M N O P Q R S T U V W X Y Z

Search the Encyclopedia for:

Search for:

☐ Articles and Tables

☐ Pictures, Flags, Maps, Charts, Sounds

☐ Websites

☐ All of the Above

If you wanted an encyclopedia article about the Statue of Liberty, you could try clicking on the letter *S*. If that doesn't work, you could try the letter *L*. Then you might get this:

Lewis, Sinclair

Lewis and Clark

Liberal Party

Liberty, Statue of

Liberty Bell

library

lichen

licorice

Try another letter:

A B C D E F G H I J K L M N O P Q R S T U V W X Y Z

Search the Encyclopedia for:

© Scott Foresman 6

When you find an article about your topic, it will probably have links to other articles. The links are often set in all capital letters that are underlined. For example, you might find an article like this about the Statue of Liberty:

Liberty, Statue of

A large statue on Liberty Island in upper New York Bay. It was given to the United States in 1886, by the Franco-American Union to commemorate the <u>AMERICAN REVOLUTION</u>. It was designed by the sculptor <u>F.A. BARTHOLDI</u>. The statue became a national monument in 1924, and was extensively restored in 1986.

<u>Click here</u> to see pictures of the Statue of Liberty.

Directions: Use the sample computer screens to answer these questions.

1. In the first and second computer screens, what happens if you click on a letter?

_____

2. Besides clicking on the letters S or L, what is another way to find information about the Statue of Liberty?

_____

3. In the second computer screen, what happens if you click on "Liberty Bell"?

_____

4. How can you get an article about the person who designed the Statue of Liberty? How can you get pictures of the Statue of Liberty?

_____

_____

5. How is a CD-ROM or online encyclopedia like and unlike a print encyclopedia?

_____

_____

_____

_____

_____

Notes for Home: Your child learned how to use a CD-ROM or online encyclopedia. ***Home Activity:*** Ask your child to list possible key words to use to search for articles about other national monuments or interesting sights, such as Mount Rushmore.

© Scott Foresman 6

Main Idea and Supporting Details

- The most important idea about the topic of a paragraph or an article is the **main idea.** Small pieces of information that tell more about the main idea are **supporting details.**

- To find the main idea, first identify the topic. Ask yourself "What is this all about?" Then look for the most important idea about the topic. If it is not stated, put the main idea in your own words.

Directions: Reread "Quilted Memories." Complete the diagram below by writing the topic of the article, its main idea, and several important details that support the main idea.

Topic

1.

↓

Main Idea

2.

↓

Supporting Detail

3.

↓

Supporting Detail

4.

↓

Supporting Detail

5.

Notes for Home: Your child identified the topic and main idea in an article. *Home Activity:* Work with your child to identify the topic and main idea of individual paragraphs in a magazine article. Then challenge your child to state the main idea of the entire article.

© Scott Foresman 6

Vocabulary

Directions: Choose the word from the box that matches each definition.
Write the word on the line.

**Check
the Words
You Know**

__ anvil
__ businessman
__ craftsman
__ horseshoes
__ ornamental
__ workshop

_____ 1. an iron or steel block on which metals
   are hammered and shaped

_____ 2. flat pieces of metal shaped like the
   letter U used to protect the hooves of
   horses

_____ 3. decorative

_____ 4. a person who is in business or who runs
   a business

_____ 5. a shop or building where work is done

Directions: Choose the word from the box that best matches each clue. Write
the word on the line.

_____ 6. They may not be fashionable, but every horse wears four of
   them.

_____ 7. You might build or make something here.

_____ 8. A person who owns a store could be called this.

_____ 9. The fancy designs on an iron gate might be called this.

_____ 10. You might see this person at a craft fair selling crafts he has
   made.

Write a Letter

On a separate sheet of paper, write a letter to a friend in which you describe
a visit to a workshop. The letter can be based on an actual workshop that you
have visited or one you imagine. Use as many vocabulary words as you can.

Notes for Home: Your child identified and used vocabulary words from *Catching the Fire.*
Home Activity: Read a story with your child and have him or her point out unfamiliar words.
Work together to try to figure out the meaning of each word using other words nearby.

© Scott Foresman 6

Main Idea and Supporting Details

- The most important idea about the topic of a paragraph or an article is the **main idea.** Small pieces of information that tell more about the main idea are **supporting details.**

- To find the main idea, first identify the topic. Ask yourself "What is this all about?" Then look for the most important idea about the topic. If it is not stated, put the main idea in your own words.

Directions: Reread this scene from *Catching the Fire* in which John Vlach and Philip Simmons admire the Snake Gate. Then answer the questions below. Think about the main idea of the passage and look for supporting details.

> Philip drove John over to East Bay Street to see his Snake Gate. It took him one month to forge that gate. He thought he'd never finish the eye. At first, it stared as if it were dead. Philip "heat and beat, heat and beat, heat and beat," until the snake looked as real as a diamond head rattler. "If it bites you," Philip joked, "you better get to the doctor fast. Blood get up to your heart, you know what happens!"
>
> John Vlach was impressed. These were no ordinary pieces of ornamental ironwork. They were sculpture! Philip Simmons was not just a blacksmith. He was an artist.
>
> Excerpt from CATCHING THE FIRE: PHILIP SIMMONS, BLACKSMITH by Mary E. Lyons. Text copyright © 1997 by Mary E. Lyons. Reprinted by permission of Houghton Mifflin Company. All rights reserved.

1. What does John Vlach think of Philip's work? _____

_____

_____

2. What is the main idea of the passage? _____

_____

_____

3.–4. List two details that support the main idea. _____

_____

_____

_____

5. On a separate sheet of paper, state the main idea of the last part of the story in which Philip attends the festival in Washington, D.C. Give specific details that support your answer.

Notes for Home: Your child identified the main idea and supporting details of an excerpt from a biography. *Home Activity:* Read a magazine article with your child. Work together to identify its main idea and several supporting details.

© Scott Foresman 6

1.	Ⓐ	Ⓑ	Ⓒ	Ⓓ
2.	Ⓕ	Ⓖ	Ⓗ	Ⓙ
3.	Ⓐ	Ⓑ	Ⓒ	Ⓓ
4.	Ⓕ	Ⓖ	Ⓗ	Ⓙ
5.	Ⓐ	Ⓑ	Ⓒ	Ⓓ
6.	Ⓕ	Ⓖ	Ⓗ	Ⓙ
7.	Ⓐ	Ⓑ	Ⓒ	Ⓓ
8.	Ⓕ	Ⓖ	Ⓗ	Ⓙ
9.	Ⓐ	Ⓑ	Ⓒ	Ⓓ
10.	Ⓕ	Ⓖ	Ⓗ	Ⓙ
11.	Ⓐ	Ⓑ	Ⓒ	Ⓓ
12.	Ⓕ	Ⓖ	Ⓗ	Ⓙ
13.	Ⓐ	Ⓑ	Ⓒ	Ⓓ
14.	Ⓕ	Ⓖ	Ⓗ	Ⓙ
15.	Ⓐ	Ⓑ	Ⓒ	Ⓓ

© Scott Foresman 6

Selection Test

Directions: Choose the best answer to each item. Mark the letter for the answer you have chosen.

Part 1: Vocabulary

Find the answer choice that means about the same as the underlined word in each sentence.

1. Where can I get some <u>horseshoes</u>?
   A. plants with spicy roots
   B. stiff fabrics made from horse hair
   C. riding crops used with horses
   D. u-shaped pieces of metal nailed to horses' hooves

2. He is a wonderful <u>craftsman</u>.
   F. person who loves to hunt
   G. person skilled in a trade
   H. person who likes to compete
   J. person trained to fly airplanes

3. Her <u>workshop</u> is quite small.
   A. strong table used for working
   B. person who is learning a trade
   C. building or room where work is done
   D. room where people exercise

4. Mr. Cole is a wise <u>businessman</u>.
   F. man who interferes in other people's business
   G. man who runs for public office
   H. man who works in a library
   J. man who owns or works in a business

5. She designed an <u>ornamental</u> gate.
   A. for decoration
   B. well-hidden
   C. made of iron
   D. without hinges

6. We bought a new <u>anvil</u>.
   F. iron or steel block on which metals are hammered and shaped
   G. small fireplace where metal is heated
   H. large, heavy hammer, usually swung with both hands
   J. device for producing a strong current of air

Part 2: Comprehension

Use what you know about the selection to answer each item.

7. Philip Simmons's best-known works are—
   A. chandeliers.
   B. plant stands.
   C. gates with animal figures on them.
   D. benches.

8. A master and an apprentice are most like a—
   F. teacher and student.
   G. father and mother.
   H. worker and tool.
   J. brother and sister.

9. The beginning of this selection is mostly about—
   A. a young boy working in his father's blacksmith shop.
   B. how to earn money as a blacksmith's apprentice.
   C. what it was like in Charleston, South Carolina, in 1923.
   D. the ancient tradition of blacksmithing that Philip Simmons followed.

10. You can tell from reading this selection that being a blacksmith like Simmons—
    F. requires little skill.
    G. is a lost art.
    H. combines physical and artistic talent.
    J. is a fairly simple way to make a lot of money.

© Scott Foresman 6

GO ON

11. When John Vlach first asked him to go to the festival, Philip—
- A. knew just what he wanted to make.
- B. wasn't sure he wanted to go.
- C. realized it was a great honor.
- D. didn't want to take his apprentices along.

12. Which title best fits the last part of the selection?
- F. "Thanking John Vlach"
- G. "Seeing Washington"
- H. "America in the 1970s"
- J. "Preserving a Lost Art"

13. You can tell from reading this selection that Philip Simmons is not only a blacksmith, he is also—
- A. an accomplished photographer.
- B. a person who knows a lot about history.
- C. a fine artist.
- D. a published author.

14. One of the major reasons that Philip survived as a blacksmith after World War II is that he—
- F. didn't charge much for his work.
- G. was able to buy iron cheaply.
- H. knew how to adapt to changes in the world around him.
- J. always worked in the same neighborhood.

15. The author's main purpose in writing this selection is to—
- A. describe the 1976 Festival of American Folklife.
- B. discuss whether blacksmithing is a dying art.
- C. entertain with an exciting story about life in the 1920s.
- D. give information about Philip Simmons, a talented blacksmith.

STOP

© Scott Foresman 6

Author's Purpose

REVIEW

Directions: Read the passage. Then read each question about the passage. Choose the best answer to each question. Mark the letter for the answer you have chosen.

Making Paint

Artists have a variety of paint choices today. Did you know that many materials in current use were also known to paintmakers in ancient times?

The substance that gives paint its color is called *pigment.* It is usually made from clay, lead, chalk, or other natural minerals that are ground into fine powder. In ancient times, people mixed vegetable and earth pigments with water or animal fat. In Colonial America, people used things like coffee, milk, and butter for pigment! Recently the paint industry has developed new chemical pigments.

To hold the color on the picture, pigments must be mixed with a sticky substance, or *binder.* A variety of materials are used, from oils to tree resins, beeswax, and even egg yolks. Recently, acrylic binders made from petroleum have also become popular. Drying time, gloss, and texture are all affected by the binder.

During the Italian Renaissance of the 1500s, painters began inventing new binders and new formulas for mixing pigments and binders. They kept their formulas secret so that other painters could not steal their ideas and profit from them. Most of the time, the new process died with the painter who invented it. Scientific analysis may yet reveal what made Italian paintings from the Renaissance so beautiful, but for now it is a mystery.

1. The topic of this article is—
   A. paintmakers of ancient times.
   B. how paint is made.
   C. finely-ground pigments.
   D. minerals and other powders.

2. The main purpose of the article is—
   F. to inform.
   G. to entertain.
   H. to persuade.
   J. to express.

3. The article's main idea is that—
   A. natural materials make the best paints.
   B. Colonial paintmakers used food substances to make pigments.
   C. paints are made from different pigments and binders.
   D. an artist's style depends upon pigments.

4. Why does the author include the mention of paintmakers of ancient times?
   F. to impress readers with his knowledge of history
   G. to show that some of their materials are still in use today
   H. to show how primitive their materials were
   J. to suggest that their materials were better than recent ones

5. The author included the last paragraph to—
   A. make the article more entertaining.
   B. inform the reader about an interesting period in the history of paintmaking.
   C. persuade the reader that the Italian painters of the Renaissance were the best painters.
   D. express the beauty of Renaissance paintings.

Notes for Home: Your child read an article and identified the author's purpose. *Home Activity:* Together, name some favorite books, TV shows, and movies. Identify the author's purpose or purposes for writing each kind of text.

© Scott Foresman 6

Word Study: Inflected Endings

Directions: If a word ends in a **consonant** and **y,** change the **y** to **i** before adding most endings. For example, **baby** becomes **babies.** You do **not** change **y** to **i** when adding **-ing. Try** becomes **trying.** If a word ends in a single consonant preceded by a single vowel, double the final consonant before adding the ending. For example, **step** becomes **stepped.** Add the given ending to each base word. Write the new word on the line.

1. drop + -ing = _____

2. strip + -ed = _____

3. family + -es = _____

4. big + -er = _____

5. factory + -es = _____

6. big + -est = _____

7. industry + -al = _____

8. stir + -ed = _____

Directions: Read each sentence. Write the base word for each underlined word below.

_____ 9. No matter how hard the ironworkers <u>tried</u>, they could not get management to give them a raise.

_____ 10. In order to have their demands met, the laborers were <u>planning</u> to go on strike.

_____ 11. In <u>counties</u> all across the state, there were no other jobs for the workers.

_____ 12. The employees were <u>running</u> out of options for the future.

_____ 13. It would be one of the biggest <u>tragedies</u> of the year if the town's factory were to close its doors.

_____ 14. In order for <u>communities</u> to survive, jobs must be plentiful.

_____ 15. It sometimes takes several <u>industries</u> to make a town a success.

Notes for Home: Your child added endings to base words. *Home Activity:* Read a newspaper with your child. Look for words with endings such as *-ing, -ed, -er, -est,* and *-es.* Have your child tell if the base word changed when the ending was added.

© Scott Foresman 6

Pictures and Captions

Pictures and captions can provide information about the characters and events in a story or information about the subject in nonfiction writing.

Directions: Use the picture and the caption to answer the questions that follow.

Quilt-making is a popular form of American folk art. Historically, quilting served as a way for women to get together in a "quilting bee." A quilt is generally made from a series of cloth patches sewn together to form a design. Story quilts include images that tell a story.

1. What does the picture show? _____

   _____

   _____

2. What is a quilting bee? _____

   _____

   _____

3. How is a quilt generally constructed? _____

   _____

   _____

4. How are "story quilts" different from other quilts? _____

   _____

   _____

5. Would this picture and caption be useful for a research essay on American folk art? Explain.

   _____

   _____

© Scott Foresman 6

Directions: Study the picture and caption from a story. Then answer the questions that follow.

John Thomas worked hard into the night. He could picture the snake in his mind and wouldn't rest until he got it right.

6. What do you learn about the character from looking at the picture? _____

_____

_____

7. What do you learn about the character from reading the caption? _____

_____

_____

8. Use what you have learned about the character to write your own caption for the picture.

_____

_____

_____

9. How can you use a picture and a caption to draw conclusions about a character?

_____

_____

_____

10. Why is it important to read captions carefully? _____

_____

_____

Notes for Home: Your child answered questions about pictures and captions. *Home Activity:* Look through a magazine or nonfiction book with your child to find pictures with captions. Discuss what you learn from these pictures and captions.

© Scott Foresman 6

Text Structure

- **Text structure** refers to the way a piece of writing is organized.

- Fiction tells of imaginary people and events. It is usually organized in chronological order, the order in which the events happen.

- Nonfiction tells of real people and events or tells information about the real world. It may be organized in chronological order, or by topic, cause and effect, problem and solution, or some other way.

Directions: Reread "Engineering the Land." Then complete the diagram.
Identify the topics and give the main idea of each paragraph related to that topic.

Topic: Terracing

First paragraph: Because much of their land was hard to farm, the Incas had to terrace and dig canals.

1. Second paragraph:

2. Topic:

3. Paragraph:

4. Topic:

5. Paragraph:

Notes for Home: Your child analyzed the way a nonfiction selection was organized. *Home Activity:* Review together the text structure of familiar textbooks. Discuss the ways the different textbook features help readers better understand and remember the information.

© Scott Foresman 6

Vocabulary

Directions: Match each word on the left with its definition on the right.
Write the letter of the definition on the line to the left of the word.

_____ 1. pharaohs

_____ 2. classical

_____ 3. tomb

_____ 4. structures

_____ 5. excavate

_____ 6. archaeologists

a. unearth; dig up

b. buildings

c. ancient Egyptian kings

d. having to do with ancient
Greece and Rome

e. scientists who study the past by
unearthing artifacts

f. grave or vault

Check the Words You Know
__ archaeologists
__ classical
__ excavate
__ pharaohs
__ structures
__ tomb

Directions: Choose the word from the box that best replaces the underlined
word or words. Write the word on the line.

_____ 7. The <u>kings</u> of ancient Egypt had huge pyramids built as a
resting place for the dead.

_____ 8. It took years and thousands of laborers just to build a single
<u>burial place</u>.

_____ 9. <u>Scientists who study</u> these <u>ancient structures</u> are still not
completely certain how these pyramids were built.

_____ 10. They continue to <u>dig</u> near these marvelous structures hoping
to learn more about the past.

Write a Journal Entry

On a separate sheet of paper, write a journal entry in which you pretend you are
an archaeologist. Describe a dig in which you discover artifacts (objects made by
humans) from an ancient civilization. Use as many vocabulary words as you can.

Notes for Home: Your child identified and used vocabulary words from *The Seven Wonders of the Ancient World*. **Home Activity:** Work with your child to write an adventure story about an archaeologist, using the vocabulary words listed above.

© Scott Foresman 6

Text Structure

- **Text structure** refers to the way a piece of writing is organized.

- Fiction tells stories of imaginary people and events. It is usually organized in chronological order, the order in which the events happened.

- Nonfiction tells of real people and events or tells information about the real world. Some ways to organize nonfiction are chronological order, cause and effect, problem and solution, or comparison and contrast.

Directions: Reread this passage about the Colossus of Rhodes from *The Seven Wonders of the Ancient World.* Then answer the questions below. Think about the way in which the events it describes are organized.

In about 226 B.C., little more than 50 years after it was completed, the Colossus fell. It was toppled by an earthquake and snapped off at the knees. The people of Rhodes were told by an oracle not to rebuild the statue, and so they left it lying where it had fallen. It stayed like this for nearly 900 years, and people would travel to Rhodes just to gaze at the ruins of the fallen sun god.

In A.D. 654 a Syrian prince captured Rhodes and stripped the statue of its bronze plates. People said that he took them back to Syria on the backs of 900 camels. The bronze was sold by merchants and probably turned into coins.

Reprinted with the permission of Macmillan Library Reference USA, a division of Ahsuog, Inc. from THE SEVEN WONDERS OF THE ANCIENT WORLD, by Reg Cox and Neil Morris. Copyright ©1996 by Silver Burdett Press, an imprint of Macmillan Library Reference.

1. What is the topic of the passage?

_____

2. About how much time does it take for all the events to happen?

_____

3. How are the events in this passage organized?

_____

4. Do you think the organization of the passage makes sense? Why or why not?

_____

_____

5. On a separate sheet of paper, explain how the information in *The Seven Wonders of the Ancient World* is organized. Explain whether you think it was effective and why.

Notes for Home: Your child identified the organization of a text. **Home Activity:** Have your child read aloud a passage from a nonfiction book. Have him or her tell how it is organized and why the author might have organized it in that way.

© Scott Foresman 6

1.	Ⓐ	Ⓑ	Ⓒ	Ⓓ
2.	Ⓕ	Ⓖ	Ⓗ	Ⓙ
3.	Ⓐ	Ⓑ	Ⓒ	Ⓓ
4.	Ⓕ	Ⓖ	Ⓗ	Ⓙ
5.	Ⓐ	Ⓑ	Ⓒ	Ⓓ
6.	Ⓕ	Ⓖ	Ⓗ	Ⓙ
7.	Ⓐ	Ⓑ	Ⓒ	Ⓓ
8.	Ⓕ	Ⓖ	Ⓗ	Ⓙ
9.	Ⓐ	Ⓑ	Ⓒ	Ⓓ
10.	Ⓕ	Ⓖ	Ⓗ	Ⓙ
11.	Ⓐ	Ⓑ	Ⓒ	Ⓓ
12.	Ⓕ	Ⓖ	Ⓗ	Ⓙ
13.	Ⓐ	Ⓑ	Ⓒ	Ⓓ
14.	Ⓕ	Ⓖ	Ⓗ	Ⓙ
15.	Ⓐ	Ⓑ	Ⓒ	Ⓓ

© Scott Foresman 6

Selection Test

Directions: Choose the best answer to each item. Mark the letter for the answer you have chosen.

Part 1: Vocabulary

Find the answer choice that means about the same as the underlined word in each sentence.

1. She wanted to <u>excavate</u> the old fort.
   A. explore
   B. lay out
   C. uncover by digging
   D. bury

2. He discovered an ancient <u>tomb</u>.
   F. fortress
   G. house
   H. earthen jar for storage
   J. grave or vault

3. They found what was left of the <u>structures</u>.
   A. paintings
   B. things that are built
   C. borders
   D. rivers and waterways

4. A team of <u>archaeologists</u> arrived.
   F. scientists who study the surface features of the earth
   G. scientists who study the people and customs of ancient times
   H. scientists who study the earth's climate
   J. scientists who study fossils of animals and plants

5. She was learning about the <u>pharoahs</u>.
   A. kings of ancient Egypt
   B. buildings in ancient Egypt
   C. statues of ancient rulers
   D. priests of an ancient religion

6. He was reading <u>classical</u> literature.
   F. originating in Asia
   G. about music
   H. of ancient Greece and Rome
   J. about school

Part 2: Comprehension

Use what you know about the selection to answer each item.

7. Which of the "Seven Wonders" is still standing today?
   A. the Mausoleum at Halicarnassus
   B. the Statue of Zeus at Olympia
   C. the Temple of Artemis at Ephesus
   D. the Great Pyramid at Giza

8. The "Seven Wonders of the Ancient World" were all located near the—
   F. Mediterranean Sea.
   G. Atlantic Ocean.
   H. Caspian Sea.
   J. Persian Gulf.

9. Why did these particular sites become known as the "Seven Wonders"?
   A. No one knew how they were made.
   B. They were built in seven different countries.
   C. A Greek poet wrote about them.
   D. Scientists today are amazed by them.

10. The main idea of this selection is that the "Seven Wonders" all—
    F. prove that ancient peoples had the same beliefs and values we do today.
    G. honored kings and queens who are no longer important.
    H. were designed and built by people who lived thousands of years ago.
    J. demonstrated the supreme power of nature.

11. The author's main purpose in this selection is to—
    A. entertain.
    B. express feelings.
    C. persuade.
    D. give information.

© Scott Foresman 6

12. The information in this selection is organized by—
    F. topic.
    G. cause and effect.
    H. problem and solution.
    J. comparison/contrast.

13. For which of these structures is the exact location **not** known?
    A. Great Pyramid at Giza
    B. Hanging Gardens of Babylon
    C. Temple of Artemis at Ephesus
    D. Pharos of Alexandria

14. Which sentence states an opinion?
    F. The Great Pyramid at Giza was built as a tomb.
    G. The main structure of the Temple of Artemis was supported by about 120 marble columns.
    H. The Statue of Zeus at Olympia stood for about 800 years.
    J. The Pharos of Alexandria was the greatest of the Seven Wonders.

15. After reading this selection, you can conclude that what we build today—
    A. is more beautiful than what people built in the past.
    B. may someday be studied by people of the future.
    C. will last much longer than buildings did in the past.
    D. differs very little from what has been built throughout history.

STOP

© Scott Foresman 6

Persuasive Devices

Directions: Read the passage. Then read each question about the passage. Choose the best answer to each question. Mark the letter for the answer you have chosen.

The Eighth Wonder of the World

The next stop on our tour is the Empire State Building. It's no longer the tallest building in New York, but it is still the best-looking. People joke about the World Trade Center being "the box the Chrysler Building came in"—no one would ever mock the Empire State Building like that!

The building is best known for its splendid view from the top of the tower. You can stay up there all day if you want, and take in the surrounding city from every direction. On clear days you can see far beyond the city limits. At night, the view is even better—everything is lit, cars drive along in rows of red and yellow lights, and the city looks magical.

The lobby is just as grand as the view. You've never seen so much marble in one place! It's as lofty as a cathedral. Even the journey to the top can be an adventure. A maze of elevators and hallways are negotiated by visitors before reaching the glorious view from the top of the tower.

No other building in New York has the personality of the Empire State. Hollywood has featured the grand building in many movies. For example, the great ape King Kong once climbed its tower! It is still the greatest tourist attraction in the city, and it deserves to be.

1. The tour guide thinks the Empire State Building is—
   A. the tallest building in New York.
   B. the smallest building in New York.
   C. the best-looking building in New York.
   D. the oldest building in New York.

2. Which words persuade the listeners that the view is great?
   F. splendid, magical
   G. all day, every direction
   H. splendid, lit
   J. clear days, far beyond

3. Which of the following is an attempt to persuade the listener?
   A. The lobby is marble.
   B. The view is splendid.
   C. King Kong once climbed the tower.
   D. The building is tall.

4. Which of the following is a sweeping generalization?
   F. No other building has a personality like that of the Empire State.
   G. From the tower, you can see a great distance on a clear day
   H. The Empire State has a marble lobby.
   J. The Empire State is no longer the tallest building in New York.

5. Which of the following is **not** an attempt to persuade the listener?
   A. The view is magnificent at night.
   B. It is the greatest tourist attraction in the city.
   C. No other building has a personality like the Empire State.
   D. On a clear day, you can see a lot from the tower.

Notes for Home: Your child identified the persuasive devices in a passage. *Home Activity:* Read a newspaper article with your child. Encourage him or her to identify persuasive devices such as generalizations and propaganda, as opposed to facts and information.

© Scott Foresman 6

Word Study: Syllabication; Common Syllable Patterns

- Knowing how to divide words into their syllable parts can help you read and understand them better

- **VCV:** If a word with two syllables has one consonant between two vowels, and the first syllable has a short vowel sound, then the word is divided after the consonant, such as **lev • er.**

- **VCV:** If a word with two syllables has one consonant between two vowels, and the first syllable has a long vowel sound, then the word is divided after the first vowel sound, such as **re • mind.**

- **VCCV:** If a word with two syllables has two consonants between two vowels, then the word is divided between the middle consonants, such as **won • der.**

- **VCCV/VCCCV:** If a word with two syllables has a consonant blend (such as **dr**) or a digraph (such as **th**) between two vowels, then the word is divided after the blend or digraph if the first vowel is short, like **fast • er,** or before the blend or digraph if the vowel is long, such as **re • think.** Follow these same rules, if there are three consonants and two of them are a blend or digraph, such as **hun • dred.**

Directions: Read the words in the box. Sort the words according to the syllable patterns. Write the words to show the syllables like this: **won • der.**

seven	organs	repaint	modern	travel
garden	terrace	chamber	farthest	workmen
destroy	merchants	Romans	worship	smother

Pattern VCV	**Pattern VCCV**	**Pattern VCCCV**
1. _____	6. _____	11. _____
2. _____	7. _____	12. _____
3. _____	8. _____	13. _____
4. _____	9. _____	14. _____
5. _____	10. _____	15. _____

Notes for Home: Your child explored vowel-consonant patterns, such as VCV in *lever,* VCCV in *wonder,* and VCCCV in *hundred,* to divide words into syllables. *Home Activity:* Together, make a list of words with two or more syllables. Use the rules above to divide each word.

© Scott Foresman 6

Name _____

Outlining

Outlining is a good way to organize information found in nonfiction texts. Outlines include main topics, subtopics, and details.

Directions: Read the nonfiction article. Think about the different civilizations described, when they lived, where they lived, and what happened to them. Then follow the directions to write an outline on the next page. Note: You may not need to fill in every line on the outline.

A **civilization** is a group of people who have a set class system of who owns and controls goods and services, political and religious structures, and people employed in a variety of positions. Scientists have classified several major ancient civilizations, among them the Sumerians, the Aegean, and the Mesoamericans.

The **Sumerians** are a people who occupied the lands of what is now called Iraq. They settled in the area about 5,000 years ago, around 3500 B.C.E. They spread northward through the Tigris-Euphrates Valley. During the early part of their civilization, the people formed small political units. As the civilization developed, these political groups began to war with each other. Eventually, the factions were united under a single ruler in the area that would later be known as Babylonia. The Sumerians lost their land and their identity when other invaders ultimately conquered the land around 2000 B.C.E.

The **Aegean** civilization arose during the Bronze Age, between 3000 and 1000 B.C.E. Early Aegean people were hunters who roamed Greece. Small settlements were then established. The first real civilization was established by the Minoan in Crete. It is believed that they used some form of writing. The next wave of the civilization's development is known as the Mycenaean. However, wars between Mycenaean states soon caused the Aegean civilization to die out.

The civilization of the **Mesoamericans** included such peoples as the Aztec, the Maya, and the Toltec. This civilization dates back to 1200 B.C.E. They lived in several areas of Mexico and Central America. Much of the Mesoamerican civilization was destroyed after the arrival of Spanish settlers in the A.D. 1500s.

- What are the three main topics of the article? Write each main topic at I, II, and III.

- What are some subtopics of the main topics I, II, III? Write each at A, B, and C.

- What details support the subtopics A, B, C? Write each at 1 and 2.

© Scott Foresman 6

Title: Three Ancient Civilizations

I. _____

   A. _____

      1. _____

      2. _____

   B. _____

      1. _____

      2. _____

   C. _____

      1. _____

      2. _____

II. _____

   A. _____

      1. _____

      2. _____

   B. _____

      1. _____

      2. _____

   C. _____

      1. _____

      2. _____

III. _____

   A. _____

      1. _____

      2. _____

   B. _____

      1. _____

      2. _____

   C. _____

      1. _____

      2. _____

Notes for Home: Your child organized information in an outline. **Home Activity:** Help your child use an outline to help study for an upcoming test. Review material to be tested and organize related information by main topics, subtopics, and details.

© Scott Foresman 6

Author's Purpose

- **Author's purpose** refers to an author's reason or reasons for writing.

- Four common purposes for writing are to inform, to persuade, to entertain, and to express. Often an author has more than one purpose for writing.

- Understanding an author's purpose can help you adjust your reading speed and can help explain the author's choice of words and writing style.

Directions: Reread "The Tortoise in the Tree." Then complete the table by writing evidence from the story that supports the purposes given. Then give an example of another folk tale that shares these purposes. Explain your choice.

Author's Purpose	Evidence for Author's Purpose
To entertain	1.
	2.
To persuade	3.
	4.
Another Folk Tale That Entertains and Persuades	
5.	

Notes for Home: Your child identified and analyzed an author's purpose for writing a folk tale. *Home Activity:* Challenge your child to write a humorous story that explains an animal's behavior or appearance, such as "How the Whale Got Its Tale" or "Why Snakes Hiss."

© Scott Foresman 6

Vocabulary

Directions: Choose the word from the box that best matches each definition.
Write the word on the line.

**Check
the Words
You Know**

__ distressed
__ impatience
__ insistent
__ recovery
__ stunned

_____ 1. continuing to demand

_____ 2. the process of regaining one's health
or well-being

_____ 3. in great pain or sorrow

_____ 4. shocked

_____ 5. a lack of patience

Directions: Choose the word from the box that best completes each sentence.
Write the word on the line to the left.

_____ 6. When the factory suddenly closed, Mr. Winters was _____ to
find out that he had lost his job.

_____ 7. He was worried and _____ about his ability to find a
new job.

_____ 8. During his first few weeks at home, Mr. Winters showed
great _____; he wanted to settle into a new job as soon
as possible.

_____ 9. Mrs. Winters knew that her husband liked learning new things,
so she was _____ that he sign up for a job training class.

_____ 10. Now Mr. Winters has a job working with computers. His
mood and his spirits have made a complete _____.

Write a News Story

On a separate sheet of paper, write a news story about
someone who has turned his or her life around. The person
can be someone you know or have heard of, or someone that
you make up. Use as many vocabulary words as you can.

Notes for Home: Your child identified and used vocabulary words from *The Gold Coin*.
Home Activity: Talk about a time when a family member recovered from an illness.
Encourage your child to use the vocabulary words to describe how the person felt.

© Scott Foresman 6

Author's Purpose

- The **author's purpose** is the reason or reasons an author has for writing.

- Four common purposes for writing are to inform, to persuade, to entertain, and to express. Often an author has more than one purpose.

Directions: Reread the scene from *The Gold Coin* in which Juan begins to change. Then answer the questions below. Think about why the author is telling this story.

> "If you'd like, I'll take you there tomorrow. But first I must gather my squash and beans."
> So Juan spent another long day in the fields. Working beneath the summer sun, Juan noticed that his skin had begun to tan. And although he had to stoop down to pick the squash, he found that he could now stretch his body. His back had begun to straighten, too.
> Later, when the little girl took him by the hand to show him a family of rabbits burrowed under a fallen tree, Juan's face broke into a smile. It had been a long, long time since Juan had smiled.
>
> From THE GOLD COIN by Alma Flor Ada. Text copyright © 1991, by Alma Flor Ada. Reprinted with permission of Atheneum Books for Young Readers, Simon & Schuster Children's Publishing Division.

1. How is Juan changing? _____

_____

2. What is Juan learning? _____

_____

3. Why does the author include the detail about the little girl and the rabbits?

_____

_____

4. What is the purpose of this passage? How do you know?

_____

_____

5. On a separate sheet of paper, explain why you think the author wrote this story. Give specific examples from the story to support your answer.

Notes for Home: Your child read a folk tale and identified the author's purpose. *Home Activity:* Encourage your child to read a movie review, a letter to the editor, and a sports article. Have your child tell you each author's purpose and explain his or her answers.

© Scott Foresman 6

1.	Ⓐ	Ⓑ	Ⓒ	Ⓓ
2.	Ⓕ	Ⓖ	Ⓗ	Ⓙ
3.	Ⓐ	Ⓑ	Ⓒ	Ⓓ
4.	Ⓕ	Ⓖ	Ⓗ	Ⓙ
5.	Ⓐ	Ⓑ	Ⓒ	Ⓓ
6.	Ⓕ	Ⓖ	Ⓗ	Ⓙ
7.	Ⓐ	Ⓑ	Ⓒ	Ⓓ
8.	Ⓕ	Ⓖ	Ⓗ	Ⓙ
9.	Ⓐ	Ⓑ	Ⓒ	Ⓓ
10.	Ⓕ	Ⓖ	Ⓗ	Ⓙ
11.	Ⓐ	Ⓑ	Ⓒ	Ⓓ
12.	Ⓕ	Ⓖ	Ⓗ	Ⓙ
13.	Ⓐ	Ⓑ	Ⓒ	Ⓓ
14.	Ⓕ	Ⓖ	Ⓗ	Ⓙ
15.	Ⓐ	Ⓑ	Ⓒ	Ⓓ

© Scott Foresman 6

Selection Test

Directions: Choose the best answer to each item. Mark the letter for the answer
you have chosen.

Part 1: Vocabulary

Find the answer choice that means about the
same as the underlined word in each sentence.

1. Everyone noticed his underline{impatience}.
   A. lack of control
   B. unwillingness to put up with delay
   C. lack of manners
   D. shyness

2. Her plea was underline{insistent}.
   F. fearless
   G. showing bad judgment
   H. unfriendly; hostile
   J. pressing; urgent

3. We were underline{stunned} by the news.
   A. shocked
   B. pleased
   C. excited
   D. angered

4. My uncle made a full underline{recovery}.
   F. act of arranging things in a new way
   G. process of repeating or summing up
   H. process of regaining one's health
   J. act of finding something out

5. The old woman looked underline{distressed}.
   A. feeling or showing scorn
   B. in high spirits; excited
   C. annoyed or angered
   D. in great pain or sorrow

Part 2: Comprehension

Use what you know about the story to answer
each item.

6. Juan looked pale because he—
   F. had been ill.
   G. worked by night.
   H. came from a cold country.
   J. had no friends.

7. Juan heard Doña Josefa say that she must
   be the—
   A. luckiest person in the world.
   B. hardest-working person in the world.
   C. busiest person in the world.
   D. richest person in the world.

8. As he tried to catch up with Doña Josefa,
   Juan first had to—
   F. cross a river.
   G. plant crops on a farm.
   H. climb a mountain.
   J. learn to ride a horse.

9. One big change that Juan noticed in
   himself was that he—
   A. followed Doña Josefa everywhere.
   B. learned to enjoy eating potatoes.
   C. smiled at a little girl.
   D. caught an illness from one of the
      people he met.

10. Why did Doña Josefa keep moving from
    house to house?
    F. She had many friends and relations.
    G. She was a house cleaner.
    H. She liked to travel to different places.
    J. She took care of sick people.

11. How is the text of this story organized?
    A. chronological order
    B. cause and effect
    C. problem and solution
    D. comparison and contrast

12. One of the author's main purposes in this
    story is to—
    F. explain farm work.
    G. compare Juan with Doña Josefa.
    H. teach a lesson.
    J. describe Doña Josefa's work.

© Scott Foresman 6

GO ON

13. Why is "The Gold Coin" a good title for this story?
    - A. The gold coin has Juan's name printed on it.
    - B. The gold coin is a symbol of Juan's greed and Doña Josefa's generosity.
    - C. Readers will be attracted to the story because people are attracted to gold.
    - D. The gold coin represents the hopes and dreams of the people in the story.

14. Which sentence best states a theme of this story?
    - F. Good things come to those who wait.
    - G. The key to happiness is giving to others.
    - H. Wealth comes to those who most deserve it.
    - J. One gold coin can make many people happy.

15. What is the most important change that has taken place between the first time Juan comes to Doña Josefa's house and the next?
    - A. Doña Josefa is not quite as willing to help her neighbors as before.
    - B. A storm is fast approaching.
    - C. Juan decides to help Doña Josefa rather than simply satisfy his own greed.
    - D. The house is now in ruins.

STOP

© Scott Foresman 6

Drawing Conclusions

Directions: Read the story. Then read each question about the story. Choose the best answer to each question. Mark the letter for the answer you have chosen.

A Frog Fable

Once three frogs lived in a shallow pond. Summer came and with it a severe drought. Their pond shrank to a mud puddle. Two of the frogs decided to search for a new home elsewhere. The third, however, claimed she'd just as soon die in their familiar puddle as some strange lake. She refused to go. Finally, her two friends left her. They promised to return as soon as the drought ended. She watched as they hopped away into the distance.

The two frogs hopped a long way, seeking water. At the end of the first day, they came to an old well. It was so dark by then that they could not see the bottom.

"Surely there is water down below. Let's hop right in!" said the first frog, leaping to the top of the wall.

"Wait, wait!" cried her friend. "We must find out for sure before you leap! What if there is no water down below? What if there is no way to climb out?"

"I know what we'll do!" said the first frog. "You will have to help me, though. We will push this pebble over the edge and listen hard. If we hear a splash, we will know there is water. We can also guess how deep it is and how far we will have to fall before we hit the water. If it is high enough, we can climb out whenever we want."

Working together, the tired frogs shoved the pebble over the side. PLUNK! It hit water almost immediately. Relieved that their suffering was over, they jumped into the well.

Suddenly, there was a booming of thunder! "Rain!" cried the first frog. "The drought is over!"

1. Why did the third frog stay behind?
   A. She was afraid of the unknown.
   B. She knew it would rain.
   C. She was happy in the mud puddle.
   D. She hated water.

2. What makes the first two frogs leave the third frog behind?
   F. They are thirstier than she is.
   G. They are braver than she is.
   H. They like to travel.
   J. They want to see the world beyond the pond.

3. Why does one frog hesitate at the side of the well?
   A. She is afraid of the dark.
   B. She is afraid leaping into the well may be dangerous.
   C. She has changed her mind and wants to go home.
   D. She is angry at the first frog.

4. The frogs know it is safe to jump in the well because—
   F. they hear the splash from the pebble right away.
   G. they hear nothing after tossing the pebble in the well.
   H. it begins to rain.
   J. they can see the water when the sun rises.

5. What will the two frogs do now that it's raining?
   A. stay in the well
   B. return to their home
   C. drown in the well
   D. push another pebble into the well

Notes for Home: Your child read a story and formed conclusions about its characters. *Home Activity:* With your child, think of other well-known folk tales or fables. Discuss why characters act a certain way and what lessons they may have learned.

© Scott Foresman 6

Word Study: Word Building

Directions: Read each sentence. Say the underlined word to yourself. Write the letters of the stressed syllable in capital letters and the unstressed syllables in lowercase letters. For example: write **garden** and **garage** as **GAR · den** and **ga · RAGE**.

_____ 1. It is sometimes <u>difficult</u> to understand how life used to be long ago.

_____ 2. <u>Imagine</u> walking five miles to school every day instead of riding in a comfortable school bus!

_____ 3. The past will become more <u>familiar</u> if you compare it to the present.

_____ 4. To learn about your family's past, talk to an older <u>relative</u>.

_____ 5. Try to keep in touch with family and <u>companions</u> in other parts of the country.

_____ 6. My aunt thinks it's <u>wonderful</u> that I keep in touch with my old friends.

_____ 7. My <u>impatience</u> to get letters often prompts me to make a telephone call.

_____ 8. Sometimes, I travel to the <u>countryside</u> to visit family members.

_____ 9. Just remember, traditions will not be <u>forgotten</u> if we work to keep them alive.

Directions: Read the pairs of related words. Say each word to yourself. Circle the stressed syllable in each word.

10. universe

11. universal

12. accident

13. accidental

14. history

15. historical

Notes for Home: Your child identified the stressed syllables in words such as *garden* (first syllable) and *garage* (second syllable). **Home Activity:** Read a poem or song lyrics with your child. Repeat individual words for your child. Work together to decide which syllable is stressed.

© Scott Foresman 6

Recipe

A **recipe** is a set of directions for preparing something to eat. It gives step-by-step instructions and may include pictures. Using recipes will strengthen your skills for following directions and understanding pictures or diagrams.

Directions: Read the recipe. Then answer the questions that follow.

Baked Chinese Egg Rolls

Ingredients:

1 cup all-purpose flour	$\frac{1}{2}$ cup diced shrimp
2 cups water	$\frac{1}{2}$ cup diced pork, cooked
2 eggs	$\frac{1}{2}$ cup chopped water chestnuts
$\frac{1}{2}$ teaspoon salt	$\frac{1}{2}$ cup bean sprouts
3 tablespoons vegetable oil	1 clove garlic, chopped
$\frac{1}{2}$ cup chopped celery	$\frac{1}{4}$ cup soy sauce
$\frac{3}{4}$ cup chopped cabbage	$\frac{1}{2}$ teaspoon sugar

4 scallions, chopped

Steps:

1. Sift flour into bowl.
2. Stir in water.
3. Beat in eggs and salt to make a smooth batter.
4. Grease a skillet with some cooking oil, butter, or margarine, and set the skillet on low heat.
5. Pour 1 tablespoon of batter into the pan to form a thin pancake. Flip so it cooks on the opposite side. Remove and set on a plate. Repeat Step 5 to make more thin pancakes. These are the outside of the egg rolls.
6. In another skillet, heat the vegetable oil.
7. Then add the celery, cabbage, and scallions. When they are nicely fried, stir in the shrimp and pork. Cook for about 3 minutes.
8. Then add the water chestnuts, bean sprouts, garlic, soy sauce, and sugar. Cook for another 5 minutes. This is the filling for the egg rolls.
9. Spoon about 4 tablespoons of filling onto each pancake.
10. Roll the pancake around the filling and fold up the ends.
11. Place on a tray in a 425°F oven for 15 minutes.
12. Serve with sweet-and-sour sauce, Chinese mustard, or soy sauce.

Makes about 12 egg rolls.

© Scott Foresman 6

1. Before starting this recipe, which cooking tools would you need to get together?

_____

_____

2. How is the list of ingredients organized? _____

_____

3. In which way are most of the vegetables prepared? _____

_____

4. What do you have to do to the pork before you can add it in Step 7? How do you know?

_____

_____

5. What part of the Baked Chinese Egg Rolls is made first? _____

_____

6. Do you think you would be able to cook the pancakes and the vegetables at the same time? Why or why not?

_____

_____

7. If you had two dozen people to serve, what would you need to do to this recipe? Why?

_____

_____

8. Why do you think the ingredients are listed separate from the steps of the recipe?

_____

_____

9. Do the pictures help you understand the recipe? Explain. _____

_____

10. Why do you think using recipes will help you strengthen your skills in following directions and understanding pictures and diagrams?

_____

_____

Notes for Home Your child read a recipe, and answered questions about its organization and contents. *Home Activity:* Help your child to write a recipe for a favorite dish by listing the ingredients and steps to follow. Work together, using the recipe to make the dish.

© Scott Foresman 6

Fact and Opinion

- A **statement of fact** can be proven true or false. You can prove it true or false by reading, observing, asking an expert, or checking it in some way.

- A **statement of opinion** tells someone's belief, judgment, or way of thinking about something. It cannot be proven true or false, but it can be supported or explained.

- Some sentences contain both facts and opinions.

Directions: Reread "Mount Everest: The Ultimate Challenge." Then complete the table. Write **X** in the proper column to show whether each statement contains a fact or an opinion.

Statement	Fact	Opinion
1. The peak of Mount Everest used to be a tough place to reach.		
2. The mountain is on the border of Nepal and China.		
3. Many climbers have come away with an incredible experience.		
4. Climbers have contributed $90 million to Nepal's economy.		
5. Modern technology makes it easier for climbers to communicate with faraway people.		
6. Too many inexperienced climbers attempt to scale Everest's treacherous terrain.		
7. About one in every thirty Everest climbers dies in the attempt.		
8. Eight climbers died in May 1996.		
9. Climbers leave behind oxygen cylinders, food remains, and other garbage.		
10. The May disaster will make climbers rethink their attitudes about climbing Mount Everest.		

Notes for Home: Your child read an article and decided whether statements were statements of fact or opinion. *Home Activity:* Have your child describe his or her school day, giving at least three statements of fact and three statements of opinion.

© Scott Foresman 6

Vocabulary

Directions: Choose the word from the box that best completes each
sentence. Write the word on the line to the left.

_____ 1. I own many books about _____ to
faraway places.

_____ 2. I've always wanted to go to the _____
and reach the North Pole.

_____ 3. I'm sure that hiking through a place like
that would be _____.

_____ 4. The icy _____ creates challenges for
even the most experienced explorers.

_____ 5. The weather conditions at that latitude
and _____ can be quite severe.

**Check
the Words
You Know**

__ Arctic
__ collide
__ expeditions
__ latitude
__ longitude
__ satellite
__ strenuous
__ terrain

Directions: Choose the word from the box that best matches each clue.
Write the word in the puzzle.

Down

6. distance north or south of the equator

8. natural features of a region

9. crash into something

Across

7. an artificial object that orbits around a planet

10. journeys to uncharted areas

Write a Story

On a separate sheet of paper, write a story about exploring an unfamiliar place.
Use as many vocabulary words as you can.

Notes for Home: Your child identified and used vocabulary words from "To the Pole." *Home
Activity:* Read a story about exploration with your child. Encourage your child to try to find
synonyms—words with similar meanings—to the vocabulary words listed above.

© Scott Foresman 6

Fact and Opinion

- A **statement of fact** can be proven true or false. You can prove it true or false by reading, observing, asking an expert, or checking it in some way.

- A **statement of opinion** tells someone's belief, judgment, or way of thinking about something. It cannot be proven true or false, but it can be supported or explained.

- Some sentences contain both facts and opinions.

Directions: Reread the part of "To the Pole" in which Will Steger describes sharing a tent with Victor. Then answer the questions below. Think about whether statements can be proven true or false.

Victor and I are sharing a tent. In our travels across Antarctica and Greenland we have tented together many nights before. He is good company—we know each other's habits well, and his optimism is always a boost to me.

We're like a little family of two, living inside a space the size of a car. Our arrangement is that I prepare dinner and he makes breakfast. In the morning, while I'm still in my sleeping bag, I know exactly what time it is by the breakfast sounds Victor is making. When I hear him stirring dried fruit and hot chocolate powder into a steaming bowl of leftover rice—my favorite on-the-ice breakfast—I know it is 6:40. Ten minutes later he will pour hot water for our tea.

From OVER THE TOP OF THE WORLD by Will Steger and Jon Bowermaster. Copyright © 1997 by Will Steger and Jon Bowermaster. Reprinted by permission of Scholastic Inc.

1. What is Will's opinion of Victor? How do you know?

_____

2. What facts are given about how chores will be done in the tent?

_____

3. Will writes, "We are like a little family . . ." Is this a statement of fact or opinion? Explain.

_____

4. Is Will's statement "I know it is 6:40" a statement of fact or opinion? Explain.

_____

5. How might the facts and opinions found in "To the Pole" be useful to another expedition? Explain your thinking on a separate sheet of paper.

Notes for Home: Your child identified statements of fact and opinion in a nonfiction text. *Home Activity:* Read the promotional material from a book or video cover with your child. Have him or her identify the statements of fact and the statements of opinion.

© Scott Foresman 6

1.	Ⓐ	Ⓑ	Ⓒ	Ⓓ
2.	Ⓕ	Ⓖ	Ⓗ	Ⓙ
3.	Ⓐ	Ⓑ	Ⓒ	Ⓓ
4.	Ⓕ	Ⓖ	Ⓗ	Ⓙ
5.	Ⓐ	Ⓑ	Ⓒ	Ⓓ
6.	Ⓕ	Ⓖ	Ⓗ	Ⓙ
7.	Ⓐ	Ⓑ	Ⓒ	Ⓓ
8.	Ⓕ	Ⓖ	Ⓗ	Ⓙ
9.	Ⓐ	Ⓑ	Ⓒ	Ⓓ
10.	Ⓕ	Ⓖ	Ⓗ	Ⓙ
11.	Ⓐ	Ⓑ	Ⓒ	Ⓓ
12.	Ⓕ	Ⓖ	Ⓗ	Ⓙ
13.	Ⓐ	Ⓑ	Ⓒ	Ⓓ
14.	Ⓕ	Ⓖ	Ⓗ	Ⓙ
15.	Ⓐ	Ⓑ	Ⓒ	Ⓓ

© Scott Foresman 6

Selection Test

Directions: Choose the best answer to each item. Mark the letter for the answer you have chosen.

Part 1: Vocabulary

Find the answer choice that means about the same as the underlined word in each sentence.

1. They struggled over the rough <u>terrain</u>.
   - A. the surface of the ocean
   - B. a ridge of high mountains
   - C. violent, rushing stream of water
   - D. the natural features of a region

2. He wanted to know the <u>latitude</u>.
   - F. distance north or south of the equator
   - G. height above the earth's surface
   - H. space in between two points
   - J. distance east or west on the earth's surface

3. We hoped the wagons wouldn't <u>collide</u>.
   - A. break apart
   - B. crash into each other
   - C. topple over
   - D. cave in

4. They traveled to the <u>Arctic</u>.
   - F. south polar region
   - G. high mountains in Asia
   - H. north polar region
   - J. desert in Africa

5. She had been on several <u>expeditions</u>.
   - A. journeys for a special purpose, such as exploration or study
   - B. long periods in outer space
   - C. visits to a zoo or museum
   - D. cruise ships

6. The journey was <u>strenuous</u>.
   - F. exciting; full of adventure
   - G. causing worry or fuss
   - H. dull and uninteresting
   - J. requiring much energy

7. The camps were at the same <u>longitude</u>.
   - A. height above the earth's surface
   - B. distance east or west on the earth's surface
   - C. space in between two points
   - D. distance north or south of the equator

8. They communicated via <u>satellite</u>.
   - F. a system of telephones connected by wires
   - G. an artificial object launched into orbit around the earth
   - H. a machine with an engine and wheels
   - J. an unidentified flying object

Part 2: Comprehension

Use what you know about the selection to answer each item.

9. Which condition presented the biggest challenge for Will Steger and his companions?
   - A. big mounds of ice
   - B. snowdrifts
   - C. open water
   - D. pressure ridges

10. The job of the "point person" is to—
    - F. ski out ahead to find a safe path.
    - G. steer the lead sled.
    - H. use the Global Positioning System.
    - J. set up the campsite.

© Scott Foresman 6

GO ON

11. Which sentence states an opinion?
    A. "We have reached the North Pole exactly as planned, on Earth Day."
    B. "Our friends have brought supplies with them—including letters and small gifts."
    C. "But I got the best present—an apple pie baked by my mother."
    D. "Victor is the first Russian to reach both the North and South poles by skis."

12. Which of the following sentences states a fact?
    F. "But then, just before we got here, it began to look like heaven."
    G. "We passed 89 degrees north latitude, which means we are less than 60 miles from the pole!"
    H. "So far, the most surprising aspect of the whole trip is all the snow."
    J. "When we left the North Pole, it seemed like a perfect day."

13. Most of the information in this selection is organized by—
    A. comparison/contrast.
    B. cause and effect.
    C. problem and solution.
    D. chronological order.

14. Which generalization seems to be based on the author's personal opinion?
    F. In most years, the Arctic has little precipitation.
    G. On most days, the ice they crossed was more than three years old.
    H. Female sled dogs are often very bright.
    J. The peoples of the Arctic have adapted to the environment.

15. Which part of this selection best supports the author's goal of showing "how all parts of the world are interconnected"?
    A. the section on pollution in the Arctic
    B. the part describing animals of the Arctic
    C. the entry for April 22, when the team reached the North Pole
    D. the section called "Facts from the Trip"

© Scott Foresman 6

Summarizing and Text Structure

Directions: Read the passage. Then read each question about the passage. Choose the best answer to each question. Mark the letter for the answer you have chosen.

Travels of the Past

The explorer and anthropologist Thor Heyerdahl went on many adventures in order to test his ideas. He believed ancient peoples regularly traveled great distances, and that this is why we find similar objects in places that are very far apart. He tested his ideas by crossing oceans in small handmade boats like those used in ancient times.

One of Thor Heyerdahl's ideas was that the native peoples of Peru were able to sail to Polynesia in the distant past. He thought that even though they did not know latitude and longitude, they were able to follow ocean currents and the stars in the sky. He tried out his idea by building a balsa raft like the ones Peruvians made long ago. His movie about this successful trip won an Academy Award in 1951. With his small crew, he led several other successful expeditions from South America to the East Pacific, to show that such long journeys would have been possible for Native American people.

Thor Heyerdahl also was able to cross the Atlantic from North Africa in a boat modeled after ancient Egyptian papyrus boats. He believed that ancient Egyptians actually did travel to South America this way and that the Egyptians are the ancestors of the Aztec and Inca people.

Thor Heyerdahl also believed that the Sumerians, who lived between the Tigris and Euphrates Rivers 5,000 years ago in what is now Iraq, traveled from their homeland to the Indian Ocean. However, war in the region kept him from testing his idea and the model reed boat he had built.

1. A summary of this article should **not** include the information about—
   A. travel from South America to Polynesia.
   B. journeys by Egyptians to America.
   C. the movie about the trip to Polynesia.
   D. Sumerian travel to the Indian Ocean.

2. A main idea of this article is that ancient peoples—
   F. followed currents and stars.
   G. were smart.
   H. did not know latitude and longitude.
   J. traveled far in simple crafts.

3. A summary of this article should include information about Thor Heyerdahl's —
   A. ways of testing his ideas about ancient travel.
   B. balsa raft.
   C. crew.
   D. education.

4. Thor Heyerdahl believed that journeys made in ancient times explain why—
   F. his film won an Academy Award.
   G. Egyptians used boats made of papyrus.
   H. similar objects are found in places great distances apart.
   J. the native peoples of Peru built such excellent boats.

5. Which text structure best describes the organization of this article?
   A. chronological order
   B. comparison-contrast
   C. problem-solution
   D. cause-effect

Notes for Home: Your child read a passage and identified its main ideas and text structure. *Home Activity:* Read a nonfiction article from a magazine with your child. Have your child identify its main ideas and then summarize it.

© Scott Foresman 6

Word Study: Prefixes

Directions: A letter or group of letters added to the beginning of a word is a **prefix.** A prefix can change the meaning of a word. Add a prefix to each word below to make a new word. Write each new word on the line.

1. re   +   heat   =   _____

2. in   +   active   =   _____

3. un   +   wrap   =   _____

4. in   +   complete   =   _____

5. re   +   place   =   _____

6. un   +   lock   =   _____

7. in   +   audible   =   _____

8. re   +   play   =   _____

Directions: Read the newspaper story below. Look for the words with the prefixes **un-, re-,** or **in-.** Circle these words. Then write the prefix and the rest of the word on the line, connected by a + sign. For example, for **undone,** you would write **un + done.**

★★★★★★★★★★★★★★★★★★
AMAZING JOURNEY!

An unlikely group has reached the North Pole. Students from a local college have journeyed with their teachers over unstable ice floes and uneven terrain to reach territory not many have seen. This unusual accomplishment was funded by a major corporation, who met the group at critical points along the way to restock their food supply and check on their health. The group made it by the end of the summer, just before the ice floes reformed and froze solid. It was an incredible show of courage and fortitude!

9. _____

10. _____

11. _____

12. _____

13. _____

14. _____

15. _____

Notes for Home: Your child formed new words by adding the prefixes *un-, re-,* and *in-* to base words. ***Home Activity:*** Read a newspaper story with your child. Help your child find words that have these prefixes. Have your child write each word and circle its prefix.

© Scott Foresman 6

Schedule

A **schedule** is a specialized chart that lists events and when they take place, side by side.

Directions: Read the schedule for cruise ships. Note the names of the cruise ships, their departure dates, routes, and arrival dates. Then answer the questions that follow.

Cruise Ship	Departure/ Anchorage, Alaska	Arrive at Prudhoe Bay (3-day stay)	Sail Through Queen Elizabeth Islands	Final Destination/ Frobisher Bay, Canada
Alaskan Princess	June 1	June 5	June 8–10	June 15
Arctic Mist	June 10	June 15	June 18–20	June 25
Northern Explorer	June 25	June 30	July 3–5	July 10
Polar Princess	July 3	July 8	July 11–13	July 18
Vancouver Vacation	July 15	July 20	July 23–25	July 30
Queen Elizabeth's Quest	July 22	July 27	July 30–August 1	August 6
Alaskan Princess	July 31	August 4	August 7–9	August 14
Arctic Mist	August 7	August 12	August 15–18	August 23
Northern Explorer	August 18	August 23	August 16–28	September 2
Polar Princess	August 29	September 3	September 6–8	September 13
Vancouver Vacation	September 10	September 15	September 18–20	September 25
Queen Elizabeth's Quest	September 20	September 25	September 28–30	October 5

1. How many days is each cruise? How can you tell? _____

_____

2. How many ships travel this route? How can you tell? _____

_____

3. If you traveled on the first sailing of the *Arctic Mist,* during which days would you cruise through the Queen Elizabeth Islands?

_____

4. What happens at Prudhoe Bay? How can you tell? _____

_____

5. If you wanted to sail on the *Polar Princess,* for which dates could you schedule a trip?

_____

© Scott Foresman 6

Directions: Use the schedule of shipboard events to answer the questions that follow.

Schedule of Activities for June 10							
Activity	7 A.M. to 9 A.M.	9 A.M. to 11 A.M.	11 A.M. to 1 P.M.	1 P.M. to 3 P.M.	3 P.M. to 5 P.M.	5 P.M. to 7 P.M.	7 P.M. to 9 P.M.
Bird Watching	✓	✓	✓				
Ship Walk	✓	✓	✓	✓	✓	✓	
Whale Watching	✓	✓	✓	✓	✓		
Shuffleboard			✓	✓	✓		
Midday Movie Feature			✓				
Iceberg Viewing	✓	✓	✓	✓	✓	✓	
Ping-Pong Tournament					✓	✓	✓
Line Dancing Instruction					✓		✓
First Dinner Seating						✓	
Talent Show							✓
Photography Class		✓		✓			✓

✓ = Activity is available.

6. What do the checkmarks on the schedule represent? How do you know?

_____

_____

7. Between which hours might you be able to watch for whales? _____

8. Which activities occur at the same time as the talent show? _____

_____

9. If you watched the Midday Movie Feature, which activities would you be missing?

_____

_____

10. How does the schedule assist passengers in planning their day? _____

_____

Notes for Home: Your child answered questions about schedules. *Home Activity:* Obtain a schedule for a bus or train route. Plan a trip with your child. Choose a destination and a departure time, and then figure out your arrival time and how long the trip would take.

© Scott Foresman 6

Context Clues

- **Context clues** are words that come before or after an unfamiliar word and help you figure out what it means.

- A context clue may be a synonym, a word with nearly the same meaning as the unknown word, or an antonym, a word with an opposite meaning.

- A context clue may also be a definition or explanation of the unknown word, or a series of examples.

Directions: Reread "For the First Time." Then complete the table. Use context clues to determine the meaning of each word or group of words from the story.

Words	Meaning
gallina rellena	1.
frijoles machacados	2.
guacamole salad	3.
bollitos	4.
tortillas	5.

Notes for Home: Your child read a story and used context clues to figure out the meaning of five words from the story. ***Home Activity:*** Read a story with your child. Prompt your child to point out unfamiliar words. Help him or her use context clues to figure out the meaning of these words.

© Scott Foresman 6

Vocabulary

Directions: Choose the word from the box that best answers each question.
Write the word on the line.

**Check
the Words
You Know**

__ bandits
__ caravans
__ conserve
__ embark
__ exiled
__ merciful

_____ 1. Which word describes people who break
the law?

_____ 2. Which word describes someone who does
not like to see other people suffer?

_____ 3. Which word has a similar meaning to the
word *begin?*

_____ 4. Which word means to save something,
such as energy or resources?

_____ 5. Which word describes groups of people
who are traveling?

Directions: Choose the word from the box that best replaces the underlined word
or words. Write the word on the line to the left.

_____ 6. Shefki was <u>banished</u> from his country because of his political
beliefs.

_____ 7. If it were not for a <u>kind, sympathetic</u> judge, he might have
been imprisoned for life.

_____ 8. Not knowing where to go, he decided to <u>set out</u> on a journey
across the desert.

_____ 9. He joined one of the <u>groups of travelers</u> that were going to
Asia to trade for silks and spices.

_____ 10. The groups traveled together for protection
against <u>outlaws</u> who might rob them.

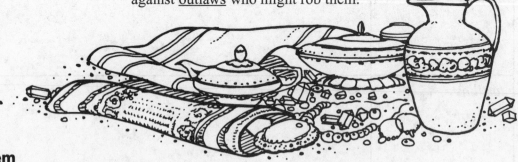

Write a Poem

On a separate sheet of paper, write a poem that tells a story of someone who must
leave his or her homeland and travel to a strange unknown place. Use as many
vocabulary words as you can in your poem.

Notes for Home: Your child identified and used vocabulary words from *El Güero*. **Home
Activity:** Act out an adventure story with your child using the listed vocabulary words.

© Scott Foresman 6

Context Clues

> • **Context clues** are words that come before or after an unfamiliar word and help you figure out what it means.
>
> • Specific types of context clues include a synonym, a word with the same or nearly the same meaning as the unfamiliar word; an antonym, a word that means the opposite of the unfamiliar word; a definition or explanation that appears before or after the unfamiliar word; or an example to explain the unfamiliar word.

Directions: Reread the passage from *El Güero* in which the characters are introduced. Then use context clues and refer to the list of types of context clues to answer the questions below.

My name is Porfirio, but nobody ever calls me by my name. It is because most people in this country have dark eyes and dark hair, while my eyes are green and my hair is yellow. It is for this reason that everyone calls me El Güero, or the Blond One. My little sister, María, is called Maruca. I call my Aunt Victoria Tía Vicky, and my mother Mamacita. Everyone in Mexico has a nickname, or a short, affectionate form of his name. Only my father, the Judge, who is so dignified and taciturn, is called by his name, Cayetano, and then only by Mamacita and Tía Vicky. I have been told to call him Papá, though the other children I know call their fathers Papacito, dear little father.

Excerpt from EL GÜERO: A TRUE ADVENTURE STORY by Elizabeth Borton de Treviño. Copyright © 1989 by Elizabeth Borton de Treviño. Reprinted by permission of Farrar, Straus & Giroux, Inc.

1. What context clues are used to explain the meaning of *El Güero* in the passage?

_____

2. Which type of context clue helps you understand the meaning of *nickname?*

_____

3. Which context clues can be used to understand what *taciturn* means? How might you check if your understanding is correct?

_____

_____

4. What does *Papacito* mean? How do you know?

_____

5. On a separate sheet of paper, list three other unfamiliar words from *El Güero* that you defined with the help of context clues. Write the meaning of each word.

© Scott Foresman 6

Notes for Home: Your child used context clues to figure out the meaning of unfamiliar words. *Home Activity:* Read a brief magazine article with your child. Help him or her to use context clues to determine the meaning of any unfamiliar words.

1.	Ⓐ	Ⓑ	Ⓒ	Ⓓ
2.	Ⓕ	Ⓖ	Ⓗ	Ⓙ
3.	Ⓐ	Ⓑ	Ⓒ	Ⓓ
4.	Ⓕ	Ⓖ	Ⓗ	Ⓙ
5.	Ⓐ	Ⓑ	Ⓒ	Ⓓ
6.	Ⓕ	Ⓖ	Ⓗ	Ⓙ
7.	Ⓐ	Ⓑ	Ⓒ	Ⓓ
8.	Ⓕ	Ⓖ	Ⓗ	Ⓙ
9.	Ⓐ	Ⓑ	Ⓒ	Ⓓ
10.	Ⓕ	Ⓖ	Ⓗ	Ⓙ
11.	Ⓐ	Ⓑ	Ⓒ	Ⓓ
12.	Ⓕ	Ⓖ	Ⓗ	Ⓙ
13.	Ⓐ	Ⓑ	Ⓒ	Ⓓ
14.	Ⓕ	Ⓖ	Ⓗ	Ⓙ
15.	Ⓐ	Ⓑ	Ⓒ	Ⓓ

© Scott Foresman 6

Selection Test

Directions: Choose the best answer to each item. Mark the letter for the answer you have chosen.

Part 1: Vocabulary

Find the answer choice that means about the same as the underlined word in each sentence.

1. The former president was exiled.
   A.   held back
   B.   assigned to a different job
   C.   imprisoned
   D.   forced to leave one's country or home

2. The family was ready to embark.
   F.   set out; start
   G.   make a decision
   H.   make their own way
   J.   take a rest

3. The merchants traveled in caravans.
   A.   small, fast sailing ships
   B.   groups of people traveling together for safety
   C.   trails marked in the woods
   D.   wagons with covers that can be taken off

4. A group of bandits approached.
   F.   pilgrims; travelers
   G.   soldiers
   H.   robbers; outlaws
   J.   peasants

5. Mr. Alexander was merciful.
   A.   showing mercy or kindness
   B.   having a stern expression
   C.   honest and truthful
   D.   tending to be cruel

6. We learned to conserve water.
   F.   be thankful for
   G.   find many uses for
   H.   make clean; purify
   J.   keep from wasting or using up

Part 2: Comprehension

Use what you know about the story to answer each item.

7. The narrator of the story is called "El Güero" because—
   A.   he is strong.
   B.   it is his name.
   C.   he is small.
   D.   his hair is yellow.

8. *Cayetano* is—
   F.   the nickname El Güero's mother uses
   G.   El Güero's father's name
   H.   a word meaning "dear little father"
   J.   the Spanish word for "judge"

9. Why was El Güero's family upset at the beginning of the story?
   A.   The President had offered El Güero's father a new job.
   B.   They were being forced to leave their home.
   C.   They had decided to move to a different country.
   D.   A war had begun, and they had to escape.

10. Why did the bandit leader decide to protect the judge and his family?
    F.   He hoped for a reward.
    G.   He was grateful for how the judge had treated him.
    H.   He was afraid of the judge.
    J.   He liked the judge's family.

11. El Güero explains, "There he had written poetry and had declaimed it before large audiences." Declaimed means—
    A.   took something back.
    B.   burned.
    C.   recited in public.
    D.   copied.

GO ON

© Scott Foresman 6

12. El Güero's father buys quinine from a pharmacist. You can figure out the meaning of the word <u>pharmacist</u> from the clue that—
    F. quinine is made from a tree in Peru.
    G. the pharmacist lives in Acapulco.
    H. quinine is a medicine.
    J. the family is staying in a hotel.

13. From the family's experiences on their journey, you can conclude that—
    A. physical health is the first thing to suffer in such situations.
    B. people tend to become very selfish when resources are limited.
    C. difficult situations can strengthen people and relationships.
    D. people who are in a faraway place really get on each other's nerves.

14. Which clue helps you understand that this story takes place in the past?
    F. The ship burns coal to power its steam engine.
    G. The judge has to pay the captain of the ship for passage.
    H. The food on the ship is heavy and salty.
    J. Tía Vicky carries scissors, thread, and cloth in her baggage.

15. At Cabo San Lucas, who seems to give up the most to help the family?
    A. El Güero
    B. Maruca
    C. Tía Vicky
    D. Mamacita

STOP

© Scott Foresman 6

Setting

Directions: Read the story. Then read each question about the story. Choose the best answer to each question. Mark the letter for the answer you have chosen.

The Endless Count

Jonelle and her friends gathered at their wooden table under the oak, each carrying a breakfast tray. None of the other people around the girls seemed aware of the awful situation they were in. The others talked excitedly about the day's activities, but Jonelle's friends did not need to talk.

No words, just numbers. Each of them was silently counting the days left until they could return to civilization. How could their parents have sent them off into the heat, the flies, the bugs, the pollen, the dust, the unfamiliar sheets, the shared bathrooms, the tiny cabins?

Jonelle's parents had been sure she would enjoy a month of camping. In spite of her protests that she would rather stay at home, they made the arrangements and bundled Jonelle into the car. "It's for your own good, honey" and "You'll thank us by the time you come home" were two sentences that stuck in Jonelle's mind. During the drive to camp, her mother told stories about her childhood summers in the hot city and her longing for a country vacation. Her father told stories about the great times he had had at camp when he was a boy. But Jonelle knew better. She would hate it!

The camp leaders had promised another day of walking through woods, looking at birds and plants. This was not life as Jonelle knew and liked it. No friends' houses, no lazy afternoons by the pool, no shopping malls, not even school. Jonelle was shocked. Could she actually be eager for the new school year to start?

1. Jonelle and her friends eat breakfast—
   A.   cold.
   B.   outside.
   C.   in a hall.
   D.   in a cabin.

2. Jonelle and the others are staying in—
   F.   a school.
   G.   a prison.
   H.   a friend's home.
   J.   a camp.

3. Which of the following is **not** part of the setting?
   A.   a swimming pool
   B.   an oak tree
   C.   tiny cabins
   D.   a wooden table

4. What effect does the setting have on Jonelle?
   F.   She hates being away from "civilization."
   G.   She misses her parents.
   H.   She wants to go on a nature walk.
   J.   She doesn't want to return to school.

5. The time of year is most likely—
   A.   spring.
   B.   summer.
   C.   fall.
   D.   winter.

Notes for Home: Your child read a story and answered questions about its setting. ***Home Activity:*** After watching a movie together, encourage your child to discuss its setting. Talk about how the setting affected the characters and their actions.

© Scott Foresman 6

Word Study: Suffixes

Directions: A letter or group of letters added to the end of a word is called a **suffix.** A suffix can change the meaning of the base word. Add a suffix to each word below to make a new word. Write each new word on the line.

1. right   +   ful   =   _____
2. flex   +   ible   =   _____
3. final   +   ly   =   _____
4. mercy   +   ful   =   _____
5. care   +   ful   +   ly   =   _____
6. fortune   +   ate   +   ly   =   _____

Directions: Read the sentences below. Look and listen for words with the suffixes **-ly, -ful,** or **-ible.** Circle these words. Then write the base word and the suffix on the line, connected by a + sign. For example, for **doubtful,** you would write **doubt + ful.**

_____ 7. Sadly, the family packed their belongings and left their home behind.

_____ 8. Being sensible, they took the first ship they could find traveling out of the country.

_____ 9. The new travelers tried to make themselves useful on board.

_____ 10. They helped prepare meals and entertained the crew willingly.

_____ 11. Once, a fog drifted in, and the ship's captain realized that the ship was slightly off course.

_____ 12. He instantly took action to correct the direction.

_____ 13. When the ship docked, the family gazed with joy at the beautiful city that would be their new home.

_____ 14. How wonderful it felt to stand on solid ground again!

_____ 15. As they made a new life for themselves, they tried to forget the painful memories of leaving their old home.

 Notes for Home: Your child formed new words by adding the suffixes *-ly, -ful,* and *-ible* to base words. *Home Activity:* Read a magazine article with your child. Help your child notice words with these suffixes. Have your child group words with the same suffix together and write them in a list.

© Scott Foresman 6

Evaluate Reference Sources

In order to decide whether a source is reliable and valid, you need to **evaluate reference sources.** You need to decide whether the information in the source is complete, unbiased, factual, and up-to-date, and ask yourself whether the source provides the kind of information you need for your research purposes.

Directions: Study the different reference sources. Then answer the questions that follow.

TRAVELING THE WORLD

Table of Contents

Getting from Here to There: A History of Travel

Contents

The World Almanac 1998, Index

World Travel

Vol. 232   Issue 9   February 1999

Features

Photo Essay

Interview

© Scott Foresman 6

Name _____

1. Read the chapter titles for *Traveling the World*. What is this book mostly about?

f _____

2. Read the chapter titles for *Getting from Here to There*. What is this book mostly about?

_____

3. Suppose you are writing a paper about exciting, yet difficult, journeys. Which of these two books would be the most helpful? Why?

_____

4. Suppose you wanted historical information about ships from long ago. Which of the resources shown would be most useful? Explain.

_____

_____

5. Would an almanac be a good place to find out the population of Jamaica? Explain.

_____

6. Suppose you wanted to read about someone's real-life travel experiences. Would the magazine *World Travel* be helpful? Explain.

_____

_____

7. Suppose you were writing a report on the invention of the airplane and you discovered that the book *Getting from Here to There* was published in 1995. Would this book still be a useful reference source? Explain.

_____

_____

8. When evaluating books, why is it important to check the copyright page?

_____

_____

9. How can an index or a table of contents help you evaluate a reference source?

_____

_____

10. Why is it important to set a purpose for your research before evaluating reference sources?

_____

_____

Notes for Home: Your child evaluated reference sources for specific research purposes. *Home Activity:* With your child, think of a topic and write questions about what you would like to know. Discuss what kinds of reference sources would be the most helpful.

© Scott Foresman 6

Steps in a Process

	First
	↓
	Then
	↓
	Next
	↓
	Last

- The actions you perform in order to make something or to reach a goal are the **steps in a process.**

- Sometimes the steps in a process will have numbers. Other clues to the order of the steps are words like *first, begin, next, then,* and *last.* If there are no clue words or numbers to help you keep the steps in order, use your common sense.

- Sometimes the steps in a process refer to a process in nature, such as the growth of a plant.

Directions: Reread "Living in Space." Then complete the flow chart to describe the process by which oxygen, water, and carbon dioxide are constantly recycled in a bottle garden. Write the steps in the flow chart in the order in which they occur. Some steps have been started for you.

1. Plants collect

↓

2. Plants convert

↓

3. The leaves also produce

↓

4.

↓

5.

Notes for Home: Your child read about a process and listed the steps in the process in the order in which they occur. ***Home Activity:*** Encourage your child to list the steps in an everyday process, such as making breakfast or playing a compact disc.

© Scott Foresman 6

Vocabulary

Directions: Choose the word from the box that best completes each
sentence. Write the word on the line to the left.

Check the Words You Know

__ commander
__ concepts
__ detected
__ organism
__ radiation

_____   1. The _____ had led many dangerous
                              missions.

_____   2. This mission was created because
                              scientists thought they had _____ life
                              on another planet.

_____   3. The commander and his crew were to
                              determine whether there was a living
                              _____ on the planet.

_____   4. The scientists were eager to find out if their _____ about
                              alien life forms were valid.

_____   5. However, when the ship got near the planet, it was
                              surrounded by dangerous levels of _____. The mission
                              could not be completed successfully.

Directions: Choose the word from the box that best matches each clue.
Write the word in the puzzle.

Down

6. ideas; notions

7. discovered; found

8. a living thing

Across

9. person in charge

10. radioactivity

Write a Brochure

A brochure is a small pamphlet that tells detailed information about
a place or a product. Use separate sheets of paper to write a brochure
advertising a tourist trip to another planet. Include as many vocabulary
words as you can.

Notes for Home: Your child identified and used vocabulary words from "Destination: Mars."
Home Activity: With your child, act out a space adventure. Try to use as many vocabulary
words as you can.

© Scott Foresman 6

Steps in a Process

- The actions you perform in order to make something or to reach a goal are the **steps in a process.**
- Sometimes the steps in a process will have numbers. Other clues to the order of the steps are words like *first, begin, next, then,* and *last.*

Directions: Reread the part of "Destination: Mars" that tells what will be done after landing on Mars. Then answer the questions below. Think about the order of steps to take in establishing life on Mars.

> Soon after landing, your crew will cover your habitat with sandbags to protect it against ultraviolet radiation and solar flares. You will set up experimental greenhouses, to see what plants can be grown without soil, *hydroponically.* You will determine what needs to be done to the Martian soil so that it can support plant life. Perhaps you will set up pools for fish, as a future source of protein. You will study the Martian weather and geology. You will investigate the possibilities of terraforming.
>
> From LIFE ON MARS by David Getz, © 1997 by David Getz.
> Reprinted by permission of Henry Holt and Company, LLC.

1. Which step will be done first and why?

   _____

   _____

2. Before trying to grow plants in Martian soil, which step should be done?

   _____

   _____

3. Which step will have to be done to provide a source of protein on Mars?

   _____

   _____

4. What are the final steps mentioned in this passage?

   _____

   _____

5. On a separate sheet of paper, explain why the steps described in the passage above are being taken. Reread that part of the selection to help you explain.

Notes for Home: Your child read a passage from a selection and identified the steps in a process. *Home Activity:* Read an instruction guide for using a simple household machine with your child. Encourage her or him to retell the steps for use in the correct order.

© Scott Foresman 6

1.	Ⓐ	Ⓑ	Ⓒ	Ⓓ
2.	Ⓕ	Ⓖ	Ⓗ	Ⓙ
3.	Ⓐ	Ⓑ	Ⓒ	Ⓓ
4.	Ⓕ	Ⓖ	Ⓗ	Ⓙ
5.	Ⓐ	Ⓑ	Ⓒ	Ⓓ
6.	Ⓕ	Ⓖ	Ⓗ	Ⓙ
7.	Ⓐ	Ⓑ	Ⓒ	Ⓓ
8.	Ⓕ	Ⓖ	Ⓗ	Ⓙ
9.	Ⓐ	Ⓑ	Ⓒ	Ⓓ
10.	Ⓕ	Ⓖ	Ⓗ	Ⓙ
11.	Ⓐ	Ⓑ	Ⓒ	Ⓓ
12.	Ⓕ	Ⓖ	Ⓗ	Ⓙ
13.	Ⓐ	Ⓑ	Ⓒ	Ⓓ
14.	Ⓕ	Ⓖ	Ⓗ	Ⓙ
15.	Ⓐ	Ⓑ	Ⓒ	Ⓓ

© Scott Foresman 6

Selection Test

Directions: Choose the best answer to each item. Mark the letter for the answer you have chosen.

Part 1: Vocabulary

Find the answer choice that means about the same as the underlined word in each sentence.

1. He was studying the effects of <u>radiation</u>.
   - A. the process of changing from a liquid to a gas
   - B. rays of light
   - C. particles or waves produced by nuclear decay
   - D. electronic signals received by radio

2. We <u>detected</u> some salt in the water.
   - F. discovered
   - G. placed
   - H. wished for
   - J. required

3. Dr. Graham found an <u>organism</u> in the bay.
   - A. sunken ship
   - B. disease that spreads from one person to another
   - C. type of musical instrument
   - D. animal, plant, or other living thing

4. We waited to hear from the <u>commander</u>.
   - F. person who takes part in combat
   - G. self-piloted space vehicle
   - H. person in charge
   - J. person who makes things

5. Janice does not understand the <u>concepts</u> of law.
   - A. documents
   - B. ideas; general notions
   - C. decisions
   - D. problems; puzzles

Part 2: Comprehension

Use what you know about the selection to answer each item.

6. The atmosphere of Mars is mainly—
   - F. oxygen.
   - G. carbon dioxide.
   - H. water vapor.
   - J. hydrogen.

7. How long will it take a spacecraft to make the trip from Earth to Mars?
   - A. 6 months
   - B. 12 months
   - C. 18 months
   - D. 30 months

8. In space there is no "down" because there is no—
   - F. floor.
   - G. returning to Earth.
   - H. air.
   - J. gravity.

9. The first step in becoming a member of the Mars mission is—
   - A. training in Antarctica.
   - B. passing the psychological testing.
   - C. participating in role playing.
   - D. going through countless interviews.

© Scott Foresman 6

GO ON

10. You are on a mission to Mars, and the spaceship is now in orbit around Earth. What is the next step?
    F. You wait for the next "launch window" before heading toward Mars.
    G. The ship slides toward Mars in a Hohman transfer.
    H. The commander fires the rockets to fling the ship away from Earth's gravity.
    J. An unmanned rocket is sent to Mars, carrying cargo you will need when you get there.

11. Why do a person's muscles become weak in outer space?
    A. They no longer need to fight gravity.
    B. There are few opportunities for exercise.
    C. The food is not healthful.
    D. The cabin of the spacecraft is small and cramped.

12. What is the same about solar flares and galactic rays?
    F. They give about an hour's warning.
    G. They are hot and bright.
    H. They are harmful to humans.
    J. They constantly bombard the spaceship.

13. People from Earth have to remain on Mars for eighteen months because—
    A. they need that long for exploring and doing experiments.
    B. they need time to readjust to living with gravity.
    C. it takes that long to make enough fuel for the return trip.
    D. it would not be possible for them to reach Earth if they tried to leave earlier.

14. Which statement is an opinion?
    F. "Thousands of people applied to join the first Mars mission."
    G. "It is one of the richest areas for finding dinosaur fossils in the world."
    H. "Most of this loss occurs in your spine and hips."
    J. "There are no magic pills for gravity yet."

15. Which is the greatest obstacle to human survival on Mars?
    A. lack of air and water
    B. lack of gravity
    C. distance from Earth
    D. lack of a native civilization

STOP

© Scott Foresman 6

Paraphrasing

Directions: Read the passage. Then read each question about the passage. Choose the best answer to each question. Mark the letter for the answer you have chosen.

The Time Machine

For centuries, people have been fascinated by the idea of time travel. Many stories from past centuries are about this concept.

Before people thought about traveling in space, they used the idea of an enchanted sleep as a way to get a person from one time period to another. In the French fairy tale "Sleeping Beauty," princess Briar Rose pricks her finger on a spindle and falls asleep. Generations pass. The prince who finally awakens her was born over a century after Briar Rose—and yet they seem to be about the same age!

A Connecticut Yankee in King Arthur's Court is a funny 19th century story of time travel by Mark Twain. In this story, an ordinary young man is knocked unconscious in a fight and awakens in Camelot in the year 528. His knowledge of everyday modern objects like forks and bicycles cause Arthur's knights and ladies to marvel.

More recent time-travel stories have involved complicated machines that literally transport people through time. In the popular film *Back to the Future,* a high school student suddenly finds himself going to class with his own mother and father. In the film, the time travel machine uses radioactive materials, lightning, and garbage as sources of fuel.

1. Which of the following is a paraphrase of the article's main idea?
   A. Time travel has been a popular subject of stories for centuries.
   B. Some time machines need lightning to travel.
   C. An enchanted sleep is one way of traveling through time.
   D. A Yankee once traveled to Camelot.

2. Which of the following best paraphrases the main idea of the second paragraph?
   F. Briar Rose pricks her finger and falls asleep.
   G. Many young men want to wake her up.
   H. The prince is 100 years younger than Briar Rose.
   J. In old stories, people travel through time by sleeping through it.

3. Which of the following best paraphrases the main idea of the third paragraph?
   A. The Yankee tells Arthur about forks.
   B. Mark Twain wrote a funny story about time travel.
   C. In the year 528, Arthur was king of Great Britain.
   D. Everyone in Camelot learns how to ride a bicycle.

4. Which of the following best paraphrases the main idea of the last paragraph?
   F. Recent time-travel stories use complicated machines to transport people through time.
   G. Characters no longer sleep through time anymore.
   H. *Back To The Future* was a popular film about time travel.
   J. Time machines can let you meet your parents as teenagers.

5. Which of the following is **not** a paraphrase of something in the article?
   A. Time-travel stories are popular.
   B. One day, a young American wakes up in King Arthur's court.
   C. Rip Van Winkle sleeps for many years.
   D. Briar Rose falls asleep when she pricks her finger.

© Scott Foresman 6

Notes for Home: Your child read a passage and identified paraphrases of statements in the passage. *Home Activity:* Tell your child a story about time travel. Have your child retell the story in his or her own words.

Word Study: Singular Possessives

Directions: Words that show ownership, or possession, are called **possessives**.
Add an **apostrophe (')** and **s** to form possessives of singular nouns: **Mom's**.
Read the phrases below. Change each phrase to form possessive nouns. Write
the new phrase on the line.

the brightness of the star   the star's brightness

1. the orders of the commander   _____

2. the surface of Earth   _____

3. the canyons of Mars   _____

4. the months of a year   _____

5. the rays of the Sun   _____

Directions: Read the paragraph below. Look for ten words with apostrophes (').
Five words are possessives. The other five words are contractions. Write each
word in the correct column to show which type of word it is.

Dr. McKay's Notes
July 2000

It's with a child's wonder and a scientist's concern that I
gaze toward the stars and speculate about the ship we've
sent into space. As a child, I'd always wanted to venture to
that great beyond and view another planet's splendor and
colors, especially Saturn's rings. But the ship doesn't carry
any crew or passengers. We'll track it by computer and
download the pictures of space.

Possessives   **Contractions**

6. _____   11. _____

7. _____   12. _____

8. _____   13. _____

9. _____   14. _____

10. _____   15. _____

Notes for Home: Your child wrote possessives and sorted contractions and possessives.
Home Activity: With your child, write ten contractions and ten possessives on separate index
cards. Take turns choosing two cards to try to get two possessives or two contractions.

© Scott Foresman 6

Technology: Electronic Media

There are two types of **electronic media**—computer and non-computer. Computer sources include computer software, CD-ROMs, and the Internet. Non-computer sources include audiotapes, videotapes, films, film strips, television, and radio.

To find information on the Internet, use a search engine and type in your key words. Be specific. It's a good idea to use two or more key words, typing AND between key words. For example, if you typed "Mars AND photographs," you might get a list of web pages like the one below. To get to a web page, click on the underlined link.

Directions: Use the Internet search results to answer the questions that follow.

You Searched For: Mars AND Photographs

Top 5 of 38 matches.

1 Ruins on Mars   Striking color photographs of what may be ancient ruins on the surface of Mars are now available.

2 Mars Home Page   All about Mars—missions to Mars, images of Mars, and plans for Mars exploration and settlement in the future.

3 Mars: Past Missions   Past missions include 1962: The first attempt to fly to Mars ended when a Russian probe was lost after traveling 66 million miles. 1964: A U.S. flyby returns 21 images of Mars to Earth. 1971–1972: America's *Mariner IX* and Russia's *Mars 3* orbit the planet, providing data and photographs.

4 Spacelink - Mars Global Surveyor   Mars Global Surveyor is a polar-orbiting spacecraft designed to provide global maps of surface topography, distribution of minerals, and monitoring of global weather.

5 Mars Pathfinder   On July 4, 1997, the Mars *Pathfinder* spacecraft arrived on the Red Planet. *Pathfinder* sent out a small rover called *Sojourner* to explore the Martian landscape. Learn more intriguing information here.

Click here to continue

© Scott Foresman 6

1. How do you get to a specific web page? _____

2. What information will web page 5 have? _____

_____

3. Which web page has information about the Mars Global Surveyor? _____

4. What key words could you use to find web pages about the history of exploration on Mars?

_____

5. Why is it important to choose your key words carefully when searching the Internet?

_____

_____

6. What are some of the advantages of using the Internet as a source of information for research?

_____

_____

7. How might you use a documentary videotape on Mars for a research report?

_____

_____

8. How might you use an audiotape of conversations between astronauts on a space mission and the mission command center?

_____

_____

_____

9. Name some ways television could be used as a research source.

_____

_____

_____

10. Is electronic media always the best choice as a research source? Explain why or why not.

_____

_____

_____

Notes for Home: Your child answered questions about the results of a web page search on the Internet and other forms of electronic media. *Home Activity:* Make a list of the different forms of electronic media. Discuss how each form could be used for research or study.

© Scott Foresman 6

Summarizing

- To **summarize** means to give a brief statement of the main idea of an article or the most important events in a story.

- When you summarize a story, include only the main actions of the characters and the outcomes of those actions.

Directions: Reread "To Surprise the Children." Then summarize the story by choosing the five sentences from the box that best describe the most important actions or events. Write the sentences in the flow chart in the correct order.

The main character asked a bricklayer what would happen if the brick fell on somebody.
The main character went somewhere and looked up.
The bricklayers supported the brick by building a whole house around it.
The main character asked what would happen if the brick fell on somebody.
Some people, including the main character, moved into the house.
The main character looked up and saw a brick sitting in the air.
Everyone was looking at the brick.
The bricklayer called for other bricklayers to come.
Some people moved into the house.

Event 1:

↓

Event 2:

↓

Event 3:

↓

Event 4:

↓

Event 5:

© Scott Foresman 6

Notes for Home: Your child summarized a story. *Home Activity:* Work with your child to summarize a story or movie. Be sure to include only the most important events.

Vocabulary

Directions: Choose the word from the box that best matches each definition. Write the word on the line.

_____ 1. place to which you are traveling

_____ 2. a gate at which money is collected before or after driving on a road

_____ 3. to find by chance

_____ 4. rules

_____ 5. good reasons for thinking that something will happen

_____ 6. put together

Check the Words You Know
__ assembled
__ destination
__ encounter
__ expectations
__ regulations
__ tollbooth

Directions: Read the diary entry. Choose the word from the box that best completes each sentence. Write the word on the matching numbered line below.

I dreamed I was in a country with strange laws. There were 7. _____ that stated how many minutes you could talk each day. If you wanted to take a trip, a court had to approve your final 8. _____. At every 9. _____ on the highway, you had to answer math word problems. Finally, I gathered the parts I needed to build a spaceship. I 10. _____ the ship and quickly escaped.

7. _____   9. _____

8. _____   10. _____

Write a Dialogue

Imagine being in a strange place and not knowing your way or the rules of the road! On a separate sheet of paper, write a dialogue between a space traveler and a toll booth attendant. Use as many vocabulary words as you can.

Notes for Home: Your child identified and used vocabulary words from the story "The Land of Expectations." **Home Activity:** Talk about a fantasy trip to outer space or some strange place in another time. Encourage your child to use vocabulary words during your discussion.

© Scott Foresman 6

Name _____

Summarizing

- **Summarizing** means giving a brief statement of the main idea of an article or the most important events in a story.

Directions: Reread the passage below in which the author introduces Milo. Then follow the instructions below. Think about which information belongs in your summary.

There was once a boy named Milo who didn't know what to do with himself—not just sometimes, but always.

When he was in school he longed to be out, and when he was out he longed to be in. On the way he thought about coming home, and coming home he thought about going. Wherever he was he wished he were somewhere else, and when he got there he wondered why he'd bothered. Nothing really interested him—least of all the things that should have.

"It seems to me that almost everything is a waste of time," he remarked one day as he walked dejectedly home from school. "I can't see the point in learning to solve useless problems, or subtracting turnips from turnips, or knowing where Ethiopia is or how to spell February." And, since no one bothered to explain otherwise, he regarded the process of seeking knowledge as the greatest waste of time of all.

From THE PHANTOM TOLLBOOTH by Norton Juster. Copyright © 1961 and renewed 1989 by Norton Juster. Reprinted by permission of Random House, Inc.

1. Write a summary of the first paragraph.

_____

2. Write a summary of the second paragraph.

_____

3. Write a summary of the third paragraph.

_____

4. Give an example of something you left out of your summary of the third paragraph. Why did you leave this information out?

_____

_____

5. Summarize the story and how Milo changes by the end. Explain your ideas on a separate sheet of paper.

Notes for Home: Your child read a story and summarized what happened in it in a few sentences. ***Home Activity:*** After watching a movie together with your child, challenge him or her to write a brief summary of it. Discuss which events were included and why.

© Scott Foresman 6

1.	Ⓐ	Ⓑ	Ⓒ	Ⓓ
2.	Ⓕ	Ⓖ	Ⓗ	Ⓙ
3.	Ⓐ	Ⓑ	Ⓒ	Ⓓ
4.	Ⓕ	Ⓖ	Ⓗ	Ⓙ
5.	Ⓐ	Ⓑ	Ⓒ	Ⓓ
6.	Ⓕ	Ⓖ	Ⓗ	Ⓙ
7.	Ⓐ	Ⓑ	Ⓒ	Ⓓ
8.	Ⓕ	Ⓖ	Ⓗ	Ⓙ
9.	Ⓐ	Ⓑ	Ⓒ	Ⓓ
10.	Ⓕ	Ⓖ	Ⓗ	Ⓙ
11.	Ⓐ	Ⓑ	Ⓒ	Ⓓ
12.	Ⓕ	Ⓖ	Ⓗ	Ⓙ
13.	Ⓐ	Ⓑ	Ⓒ	Ⓓ
14.	Ⓕ	Ⓖ	Ⓗ	Ⓙ
15.	Ⓐ	Ⓑ	Ⓒ	Ⓓ

© Scott Foresman 6

Selection Test

Directions: Choose the best answer to each item. Mark the letter for the answer you have chosen.

Part 1: Vocabulary

Find the answer choice that means about the same as the underlined word in each sentence.

1. Dad stopped at the <u>tollbooth</u>.
   A. place where people sit to watch a game or contest
   B. vehicle for traveling
   C. booth or gate at which money is collected from travelers
   D. place for selling maps

2. Diana had few <u>expectations</u>.
   F. things that are looked forward to
   G. reasons to remember something
   H. things that are decided beforehand
   J. observations

3. The team <u>assembled</u> it quickly.
   A. performed
   B. put together
   C. opened
   D. broke apart

4. Our <u>destination</u> was near.
   F. source of ideas
   G. place where someone lives
   H. fortune; luck
   J. place to which someone or something is going

5. We read the <u>regulations</u>.
   A. rules
   B. tools
   C. letters
   D. guides

6. Did you <u>encounter</u> anyone on the hike?
   F. go along with
   G. meet unexpectedly
   H. watch closely
   J. lose track of

Part 2: Comprehension

Use what you know about the story to answer each item.

7. Why was Milo hurrying to get home from school?
   A. He always liked to get places as quickly as possible.
   B. He never seemed to have enough time to do all the things he wanted to.
   C. He was eager to find out what was waiting for him at home.
   D. He felt nervous and afraid of what he might run into on the way home.

8. What was odd about the map Milo found in the surprise package?
   F. Milo had to unfold it to see what it looked like.
   G. It showed roads, rivers, and seas.
   H. Milo had never heard of any of the places on the map.
   J. The places on the map were beautiful and historic.

9. Milo got into the Doldrums by—
   A. following the map.
   B. making a foolish choice.
   C. listening to the Whether Man.
   D. not thinking.

10. Which sentence best summarizes what happens to Milo?
    F. He meets a dog with a clock for a body.
    G. He takes an unexpected trip to a very unusual place.
    H. He talks with the Whether Man.
    J. He finds a package in his room.

© Scott Foresman 6

GO ON

11. Which of these events would be important to include in a summary of this story?
    A. The Whether Man released a dozen balloons that sailed off into the sky.
    B. The Lethargarians described their busy schedule to Milo.
    C. Tock the watchdog helped Milo get out of the Doldrums.
    D. Tock explained that it is traditional for watchdogs to be ferocious.

12. What can you tell about the Whether Man?
    F. He enjoys life to the fullest.
    G. He does not know where he is.
    H. He doesn't like to make up his mind.
    J. He is Milo's best friend.

13. Where will Milo probably go next?
    A. back to the Doldrums
    B. to Dictionopolis
    C. back to his apartment
    D. to Tock's home

14. In Tock's view, the most valuable thing in the world is—
    F. time.
    G. diamonds.
    H. sleep.
    J. weather.

15. One thing that Tock likes to do is—
    A. chase after cars.
    B. kill time.
    C. socialize with the Lethargarians.
    D. tell long stories about his family.

STOP

© Scott Foresman 6

Cause and Effect

Directions: Read the story. Then read each question about the story. Choose the best answer to each question. Mark the letter for the answer you have chosen.

The Monster, the Maze, and the Fall

King Minos of Crete asked the architect Daedalus to build a maze. The maze was to be a prison for the Minotaur, a fierce monster who was half human and half bull. Minos wanted a maze from which the monster would never be able to escape. Daedalus created a maze, so full of twists and turns that the Minotaur could never find his way out.

Minos' daughter Ariadne had fallen in love with the hero Theseus. When Minos threatened to feed Theseus to the Minotaur, Ariadne thought of a way to save his life. She told Theseus to fasten a thread to the maze's entrance. If he kept hold of the thread's other end, he would be able to find his way out. Theseus killed the Minotaur and escaped from the maze.

King Minos was so angry about Theseus's escape that he imprisoned Daedalus and his son Icarus in a tower. Daedalus made wings of wood, wax, and feathers for himself and his son so that they could fly away from their prison. Daedalus warned Icarus not to fly too close to the sun. If the wax melted, the feathers would fall from the frames.

Icarus enjoyed flying so much that he forgot his father's warning. He flew too close to the sun. The wax on his wings melted, and he fell into the sea. Grief-stricken, Daedalus recovered his son's body and buried it on a nearby island.

1. The Minotaur cannot escape because—
   A. the maze is too complicated.
   B. it is part animal.
   C. it will be killed if it escapes.
   D. Ariadne refuses to help it.

2. Because Daedalus is an excellent architect—
   F. he is put in prison.
   G. he traps King Minos.
   H. he is asked by the King to build a flying machine.
   J. he is asked by the King to build an escape-proof maze.

3. Thanks to the help of Ariadne—
   A. Icarus escapes.
   B. Daedalus escapes.
   C. Theseus escapes.
   D. King Minos kills Theseus.

4. Daedalus makes wings in order to—
   F. escape the tower.
   G. teach his son to fly.
   H. kill the monster.
   J. challenge the king.

5. Icarus is killed because—
   A. he flies into the sea.
   B. he forgets his father's warning.
   C. the wings don't work very well.
   D. the king is angry with him.

Notes for Home: Your child read a story and identified the causes and effects of its events. *Home Activity:* Read a myth or folk tale with your child. Encourage him or her to tell what happens in the story (effects) and why these events happen (causes).

Word Study: Suffixes

Directions: A letter or group of letters added to the end of a word is called a **suffix.** A suffix can change the meaning of the base word. The words below have been formed by adding suffixes. Read each word pair. Write the suffix on the line.

1. useless, endless _____

2. traditional, logical _____

3. silvery, rusty _____

4. historic, apologetic _____

5. festive, massive _____

6. magical, natural _____

7. meaningless, clueless _____

8. classy, showy _____

9. hypnotic, idiotic _____

10. preventive, inventive _____

Directions: Read the letter below. Look and listen for words that have the suffixes **-less, -al, -y, -ic,** and **-ive.** Circle these words. Then write the base word and the suffix on the line, connected by a + sign. For example, for **restless,** you would write **rest + less.**

Dear Marisa,

You'll never believe what happened to me! I went on a magical journey. It was quite dreamy and fantastic. You see, I haven't been very active these days. So when my uncle suggested that I join him on his traditional yearly trip, I said sure. But where he went and what I saw made me speechless! He took me up in a hot-air balloon. Wish you had been there. I could see for endless miles. My head was spinning. Even my uncle got emotional. It felt like a historic moment in my life. I'm so lucky.

Your friend,

Dianne

11. _____

12. _____

13. _____

14. _____

15. _____

16. _____

17. _____

18. _____

19. _____

20. _____

Notes for Home: Your child identified and wrote words with the suffixes *-less, -al, -y, -ic,* and *-ive. Home Activity:* Read a short story with your child. Encourage your child to find words with these suffixes. Have your child write down the words and underline the suffixes.

© Scott Foresman 6

Manual

A **manual** is usually in the form of a booklet or book. It contains a written set of directions that help the reader understand, use, or build something.

Directions: Study the table of contents and diagram from a manual for a VCR (video cassette recorder). Then answer the questions that follow.

Table of Contents for Your VCR

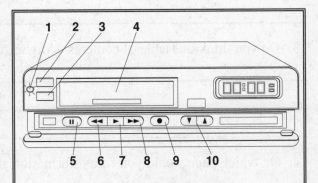

Front Panel Features

1. Power Indicator Light—A red light appears when the VCR is on.
2. Power Button—Use to turn the VCR on and off.
3. Stop/Eject Button—Press to stop videotape. Then press again to eject tape.
4. Tape Compartment—Insert videotaope here.
5. Pause Button—Use to view single frame or picture while playing a videotape.
6. Rewind Button—Press to rewind tape after pressing stop. If pressed during playback, video may be viewed in rapid reverse.
7. Play Button—Press to play videotape.
8. Fast Forward Button—Press to advance the tape. If pressed during playback, video may be viewed in rapid forward.
9. Record Button—Use for recording.
10. Channel Up/Channel Down Buttons— Use to select TV channels on VCR.

© Scott Foresman 6

Name _____

1. What is the purpose of this manual? _____
_____
_____

2. When might you use this manual? Give an example. _____
_____
_____

3. Do you think this table of contents is organized well? How might it help you use the manual?
_____
_____
_____

4. On which page would you find information about setting the clock? _____

5. Suppose you wanted to record a TV program about space travel. Which page would you turn to in the manual to see how to do this? Which front panel features would you most likely use?
_____
_____

6. Which front panel feature confirms that the VCR is actually on? _____
_____

7. What does the rewind button do? _____
_____

8. If you were unable to make the VCR work properly, on what page would you find a phone number to get help?
_____

9. Why do you think a diagram was included in this manual? _____
_____

10. Why is it important to be able to follow directions carefully and correctly when using a manual?
_____
_____
_____

Notes for Home: Your child studied a sample page from an instruction manual and answered questions about it. *Home Activity:* With your child, look at an instruction manual. Discuss the information in it, such as the table of contents, diagrams, and instructions.

© Scott Foresman 6

Character

- **Characters** are the people or animals who take part in the events of a short story, novel, play, or other form of fiction.

- You can learn about characters by noticing what they think, say, and do. You can also learn about characters by paying attention to how other characters treat them and what others say about them.

- The lasting qualities of a character's personality are called character traits. *Brave, stubborn,* and *honest* are examples of character traits.

Directions: Reread "The Pleasantest Days." Complete the web by writing about what Sam likes. Then write a sentence describing Sam.

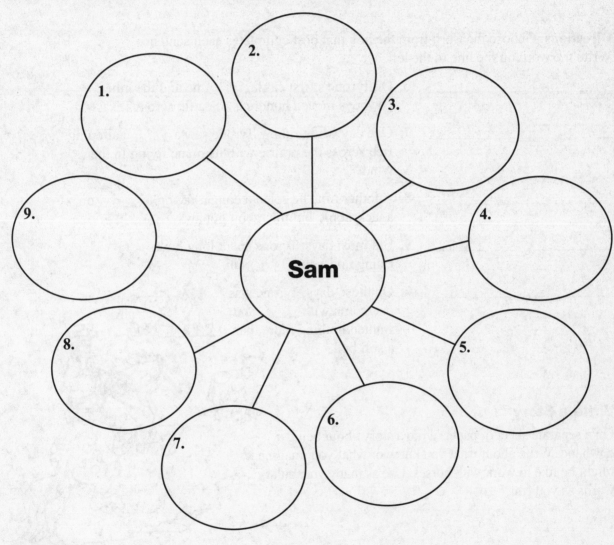

10. Sam is _____.

© Scott Foresman 6

Notes for Home: Your child described a story character. *Home Activity:* Encourage your child to make a list of character traits for different characters in stories, movies, and TV programs. Work together to draw a picture and write a caption that describes each character.

Vocabulary

Directions: Choose the word from the box that best matches each definition.
Write the word on the line.

_____ 1. a small, wild horse

_____ 2. to attack suddenly, usually from above

_____ 3. exhaustion

_____ 4. the act of moving cattle overland to a
shipping point

_____ 5. very hot

Check the Words You Know
__ drive
__ mustang
__ pounce
__ scorching
__ weariness

Directions: Choose the word from the box that best completes each sentence.
Write the word on the line to the left.

_____ 6. On Tyrone's first cattle _____, he and the other
cowboys moved hundreds of cattle across Texas.

_____ 7. One day while riding, Tyrone saw a _____ galloping
free across the prairie with its mane flying in the
wind.

_____ 8. Another time he spied a cougar trying to _____ on
a jackrabbit, but the rabbit got away.

_____ 9. But most days, Tyrone spent long hours
riding under the _____ sun.

_____ 10. On those days, Tyrone was
overcome with _____ and
wanted nothing more than
a soft bed.

Write a Story

On a separate sheet of paper, write a story about being a
cowhand. Write about what you know or what you imagine it
might be like to work with horses. Use as many vocabulary
words as you can.

Notes for Home: Your child identified and used vocabulary words from "The Trail Drive."
Home Activity: Act out a conversation between two cowhands. Try to use as many listed
vocabulary words as you can.

© Scott Foresman 6

Character

- **Characters** are the people or animals who take part in the events of a short story, novel, play, or other form of fiction.

- You can learn about characters by noticing what they think, say, and do.

- You can also learn about characters by paying attention to how other characters in the story treat them and what these other characters say about them.

Directions: Reread the part of "The Trail Drive" about Midnight's first day on the drive. Then answer the questions below. Think about what the passage tells you about the characters.

> One by one Midnight tethered six ponies to the picket line. He worked on, not paying attention to anyone or anything else. Sweat rolled down his temples. He licked the salty taste off his lips and kept going. Six more. At last he tied Dahomey to the line and stood to wipe his forehead. Midnight looked back at the work he'd done. The horses hadn't really given him any trouble. His first day on the drive was over, and he was satisfied.
>
> "Good job for your first time." Joe B. strolled up and tugged on the last rope line Midnight had stretched. It was so tight that the rope bounced against Joe's hand. He nodded and looked at Midnight.

From THE ADVENTURES OF MIDNIGHT SON by Denise Lewis Patrick, © 1997 by Denise Lewis Patrick. Reprinted by permission of Henry Holt and Company, LLC.

1. What action tells you that Midnight feels that working hard is more important than socializing or watching the others?

_____

2. How does Midnight feel about his first day on the drive?

_____

3. What do Joe B.'s words tell you about how he feels about Midnight's work?

_____

_____

4. What action by Joe B. suggests that he feels Midnight did a good job tying the ropes?

_____

5. On a separate sheet of paper, describe what you learn about the character of Midnight from reading the story. Give examples from the story to support your answer.

Notes for Home: Your child read a story and analyzed its characters. *Home Activity:* Read a short story with your child. Encourage your child to describe what he or she learns about its characters.

© Scott Foresman 6

1.	Ⓐ	Ⓑ	Ⓒ	Ⓓ
2.	Ⓕ	Ⓖ	Ⓗ	Ⓙ
3.	Ⓐ	Ⓑ	Ⓒ	Ⓓ
4.	Ⓕ	Ⓖ	Ⓗ	Ⓙ
5.	Ⓐ	Ⓑ	Ⓒ	Ⓓ
6.	Ⓕ	Ⓖ	Ⓗ	Ⓙ
7.	Ⓐ	Ⓑ	Ⓒ	Ⓓ
8.	Ⓕ	Ⓖ	Ⓗ	Ⓙ
9.	Ⓐ	Ⓑ	Ⓒ	Ⓓ
10.	Ⓕ	Ⓖ	Ⓗ	Ⓙ
11.	Ⓐ	Ⓑ	Ⓒ	Ⓓ
12.	Ⓕ	Ⓖ	Ⓗ	Ⓙ
13.	Ⓐ	Ⓑ	Ⓒ	Ⓓ
14.	Ⓕ	Ⓖ	Ⓗ	Ⓙ
15.	Ⓐ	Ⓑ	Ⓒ	Ⓓ

© Scott Foresman 6

Selection Test

Directions: Choose the best answer to each item. Mark the letter for the answer
you have chosen.

Part 1: Vocabulary

Find the answer choice that means about the
same as the underlined word in each sentence.

1. Those cowboys saw the <u>drive</u>.
   A. a public sale of animals
   B. act of moving cattle overland
   C. a rodeo show
   D. fenced-in area for cattle

2. <u>Weariness</u> overtook them.
   F. state of being confused
   G. nervousness; fear
   H. state of being alert
   J. deep tiredness

3. It was <u>scorching</u> weather.
   A. very hot
   B. unpredictable
   C. very wet
   D. unpleasant

4. He kept his eye on the <u>mustang</u>.
   F. leader in a group of horses
   G. group of spare horses
   H. small wild stray horse
   J. horse used for carrying loads

5. The cat was about to <u>pounce</u>.
   A. begin eating
   B. hunch down with eyes alert
   C. turn over on its back
   D. leap suddenly and seize something

Part 2: Comprehension

Use what you know about the story to answer
each item.

6. This story begins with—
   F. Midnight's first day on a long trip.
   G. a river crossing.
   H. the last day of a long trip.
   J. a terrible storm.

7. What is Midnight's job in the evenings?
   A. watching the edges of the herd
   B. helping to make dinner
   C. taking care of the spare horses
   D. finding water for the herd

8. What is Slim's job on the drive?
   F. boss
   G. cook
   H. scout
   J. guard

9. Why did Midnight tie Rusty to the picket
   line before the other horses?
   A. He noticed that other horses seemed
      to follow her.
   B. She was the horse he rode on the
      drive.
   C. He could tell she was hungry.
   D. He thought she was the one most
      likely to give him trouble.

10. You can tell that Slim was a little worried
    about—
    F. the horses.
    G. whether there was enough food.
    H. the weather.
    J. how things were going for Midnight.

11. Midnight showed he was brave and
    determined when he—
    A. set up a picket line for the first time.
    B. took the horses across the Red River.
    C. avoided talking to Lou Boy about
       Curly.
    D. fell asleep on the bare ground.

12. Nighttime reminded Midnight of—
    F. the first time he saw a horse.
    G. his escape from slavery.
    H. crossing large bodies of water.
    J. his arrival in Mexico.

© Scott Foresman 6

GO ON ▶

13. What feeling deep inside Midnight was the main cause of his fight with the cougar?
   A. fear that he would lose his job if he wasn't brave enough
   B. love for the horses in his care
   C. anger over things that happened in the past
   D. hatred of wild cats

14. In some parts of the story, the author uses *italic* type to call attention to—
   F. Midnight's thoughts.
   G. important ideas.
   H. events from the past.
   J. make-believe events.

15. Slim cautions Midnight not to—
   A. risk his life for a horse.
   B. leave camp without a partner.
   C. get too friendly with the other cowboys.
   D. let bad memories control him.

© Scott Foresman 6

Generalizing

Directions: Read the passage. Then read each question about the passage. Choose the best answer to each question. Mark the letter for the answer you have chosen.

Explosive Earth

Most volcanoes are made out of lava flows, or streams of melted rock, and other materials. The lava shoots upward in the eruption and falls back again. It lands as cinders or ashes and is shot into the air again. This rise and fall happens many times and forms the cone shape common to most volcanoes. Mount Vesuvius in Italy is a famous volcano of this kind.

A number of volcanoes have deep basins, called calderas, which become filled with water over a long period of time. Crater Lake in Oregon is an example. Forceful explosions that destroy the volcano itself form some calderas.

Many volcanoes are born underwater on the sea floor. Mount Etna and Mount Vesuvius began as underwater volcanoes. So did the huge cones found in the Hawaiian Islands.

Some volcanoes are much more active than others. A number of constantly active volcanoes are found in a belt called the Ring of Fire that encircles the Pacific Ocean. Other volcanoes become inactive, or dormant, for months or years. The eruption that follows a long dormant period is usually violent. This was true in the state of Washington when Mount Saint Helens erupted violently after a 123-year period of quiet.

One reason scientists study volcanoes is that they can be dangerous to life forms. In addition to the dangers of lava and ash, the eruptions can melt ice and snow and cause deadly mud flows. Harmful gases can pour out of volcanoes long after they have erupted.

1. Which of the following statements is **not** a generalization?
   A. Most volcanoes are made out of lava flows and other materials.
   B. Mount Vesuvius is a famous volcano in Italy.
   C. A number of volcanoes have deep basins.
   D. Most volcanoes have a cone shape.

2. Underwater volcanoes are born—
   F. only in Italy.
   G. inactive.
   H. on the sea floor.
   J. only in the Ring of Fire.

3. Many active volcanoes are found—
   A. only on the sea floor.
   B. in Oregon.
   C. in a rim around the Pacific.
   D. everywhere on Earth.

4. An eruption after a period of inactivity usually—
   F. occurs in the Ring of Fire.
   G. is violent.
   H. creates a cone-shaped volcano.
   J. forms a caldera.

5. Which statement below is a valid generalization?
   A. All volcanoes become active again after a quiet time.
   B. Few volcanic eruptions are dangerous.
   C. Danger from volcanoes ends with the eruptions.
   D. Some volcanoes are more active than others.

Notes for Home: Your child identified generalizations—broad statements about several things or people—in a passage. *Home Activity:* Read a brief magazine article with your child. Challenge him or her to write one or two generalizations that are supported by the facts in the article.

© Scott Foresman 6

Word Study: Plural Possessives

Directions: Add an apostrophe (') to form the possessive of plural nouns that end in **s: sisters'.** For plural nouns that do not end in **s**, add an **apostrophe (')** and **s** to form the possessive: **oxen's.** Read the phrases below. Change each phrase to form a possessive noun. Write each new phrase on the line.

the scales of the fish   the fish's scales

1. the chores of the men   _____

2. the toys of the boys   _____

3. the experiences of the women   _____

4. the squeaks of the mice   _____

5. the heavy loads of the trucks   _____

Directions: Read each sentence. Use the possessive form of the noun in ( ) to complete each sentence. Write the possessive noun on the line.

_____ 6. Before they fell asleep, the (girls) last thoughts were of the next day's trail drive.

_____ 7. The next morning, the (horses) whinnies sounded clearly across the field.

_____ 8. The (children) excitement was infectious as they gathered around the horses.

_____ 9. The (parents) concerns had been that their children might get hurt.

_____ 10. But the (families) worries were laid to rest when they saw how gentle the horses were.

_____ 11. The (trails) rocky terrain made the ride a little rough for those not used to traveling on horseback.

_____ 12. Even the (men) warnings of dangers along the trail could not dampen the group's enthusiasm.

_____ 13. Everyone kept a sharp eye out looking for the (moose) tracks.

_____ 14. They saw marks on the ground where the (elk) hooves had dug in the dirt.

_____ 15. The guide pointed to scratches where the (deer) antlers had rubbed against the tree bark.

Notes for Home: Your child formed plural possessives, such as *sisters'* and *oxen's.* **Home Activity:** Read a biography with your child about a person she or he finds interesting. Look for possessive nouns. Have your child write the words and notice how they were formed.

© Scott Foresman 6

Interpret Information/Draw Conclusions

To interpret information and draw conclusions about it, you need to decide what the information means and whether it suits your research purposes.

Directions: Read the passage. Next, complete the web by telling what you learned from reading the passage. Then answer the questions that follow the web.

The True Life of the Cowboy

Imagine working up to 20 hours a day in grueling weather with unpredictable animals. Now imagine you only got paid about $25 to $40 a month! Even back then, this wasn't a lot of money. This was what a cowboy's life was really like.

Cowboys have become almost legendary in American history as bold, heroic figures who led glamorous lives in the Old West. However, the cowboy's life was anything but glamorous. Besides being poorly paid, the work they did was very strenuous and very difficult, not to mention dirty and dangerous. A cowboy's job was to take a herd of cattle from one place to another, usually from Texas into either Kansas, Nebraska, or Wyoming. Each minute of every hour of every day cowboys needed to stay constantly alert in order to avoid disaster. They had to guard the cattle from predators—both animal and human. They also had to prevent, if possible, cattle stampedes. They had to round up any stray cattle, as well as take care of the ones already in their possession.

The era of the cowboy spanned about 25 years from 1865–1890. With the expansion of the railroad, these underpaid workers were no longer needed to do long cattle drives. However, "cowboys" continue to live on through the many western stories written about them and the TV shows and movies made about them.

©Scott Foresman 6

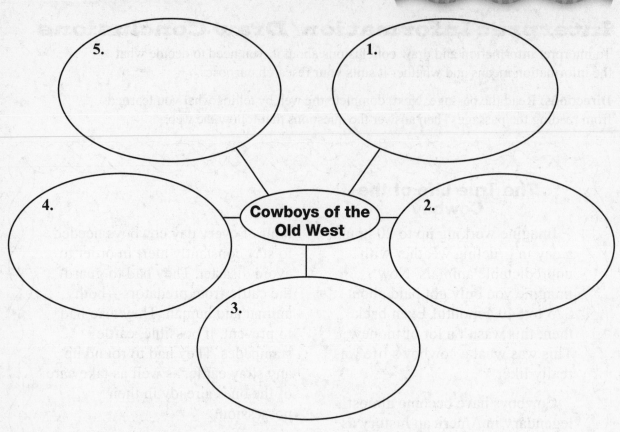

Cowboys of the Old West

5.

1.

4.

2.

3.

6. Does the passage contain mostly statements of fact or opinion? _____

_____

7. What is the main idea of the passage? _____

_____

_____

8. Why were cowboys not needed for cattle drives after the expansion of the railroad?

_____

_____

9. Would the information in this passage be useful for a research report on the work that
cowboys did? Explain.

_____

_____

10. Would the information in this passage help you answer the question: "What is life like for
cowboys on ranches today?" Explain.

_____

_____

Notes for Home Your child read a nonfiction passage, interpreted information in it, and drew
conclusions about it. *Home Activity:* Challenge your child to read a newspaper article and tell
you the main idea of the article.

© Scott Foresman 6

Generalizing

- A broad statement about what several people or things have in common is a **generalization.**

- Some generalizations contain clue words such as *most, many, all, sometimes, generally, always,* or *never.*

- A valid generalization is supported by facts and agrees with what you already know. A faulty generalization is not supported by facts.

Directions: Reread "Almost Ready for School." Then complete the table. Circle **Yes** if the statement is a generalization. Circle **No** if it is not. Explain your answer. Identify any clue words that signal a generalization.

Statement	Generalization?	Explanation
Sixth-graders were always chosen to help out in the office or in the halls.	**1.** Yes No	**2.**
Dad made an appointment for me with a new dentist.	**3.** Yes No	**4.**
Dentists always slip into the room so quietly you don't even know they're there.	**5.** Yes No	**6.**
I immediately opened my mouth.	**7.** Yes No	**8.**
People grind their teeth when they're tense.	**9.** Yes No	**10.**

Notes for Home: Your child read a story and identified generalizations. *Home Activity:* Take turns using *always, sometimes,* and *never* to make generalizations. Discuss whether each generalization is valid or faulty.

© Scott Foresman 6

Vocabulary

Directions: Draw a line to connect each word on the left with its definition on the right.

Check the Words You Know

__ calligraphy
__ circumstances
__ committee
__ generation
__ handwriting
__ stationery

1. handwriting   a group of people who plan something

2. generation   writing materials, such as paper and envelopes

3. stationery   writing by hand

4. calligraphy   people born about the same time

5. committee   a style of handwriting

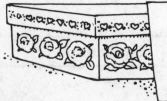

Dear Friend

Directions: Choose the word from the box that best completes each sentence. Write the word on the line.

_____   6. Before there were typewriters or computers, well-educated people learned an elegant style of writing called _____ to make their letters beautiful.

_____   7. Since their _____ was too expensive to waste, they wrote carefully.

_____   8. This older _____ who wrote so carefully may criticize the way young people write now.

_____   9. They might like to set up a _____ to suggest changes, but it probably would not do much good.

_____   10. The _____ of modern life have changed, and most people type or e-mail their letters today.

Write a Comparison

On a separate sheet of paper, write a paragraph that compares e-mail messages to conventional letters. Think about the benefits of both forms of communication. Do you think the advantages of one type of writing outweighs the other type? Use as many vocabulary words as you can in your comparison.

Notes for Home: Your child identified and used vocabulary words from the story. "Noah Writes a B & B Letter." **Home Activity:** Discuss which is more important: improving one's handwriting or typing skills.

© Scott Foresman 6

Generalizing

- A broad statement about what several people or things have in common is a **generalization.**

- Some generalizations contain clue words such as *most, many, all, sometimes, generally, always,* or *never.*

- A valid generalization is supported by facts and agrees with what you already know. A faulty generalization is not supported by facts.

Directions: Reread what happens in "Noah Writes a B & B Letter" when Noah begins to write a letter to his grandparents. Then answer the questions below. Think about how generalizations sum up the story details.

I took a box of notepaper out of my desk drawer. The notes were bigger than postage stamps, but not by much. I took out a ballpoint pen and started pressing it against a piece of scrap paper, making dents in the paper but not making a mark. Ballpoint pens sometimes take a while to get started. When I was down in Florida, Tillie Nachman had said, "The ballpoint pen has been the biggest single factor in the decline of Western Civilization. It makes the written word cheap, fast, and totally without character." My mother and Tillie should get together. Between them, they have come up with the two major reasons why Western Civilization is about to collapse.

Reprinted with the permission of Atheneum Books for Young Readers, an imprint of Simon & Schuster Children's Publishing Division from THE VIEW FROM SATURDAY by E.L. Konigsburg. Copyright © 1996 E.L. Konigsburg.

1. What is Noah's first generalization?

_____

2. What clue word did you use to identify this generalization? _____

3. Does Noah support his generalization? Explain.

_____

_____

4. If Noah had said, "ballpoint pens always get started easily," would this be a valid or faulty generalization? Explain.

_____

_____

5. On a separate sheet of paper, write a valid generalization about the people of Century Village. Give evidence from the story to support your generalization.

Notes for Home: Your child identified generalizations and decided if they were valid or faulty. *Home Activity:* Take turns using *most, all, always,* and *never* to make generalizations about your neighborhood. Discuss whether each generalization is valid or faulty.

© Scott Foresman 6

1.	Ⓐ	Ⓑ	Ⓒ	Ⓓ
2.	Ⓕ	Ⓖ	Ⓗ	Ⓙ
3.	Ⓐ	Ⓑ	Ⓒ	Ⓓ
4.	Ⓕ	Ⓖ	Ⓗ	Ⓙ
5.	Ⓐ	Ⓑ	Ⓒ	Ⓓ
6.	Ⓕ	Ⓖ	Ⓗ	Ⓙ
7.	Ⓐ	Ⓑ	Ⓒ	Ⓓ
8.	Ⓕ	Ⓖ	Ⓗ	Ⓙ
9.	Ⓐ	Ⓑ	Ⓒ	Ⓓ
10.	Ⓕ	Ⓖ	Ⓗ	Ⓙ
11.	Ⓐ	Ⓑ	Ⓒ	Ⓓ
12.	Ⓕ	Ⓖ	Ⓗ	Ⓙ
13.	Ⓐ	Ⓑ	Ⓒ	Ⓓ
14.	Ⓕ	Ⓖ	Ⓗ	Ⓙ
15.	Ⓐ	Ⓑ	Ⓒ	Ⓓ

© Scott Foresman 6

Selection Test

Directions: Choose the best answer to each item. Mark the letter for the answer you have chosen.

Part 1: Vocabulary

Find the answer choice that means about the same as the underlined word in each sentence.

1. Emma practiced her handwriting.
   A. a method of painting on paper with fingers instead of brushes
   B. using hand and finger movements to spell out words in the air
   C. making letters or words with a pen, pencil, or other writing tool
   D. any means of communicating that involves the hands

2. Martin used a calligraphy pen.
   F. expressing meaning without words
   G. writing in code
   H. of or related to black
   J. beautiful handwriting

3. Dad checked his stationery supplies.
   A. writing materials, such as paper, cards, and envelopes
   B. staying in one place
   C. furniture, such as desks, chairs, and file cabinets
   D. related to weather

4. Considering the circumstances, she was doing well.
   F. difficulties
   G. conditions for an act or event
   H. goals
   J. time left to complete something

5. My dad just doesn't understand our generation.
   A. method of getting something done
   B. the people on one side of a family
   C. standards of taste or style
   D. all the people born at about the same time

6. They formed a committee.
   F. group of persons elected to make laws
   G. business
   H. group of persons appointed or elected to do a certain task
   J. large circle

Part 2: Comprehension

Use what you know about the story to answer each item.

7. What is a "B & B letter"?
   A. an invitation
   B. a thank-you letter
   C. a business letter
   D. a story in letter form

8. Why did Noah go to Florida to stay with his grandparents?
   F. His parents were away on a cruise.
   G. His grandparents needed his help.
   H. He wanted to meet his grandparents' friends.
   J. He wanted to visit a theme park in Florida.

9. What kind of place is Century Village?
   A. a small town
   B. a nursing home
   C. a vacation resort
   D. a retirement community

10. What generalization can you make about the residents of Century Village based on the information in the story?
    F. Most came to Florida from Epiphany, New York.
    G. Many have grandchildren living with them.
    H. Most like to grow flowers.
    J. Many get involved in community events.

© Scott Foresman 6

GO ON

11. Which sentence from the story is a valid generalization?
    A. "The ball-point pen has been the biggest single factor in the decline of Western Civilization."
    B. "Almost everyone who lives there is retired."
    C. "I looked totally presentable in my tuxedo T-shirt, which was a real work of art."
    D. "Fortunately, Grandpa Nate took its picture right after she finished it."

12. What did everyone at Century Village believe about Tillie Nachman?
    F. She was a great artist.
    G. She should become a professional calligrapher.
    H. She did not make mistakes.
    J. She was unhappy living in Florida.

13. During the preparations for the wedding, Noah seems to think that almost everything is—
    A. educational.
    B. unnecessary.
    C. extremely annoying.
    D. going wrong in some way.

14. The author's purpose in writing this story was to—
    F. describe life in southern Florida.
    G. tell an amusing story.
    H. help the reader distinguish between facts and opinions.
    J. show that young people are not good judges of adults.

15. Noah's mother thinks the decline of Western Civilization will come about because—
    A. young people don't do things the way they used to be done.
    B. boys wear T-shirts instead of tuxedos.
    C. young people do not learn calligraphy.
    D. children let computers think for them.

STOP

© Scott Foresman 6

Character and Visualizing

Directions: Read the story. Then read each question about the story. Choose the best answer to each question. Mark the letter for the answer you have chosen.

A Hoop, a Game Show, and a Good Idea

"I know you'll find a way to help me out, Desirée," said Desi's mother as she turned back to the work on her desk. When Mom spoke in that tone of voice, Desi knew she meant what she said. Her mother, she knew, had a deadline to meet with her publisher, and she couldn't stop working until their relatives actually arrived in an hour. But how was Desi to entertain her four little cousins on a rainy day?

Desi surveyed her cluttered room. A huge, striped hoop, five dusty sneakers, and colorful scarves sat in one corner. Wads of crumpled paper crowded her wastebasket, like so much popcorn, and her closet and shelves overflowed with toys and books. Old prizes from parties—cheap plastic rings, whistles, and so on—looked like crickets escaping from the tipped box nearby. An old box of cards with trivia questions and answers had spilled like a waterfall onto the carpet. Only her compact discs were carefully arranged on her desk by the CD player, like soldiers lined up for inspection. It was the one corner of the room Desi always kept neat, dusted, and organized.

"Maybe I can make an obstacle course in the basement," thought Desi. "The hoop, scarves, and shoes will be handy for that. The plastic prizes will be useful too, but I'll also need a timer." Surely Desi could find one in an old game box! Now, how could she use those worn-out trivia cards? "Hmmm. I'll set up my room as a TV game show. The kids can answer trivia questions and win play money. Perfect, but I'd better get busy! They'll be here in an hour!"

1. Desi's thoughts show that she is—
   A. puzzled by her mother's request.
   B. good at solving problems.
   C. easily upset by a change of plans.
   D. a constant complainer.

2. Desi's CDs are neatly arranged because—
   F. she likes to keep her room neat.
   G. she likes loud music.
   H. the CDs are important to her.
   J. her mother likes to see things neat and orderly.

3. The word *crickets* is used to describe how—
   A. bugs could be heard outside.
   B. the plastic prizes were all one color.
   C. the prizes jumped around the room.
   D. the prizes were scattered about.

4. The CDs were compared to soldiers to show—
   F. how much Desi likes toy soldiers.
   G. how neat and orderly they were.
   H. the kinds of music recorded on them.
   J. the similarity of their cover designs.

5. In the next hour, Desi will probably—
   A. set up games for her cousins.
   B. make lunch for her cousins.
   C. reorganize her CD collection.
   D. help her mom with her work.

Notes for Home: Your child identified a character's traits and visualized the setting based on images from a passage. *Home Activity:* Take turns describing the bedrooms or favorite rooms of family members. Discuss how each room reveals something about that person.

© Scott Foresman 6

Character and Visualizing 257

Phonics: Vowel Digraphs

Directions: Read the words in the box. Each word contains the vowel combination **oo.** Say each word to yourself. Listen for those words with the same vowel sound as **choose** and those words with the same vowel sound as **stood.** Write each word in the correct column.

bedroom	fishhook	look
books	fooling	moon
cook	good	pooled
cookie	groom	stool

Vowel sound in *choose*

1. _____
2. _____
3. _____
4. _____
5. _____
6. _____

Vowel sound in *stood*

7. _____
8. _____
9. _____
10. _____
11. _____
12. _____

Directions: Read the words below. Each word contains the vowel combination **ow.** Circle the words that have the same vowel sound as **grow.**

13. row   now   slowly   however   brown   sowing   cowboy

14. down   grown   gown   towns   tow   mowing   lowly

15. owed   flowers   stow   show   know   Howard   below

Directions: For each word below, give three more words that have the same vowel sound and spelling.

16. throat   _____   _____   _____

17. weight   _____   _____   _____

18. flow   _____   _____   _____

19. room   _____   _____   _____

20. good   _____   _____   _____

Notes for Home: Your child distinguished vowel digraphs, such as *oo* in *room, ow* in *owe, oa* in *toast,* and *ei* in *weight.* **Home Activity:** With your child, read a letter or card you have received from family or friends. Look for these vowel sounds and spellings.

© Scott Foresman 6

Dictionary

A **dictionary** is a book of words, listed in alphabetical order, and their meanings. Guide words appear at the top of each page that tell the first and last words that appear on the page. Each entry shows a word's spelling, syllable parts, pronunciation, definitions, and parts of speech. Some entries will also include illustrative, or sample, phrases or sentences, and an etymology that tells how the word came into the English language from other languages.

Directions: Use the dictionary entries to answer the questions that follow.

---

re • la • tion • ship (ri lā´ shən ship), **1** a connection: *What is the relationship of clouds to rain?* **2** the condition of belonging to the same family. **3** the state that exists between people or groups that deal with each other: *I have good relationships with all of my teachers this year. noun.*

rel • a • tive (rel´ ə tiv), **1** a person who belongs to the same family as another, such as a father, brother, aunt, nephew, or cousin. **2** compared to each other: *We discussed the relative advantages of city and country life.* **3** depending for meaning on a relation to something else: *East is a relative term; for example, Chicago is east of California but west of New York.* **1** *noun,* **2, 3** *adjective.* **relative to, 1** about; concerning: *The teacher asked me some questions relative to my plans for the summer.* **2** in comparison with; in proportion to; for: *He is strong relative to his size.*

rel • a • tive • ly (rel´ ə tiv lē), in relation to something else; comparatively: *You are relatively tall for your age. adverb.*

re • lax (ri laks´), **1** to loosen up; make or become less stiff or firm: *Relax your muscles to rest them. Relax when you dance.* **2** to make or become less strict or severe; lessen in force: *Discipline is relaxed on the last day of school.* **3** to relieve or be relieved from work, effort, or worry: *We relaxed during the holidays. Relax! Everything will be all right. verb.*

re • lax • a • tion (rē´ lak sā´ shən), **1** a loosening: *the relaxation of the muscles.* **2** a lessening of strictness, severity, or force: *the relaxation of discipline over the holidays.* **3** recreation; amusement: *Walking and reading are relaxations. noun.*

re • lay (rē´ lā *for 1;* rē´ lā´ *or* ri lā´ *for 2*), **1** a fresh supply: *New relays of firefighters were sent in.* **2** to take and carry farther: *Please relay this message to your parents.* **1** *noun,* **2** *verb,* **re • lays, re • layed, re • lay • ing.**

re • lay race (rē´ lā rās´), a race in which each member of a team runs or swims only a certain part of the distance.

From SCOTT FORESMAN BEGINNING DICTIONARY by E.L. Thorndike and Clarence L. Barnhart.
Copyright © 1997 by Scott Foresman and Company.

© Scott Foresman 6

1. Does the *e* in *relationship* sound like the first *e* in *relative* or the *e* in *relax?* Explain.

_____

_____

2. Find the word that can be used as both a noun and a verb. Write two sentences using the word, one for each part of speech.

_____

_____

3. How many syllables does *relative* have?_____

4. Which meaning of the word *relax* best refers to rules or enforcers of rules?

_____

5. If the guide words *reign* and *relay race* were shown above the entries, list three words that might appear on this page before the word *relationship*.

_____

6. Which meaning of *relationship* is being used in the following sentence?
   The relationship between the two old friends was as strong today as it was twenty years ago.

_____

7. Are the spellings of the underlined words in the following sentence correct? If not, identify and correct any misspelled words.
   My <u>relatives</u> were <u>relativly</u> <u>relaxed</u> given that the groom was rather late.

_____

8. Why are guide words helpful when you are searching for a specific entry?

_____

_____

_____

9. Do you think the illustrative phrases are helpful? Explain. _____

_____

10. How might you use a dictionary to help you as you read and write?

_____

_____

_____

Notes for Home: Your child answered questions about several dictionary entries. *Home Activity:* Play a dictionary game in which one person picks a word from a dictionary and uses it in an illustrative sentence. The other players write down what they think the word means.

© Scott Foresman 6

Author's Viewpoint/Bias

- **Author's viewpoint** is the way an author thinks about the subject of his or her writing.

- You can identify an author's viewpoint by looking at the words an author uses. Some authors use loaded words, such as *terrible* or *wonderful,* to express a strong preference, or bias.

- *Balanced writing* presents both sides of an issue. *Biased writing* shows strong feeling for or against someone or something and presents only one side of an issue. You should read biased writing critically.

Directions: Reread "Normal." Then complete the table. Write whether you think the author would agree or disagree with each statement below. Explain your thinking with evidence from the article.

Statement	Agree or Disagree? Explain.
Normal is different for each individual.	1.
Students cannot learn anything from a person in a wheelchair.	2.
A person can learn to overcome any problem.	3.
When something is *normal* to a person, that person does not think about it.	4.
Normal is what is average or what the majority accepts.	5.

Notes for Home: Your child read an article and analyzed the author's viewpoint. *Home Activity:* Have a family debate. Write topics on slips of paper. Take turns choosing one and expressing a viewpoint on the topic. Later, discuss whether any speaker used loaded words.

© Scott Foresman 6

Vocabulary

Directions: Choose the word from the box that best matches each definition. Write the word on the line.

_____ 1. of, for, or by sight

_____ 2. worth or value; quality

_____ 3. favorable notice

_____ 4. benefits

_____ 5. things strongly desired

_____ 6. condition of being without sight

Check the Words You Know

__ advantages
__ ambitions
__ blindness
__ complicated
__ merit
__ recognition
__ visual

Directions: Read the diary entry of an inventor. Choose the word from the box that best completes each sentence. Write the word on the matching numbered lines below.

> Tomorrow I will show off my new invention. I hope everyone will see the **7.** _____ of making a device that makes it easier for people to open cans and jars. For this invention to be a success, it can't be too **8.** _____, or people won't want to use it. If tomorrow's test goes well, my ideas will soon get the **9.** _____ they deserve. My friends tell me that my **10.** _____ are too high, but I know that this invention could change people's lives for the better. I'm sure of it!

7. _____   9. _____

8. _____   10. _____

Write a Commercial

On a separate sheet of paper, write a television or radio commercial for a new invention. Your commercial should briefly tell what your invention can do and convince people of its merit. Use as many vocabulary words as you can.

Notes for Home: Your child identified and used vocabulary words from *Louis Braille*. ***Home Activity:*** Talk to your child about an invention that has changed the lives of those who use it. Make a two-column list that shows the advantages and drawbacks of the invention.

© Scott Foresman 6

Author's Viewpoint/Bias

- **Author's viewpoint** is the way an author thinks about the subject of his or her writing. You can identify an author's viewpoint by looking at the words an author uses. Some authors use loaded words, such as *terrible* or *wonderful,* to express a strong preference, or bias.

- *Balanced writing* presents both sides of an issue. *Biased writing* shows strong feeling for or against someone or something and presents only one side of an issue. You should read biased writing critically.

Directions: Reread the passage from *Louis Braille* which describes the governor's reaction to the Braille system. Then answer the questions below. Think about the words the author uses to support his viewpoint.

> Although Braille's system was brilliant, and although it was supported by all the pupils and many of the teachers at the National Institute for Blind Youth, it was disliked by the Institute's governors. They supported other systems of reading and writing, such as Haüy's raised wooden letters, which they knew how to read themselves but which was far too cumbersome to be efficient when used by the blind.
>
> Because the governors of the Institute were not blind themselves, they couldn't understand the tremendous advantages of Braille. They did not realize its simplicity and the fact that it allowed blind people to write as well as to read. They distrusted a new system that they were unable to use without first having to learn Braille's language of dots.
>
> From LOUIS BRAILLE by Stephen Keeler. Copyright ©1986 by Wayland Publishers, Ltd. Reprinted by permission.

1. What word or words indicate the author's view of Louis Braille's system?

_____

2. What word or words indicate the author's view of Haüy's system?

_____

3. Why does the author think the governors favor Haüy's system?

_____

_____

4. Which system of reading does the author favor?

_____

5. On a separate sheet of paper, explain the author's viewpoint of Louis Braille and his invention. Is the author biased? Explain.

Notes for Home: Your child analyzed the way an author presented his viewpoint. **Home Activity:** Discuss the viewpoint presented in a newspaper editorial. Think about the bias of the writer and how convincing and valid the evidence is.

© Scott Foresman 6

Name _____

1.	Ⓐ	Ⓑ	Ⓒ	Ⓓ
2.	Ⓕ	Ⓖ	Ⓗ	Ⓙ
3.	Ⓐ	Ⓑ	Ⓒ	Ⓓ
4.	Ⓕ	Ⓖ	Ⓗ	Ⓙ
5.	Ⓐ	Ⓑ	Ⓒ	Ⓓ
6.	Ⓕ	Ⓖ	Ⓗ	Ⓙ
7.	Ⓐ	Ⓑ	Ⓒ	Ⓓ
8.	Ⓕ	Ⓖ	Ⓗ	Ⓙ
9.	Ⓐ	Ⓑ	Ⓒ	Ⓓ
10.	Ⓕ	Ⓖ	Ⓗ	Ⓙ
11.	Ⓐ	Ⓑ	Ⓒ	Ⓓ
12.	Ⓕ	Ⓖ	Ⓗ	Ⓙ
13.	Ⓐ	Ⓑ	Ⓒ	Ⓓ
14.	Ⓕ	Ⓖ	Ⓗ	Ⓙ
15.	Ⓐ	Ⓑ	Ⓒ	Ⓓ

© Scott Foresman 6

Selection Test

Directions: Choose the best answer to each item. Mark the letter for the answer you have chosen.

Part 1: Vocabulary

Find the answer choice that means about the same as the underlined word in each sentence.

1. Her <u>blindness</u> was caused by a childhood illness.
   A. condition of being slow to learn
   B. condition of being unable to see
   C. condition of having weak muscles
   D. condition of being unable to hear

2. John spoke of his <u>ambitions</u>.
   F. plans for a building
   G. ideas about education
   H. things that are strongly desired
   J. places where students are taught

3. Dr. Casey gained <u>recognition</u> for his ideas.
   A. favorable notice; acceptance
   B. award of money
   C. distrust; lack of faith
   D. permission to change

4. Candace got a raise based on <u>merit</u>.
   F. time spent on a job
   G. ability to plan ahead
   H. condition of being older than others
   J. something that deserves praise or reward

5. Maureen has great <u>visual</u> skills.
   A. used for teaching; educational
   B. related to sight
   C. from a certain time in history
   D. related to machines

6. These instructions are <u>complicated</u>.
   F. freely offered
   G. hard to understand
   H. providing correct information
   J. well organized

7. Her plan had some <u>advantages</u>.
   A. unfavorable conditions
   B. supporters
   C. causes of cancellation or delay
   D. benefits

Part 2: Comprehension

Use what you know about the selection to answer each item.

8. The school in Paris that Louis Braille attended in 1819 was—
   F. the first school for boys and girls with special needs.
   G. a school for children who were gifted.
   H. the only school for blind children in France.
   J. a school for music students.

9. At the National Institute for Blind Youth, students learned mainly by—
   A. listening and remembering.
   B. reading books published in "Night Writing."
   C. going on field trips.
   D. making things and doing experiments.

10. The writing system developed by Charles Barbier was easier to read than embossed books because—
    F. it was first developed for sighted people to use at night.
    G. dots and dashes are easier to recognize by touch than the shapes of letters.
    H. it was based on sounds rather than spelling.
    J. each letter could be quickly recognized by a single touch of the finger.

© Scott Foresman 6

11. In his efforts to improve Charles Barbier's system, Louis Braille's major breakthrough came when he—
    A.   dropped all dashes from the system.
    B.   learned to write with a stylus.
    C.   invented a system of only six dots to represent letters.
    D.   talked to Dr. Pignier, the school principal, about his experiments.

12. The author of this selection seems to think that—
    F.   Louis Braille was a truly remarkable person.
    G.   schools in the past gave students more opportunities to be creative than those of today.
    H.   Louis Braille has been given too much credit for something another man invented.
    J.   Louis Braille's success was based largely on luck.

13. Which words do you think the author would use to describe school principal Dr. Pignier?
    A.   creative and fun
    B.   mean-spirited
    C.   thoughtful and open-minded
    D.   stubbornly proud

14. Which of these statements would be impossible to verify as a fact?
    F.   Gabriel Gauthier went to school with Louis Braille.
    G.   Boys who broke the rules were kept after school and made to write punishment papers.
    H.   Charles Barbier had invented a secret military code based on dots and dashes.
    J.   Louis's face lit up with excitement when he realized what a great opportunity he had.

15. In writing this selection, the author has combined known facts with—
    A.   fictional characters and events.
    B.   exaggerated statements and humor.
    C.   what he imagines the characters may have thought and felt.
    D.   poetic language and rhythms.

© Scott Foresman 6

Persuasive Devices

Directions: Read the passage. Then read each question about the passage. Choose the best answer to each question. Mark the letter for the answer you have chosen.

Simply Speaking

Hands off that keyboard! Make editing and spell-checking things of the past. Join the revolution that has everyone talking—and all the computers listening!!

From stressed typists to keyboard klutzes, every computer-user can find a use for this advanced technology. Known in the industry as *continuous-speech recognition,* these programs can turn natural speech into typed pages almost instantly. (This means that you speak and your words appear automatically on the screen. Over 90 percent of the time, they appear correctly spelled and punctuated.) Many of these high-powered programs also come with simple voice commands that make formatting, editing, and moving through files a breeze. When combined with other programs, some products can sort through records, search for data, even send messages and read them aloud, simply based on voice commands. As a result, all office workers can increase their speed and output, as can students, researchers, and anyone else who talks!

The sharpest minds in the business are already switching to speech recognition programs, so don't be left out of the conversation. Speak up and install your own right away!

1. The author believes that the product is best suited for—
   A. people who are poor spellers.
   B. everyone needing to search for data.
   C. those who write exactly the way they speak.
   D. anyone who owns a computer and can talk.

2. Which of the following claims is an attempt to persuade you?
   F. The programs can turn natural speech into typed pages.
   G. The smartest people are using it already.
   H. Some programs can even send messages and read them aloud.
   J. Some products can sort through records.

3. Loaded words used to influence the reader include—
   A. keyboard and voice commands.
   B. commands and technology.
   C. revolution and high-powered.
   D. recognition and punctuated.

4. Which of the following is a sweeping generalization?
   F. As a result, all office workers can increase their speed and output.
   G. Some products can sort through records.
   H. Continuous-speech recognition programs turn natural speech into typed pages.
   J. Continuous-speech recognition programs come with simple voice commands.

5. The purpose of this passage is to persuade readers to—
   A. quit using computers.
   B. install continuous-speech recognition programming.
   C. spell-check more often.
   D. increase their speed and output.

Notes for Home: Your child analyzed various persuasive techniques in an advertisement. *Home Activity:* Have your child find examples of persuasive language in magazine advertisements and identify what evidence, if any, is given to support the claims made.

© Scott Foresman 6

Phonics: Diphthongs and Digraphs

Directions: Read the word pairs below. Each word contains the vowel combination **ou.** For each pair, circle the word that has the same vowel sound as **out.**

1. house   tough

2. through   trousers

3. though   mountains

4. announcements   thorough

5. bought   bound

6. astound   thought

Directions: Read each sentence below. Each sentence has two words with the letters **ou,** but only one of the words has the same vowel sound as **out.** Circle that word and write it on the line.

_____ 7. The group of science students was experimenting with the principles of sound.

_____ 8. They wanted to learn about how music travels through water.

_____ 9. They brought a stereo speaker up to the outside of an aquarium tank filled with water.

_____ 10. Then they turned up the stereo, loud enough to feel the vibrations on the speaker.

_____ 11. By noticing the vibrations in the water, the students proudly concluded that music could travel underwater.

Directions: Read the paragraph below. Look and listen for words that have the letters **au** with the same vowel sound as in **sauce;** the letters **ew** with the same vowel sound as in **threw;** or the letters **oi** with the same vowel sound as in **moist.** Circle the words and write them on the lines.

> The students did not want to be disappointed again. They'd been extra cautious this time, adjusting a few dials and pointing out any possible problems. They'd trusted the voices inside their heads, as well as the science lessons their teacher had taught them. Now they were ready. Because they'd followed each step to the letter, their anticipation grew. Their hopes had been renewed that this time their invention would be a success.

au as in *sauce*	**ew as in *threw***	**oi as in *moist***
12. _____	15. _____	18. _____
13. _____	16. _____	19. _____
14. _____	17. _____	20. _____

Notes for Home: Your child sorted words with the vowel sounds heard in *sauce, threw, moist,* and *out.* **Home Activity:** Together, write other words with *au, ew, oi,* and *ou.* Take turns using these words in sentences.

© Scott Foresman 6

Chart/Table/Time Line

A **chart** organizes information visually, such as in a list, table, or diagram.
A **table** is a special kind of chart that shows information in rows and columns.
A **time line** is a bar divided into periods of time that shows a sequence of events.

Directions: Use the time line to complete the table on the next page. List in the table's second column the different types of transportation shown on the time line. Then answer the questions that follow.

Transportation Time Line

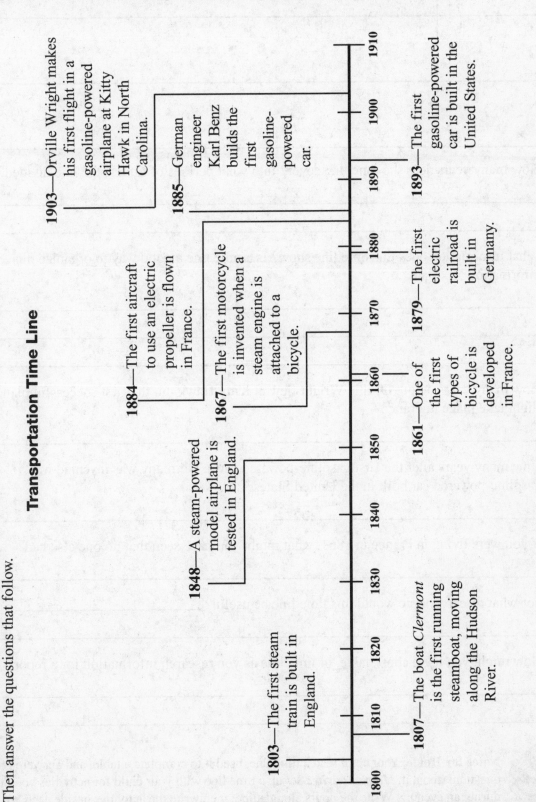

1803—The first steam train is built in England.

1807—The boat *Clermont* is the first running steamboat, moving along the Hudson River.

1848—A steam-powered model airplane is tested in England.

1861—One of the first types of bicycle is developed in France.

1867—The first motorcycle is invented when a steam engine is attached to a bicycle.

1879—The first electric railroad is built in Germany.

1884—The first aircraft to use an electric propeller is flown in France.

1885—German engineer Karl Benz builds the first gasoline-powered car.

1893—The first gasoline-powered car is built in the United States.

1903—Orville Wright makes his first flight in a gasoline-powered airplane at Kitty Hawk in North Carolina.

1800 1810 1820 1830 1840 1850 1860 1870 1880 1890 1900 1910

© Scott Foresman 6

Travel by . . .	Transportation Invention
Land	1.
Sea	2.
Air	3.

4. How many years does the time line cover? Into what periods of time is the line divided?

_____

_____

5. What information does this time line show? Is a time line a good way to organize this information? Explain.

_____

_____

_____

6. How many years before Orville Wright flew at Kitty Hawk did the first successful plane flight take place in France?

_____

7. How many years after the first gasoline-powered car in Germany was invented was a gasoline-powered car built in the United States?

_____

8. If you were living in France in 1861, what might you have seen that no one else had?

_____

9. For what research topic would this time line be useful? _____

_____

10. How might you use a chart, table, or time line as you research information for a report?

_____

_____

Notes for Home: Your child read a time line, used it to complete a table, and answered questions about it. ***Home Activity:*** Set up a time line with your child for activities you do during an evening. Write the hours along a line; then write the activities beside each hour.

© Scott Foresman 6

Graphic Sources

- A **graphic** or **graphic source** of information is something that shows information visually.
- Some common graphic sources of information are pictures, charts, maps, graphs, and diagrams.
- A graphic source can present new information in the text differently or show more information.

Directions: Reread "Ptolemy—An Early Map Maker," and review the maps. Then follow the directions below to mark the map to show areas Ptolemy did and did not know about. You may need to refer to another map to complete the last two directions.

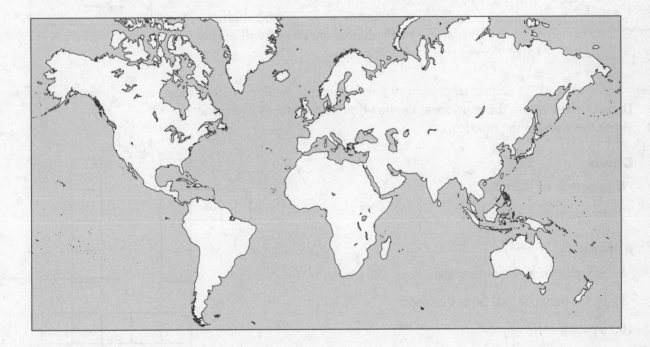

1. Label the city where Ptolemy was from.

2. Shade the land areas that Ptolemy knew about.

3. Use a different color to shade the areas of water that Ptolemy knew about.

4. Label the two continents that Ptolemy did not know about.

5. Label the ocean that Ptolemy did not know about.

Notes for Home: Your child marked a map to show his or her understanding of the material. *Home Activity:* With your child, find a newspaper or magazine article that includes a picture, map, or graph. Discuss how the graphic source of information relates to the article.

© Scott Foresman 6

Vocabulary

Directions: Choose the word from the box that best completes each
sentence. Write the word on the line to the left.

_____ 1. Scientists can make _____ predictions
about a satellite's path.

_____ 2. They can make an _____ based on
what they know about space flight.

_____ 3. Sometimes, scientists _____ an exact
answer.

_____ 4. They use a _____ in which symbols
stand for different pieces of data.

_____ 5. Sometimes, a _____ who studies
mathematics or science will discover a
new formula.

> **Check
> the Words
> You Know**
>
> __ accurate
> __ angle
> __ arc
> __ calculate
> __ estimate
> __ formula
> __ scholar
> __ sphere

Directions: Choose the word from the box that best matches each clue.
Write the word in the puzzle.

Down

6. a person of learning

7. to compute information

Across

8. any part of a circumference

9. space between two lines that meet

10. a round solid object

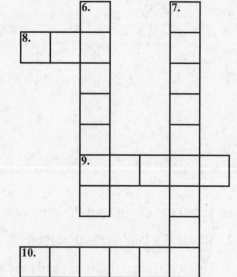

Write an E-mail Message

On a separate sheet of paper, write an e-mail message.
Imagine you are a scientist who has made a new discovery
and that you are describing your discovery to another
scientist. Use as many vocabulary words as you can.

Notes for Home: Your child identified and used vocabulary words from *The Librarian Who
Measured the Earth*. **Home Activity:** Talk with your child about math in everyday life.
Encourage him or her to use vocabulary words during the discussion.

© Scott Foresman 6

Graphic Sources

- A **graphic** or **graphic source** of information is something that shows information visually.
- Some common graphic sources of information are pictures, charts, maps, graphs, and diagrams.
- A graphic source can present new information in the text differently or show more information.

Directions: Reread the passage from *The Librarian Who Measured the Earth* in which the author explains how to find Earth's circumference. Then follow the instructions below.

Perhaps [Eratosthenes] imagined the earth as a grapefruit. If [a grapefruit] is sliced in half, you can see its sections. In order to measure the distance all the way around the edge of the grapefruit (the circumference), you would need to know only the distance along the edge of one section (the arc) and how many of these same-size sections it would take to make up the whole grapefruit.

From THE LIBRARIAN WHO MEASURED THE EARTH by Kathryn Lasky.
Copyright ©1994 by Kathryn Lasky; Illustrations © by Kevin Hawkes.
By permission of Little, Brown and Company.

1. Use the description in the passage and the picture of the grapefruit to trace the circumference of the grapefruit. Label the circumference you traced.

2. Draw and label an arc on the picture of the grapefruit.

3. Shade in one section.

4. How does the image of the grapefruit help you better understand the main idea of the passage?

_____

_____

_____

5. Reread the story. Are there other places in the story where a picture helps you better understand the text? Explain your thinking on a separate sheet of paper.

Notes for Home: Your child used a graphic source of information to help him or her understand the passage's main idea. *Home Activity:* Look at some newspaper graphics. Ask each other questions that can be answered using the graphic source.

© Scott Foresman 6

1.	Ⓐ	Ⓑ	Ⓒ	Ⓓ
2.	Ⓕ	Ⓖ	Ⓗ	Ⓙ
3.	Ⓐ	Ⓑ	Ⓒ	Ⓓ
4.	Ⓕ	Ⓖ	Ⓗ	Ⓙ
5.	Ⓐ	Ⓑ	Ⓒ	Ⓓ
6.	Ⓕ	Ⓖ	Ⓗ	Ⓙ
7.	Ⓐ	Ⓑ	Ⓒ	Ⓓ
8.	Ⓕ	Ⓖ	Ⓗ	Ⓙ
9.	Ⓐ	Ⓑ	Ⓒ	Ⓓ
10.	Ⓕ	Ⓖ	Ⓗ	Ⓙ
11.	Ⓐ	Ⓑ	Ⓒ	Ⓓ
12.	Ⓕ	Ⓖ	Ⓗ	Ⓙ
13.	Ⓐ	Ⓑ	Ⓒ	Ⓓ
14.	Ⓕ	Ⓖ	Ⓗ	Ⓙ
15.	Ⓐ	Ⓑ	Ⓒ	Ⓓ

© Scott Foresman 6

Selection Test

Directions: Choose the best answer to each item. Mark the letter for the answer
you have chosen.

Part 1: Vocabulary

Find the answer choice that means about the
same as the underlined word in each sentence.

1. We asked him to <u>estimate</u> the cost.
   A. agree to pay on a fixed schedule
   B. make a judgment or guess based on
      available facts
   C. pay no attention to
   D. say that something is larger or
      greater than it is

2. I knew that the news story was not
   <u>accurate</u>.
   F. interesting
   G. well written
   H. recent
   J. correct; exact

3. I need to <u>calculate</u> the distance.
   A. make shorter and narrower
   B. increase
   C. find by using numbers
   D. imagine

4. She found the <u>formula</u> she needed.
   F. combination of symbols used in
      mathematics to state a rule or
      principle
   G. list of ingredients and procedures for
      preparing food
   H. a formal written or oral discussion of
      a topic
   J. an explanation based on observation
      only

5. The moon is a <u>sphere</u>.
   A. figure shaped like an oval
   B. a round solid object; globe
   C. object that revolves around a planet
   D. solid block

6. He needed to know the distance along the
   <u>arc</u>.
   F. one side of a triangle
   G. a curved structure capable of
      carrying weight
   H. a type of boat
   J. any part of a circle's circumference

7. She measured the <u>angle</u>.
   A. space between two lines or surfaces
      that meet
   B. distance along the curve of a circle
   C. point where two lines meet
   D. side of a square or rectangle

8. His mother is a famous <u>scholar</u>.
   F. person who writes plays
   G. person who has much knowledge
   H. woman who sings with a high voice
   J. person who practices magic

Part 2: Comprehension

Use what you know about the selection to
answer each item.

9. When did Eratosthenes live?
   A. less than 900 years ago
   B. about 1,000 years ago
   C. more than 2,000 years ago
   D. about 4,000 years ago

10. At the gymnasium, Eratosthenes wrote
    with—
    F. charcoal on slate tablets.
    G. pen and ink on paper.
    H. sharp sticks on wax tablets.
    J. brushes and ink on papyrus.

© Scott Foresman 6

GO ON

11. Why was Eratosthenes glad to go to Alexandria to tutor the king's son?
  A. Life in Cyrene offered few challenges for him.
  B. It was near the place where he had grown up as a boy.
  C. It was a great honor to teach the son of the king.
  D. Alexandria was the best place in the world to study and learn.

12. In this selection, the pictures of a circle and a grapefruit help to show—
  F. why the sun's rays strike only one section of the earth at a time.
  G. how applying geometry to everyday objects could help Eratosthenes figure out the size of the earth.
  H. why circles are measured in degrees.
  J. how Eratosthenes measured the distance from Alexandria to Syene.

13. The picture of Eratosthenes measuring the shadow of a pole helps to show how he—
  A. measured the angle of the sun's rays.
  B. organized books in the library.
  C. traveled to Syene.
  D. demonstrated to others that his numbers were correct.

14. Which statement would be most difficult to verify as a fact?
  F. "He would crawl across the kitchen floor to follow the path of ants."
  G. "He also made a list of all the winners of the Olympic Games."
  H. "At the museum there were laboratories and libraries, dining halls and private studios."
  J. "Eratosthenes dedicated the solution to the king."

15. In order to write this selection, the author most likely spent a lot of time—
  A. visiting Athens, Alexandria, and other cities named in the selection.
  B. solving geometry problems.
  C. talking with people who knew Eratosthenes.
  D. doing historical research.

STOP

© Scott Foresman 6

Context Clues

Directions: Read the passage. Then read each question about the passage. Choose the best answer to each question. Mark the letter for the answer you have chosen.

Before Chemistry

Over 800 years ago, some European scholars practiced alchemy, an early form of chemistry. These alchemists had three main goals. They wanted to discover the secret of <u>transmutation</u>, a process in which <u>base metals</u> such as iron or lead could be turned into costly silver or gold. They also hoped to discover the philosopher's stone, an unusual substance that would make transmutation easier. Additionally, many alchemists <u>aspired</u> to discover the proper chemical mix for a potion to cure all diseases and prolong lives by hundreds of years.

Some alchemists were <u>charlatans</u> who claimed that their discoveries gave them magical powers. Other more honest scholars devoted their entire lives to their experiments. They learned about the <u>properties</u> of various substances. After all, knowing the characteristics of a chemical —its hardness and melting point, and the ways it reacts with other substances—might one day be the key to a success. As a result, alchemists added new information to the pool of knowledge about chemicals. New kinds of tools and equipment were needed to aid them in their work, so they invented special scales, tools to melt metals, and other equipment. Alchemy may seem foolish by today's standards, but alchemists' research helped lay the foundations of modern chemistry.

1. <u>Transmutation</u> is a process that alchemists believed could—
   A. remove the metal found in rocks.
   B. help them live longer.
   C. change lead into gold.
   D. change gold into base metals.

2. In this passage, <u>base metals</u> are those that are—
   F. low in weight.
   G. the supporting layers for other metals.
   H. the most important ingredients in the philosopher's stone.
   J. low in cost or value.

3. In this passage, the word <u>aspired</u> means—
   A. hoped to achieve a goal.
   B. expressed a thought clearly.
   C. took for granted.
   D. worried or annoyed.

4. In this passage, the word <u>charlatans</u> means—
   F. street actors.
   G. frauds.
   H. scientists.
   J. cure-alls.

5. In this passage, the word <u>properties</u> means—
   A. rightful owners.
   B. magic powers.
   C. characteristics of chemical substances.
   D. owned pieces of land.

© Scott Foresman 6

Notes for Home: Your child figured out the meaning of unfamiliar words by using context clues. *Home Activity:* Encourage your child to use context clues to figure out the meanings of unfamiliar words in stories he or she reads. Together, use a dictionary to check these words.

Phonics: *r*-Controlled Vowels

Directions: Read the diary entry below. Look and listen for words with **ar** that sound like **garden.** Circle the words and write them on the lines.

January 9

    As I gaze at the stars, I am bombarded with

all sorts of questions. How did these

outer-space lights find their place in the sky?

Could they be as random as marbles thrown

across a playing field? Or is there a pattern,

something no one has yet discovered? Several

look closer together while others seem far

from each other. You need to be sharp to

study the universe. I wonder if I am smart

enough to figure out such cosmic mysteries?

1. _____
2. _____
3. _____
4. _____
5. _____
6. _____

Directions: Read the word pairs below. Each word contains the letters **or.** For each pair, circle the word that has the same vowel sound as **for.**

7. born   working
8. word   morning

9. worthless   formula
10. transport   worm

Directions: Read each sentence below. Listen for a word that has the same vowel sound as **shirt.** Hint: This vowel sound can be spelled different ways. Circle the word and write it on the line.

_____ 11. Thousands of years ago, it seemed impossible to find out exactly how big our world was.

_____ 12. Only those with the desire and skill could calculate Earth's size.

_____ 13. Thanks to the research of one ancient scholar, this was solved long ago.

_____ 14. Who knows who else might have been the first to find out some of the very basic things?

_____ 15. Much of the work of scholars in ancient times has not been recorded in history.

Notes for Home: Your child identified words with *r*-controlled vowels, such as *garden, for,* and *shirt.* **Home Activity:** Read a nonfiction book with your child. Help your child find words with these sounds. Make a chart to record the words you find.

© Scott Foresman 6

Name _____

Diagram

A **diagram** is a special drawing with labels. A diagram usually shows how
something is made or how it works.

Directions: Study the diagram of a tree house. Then use it to answer the
questions that follow.

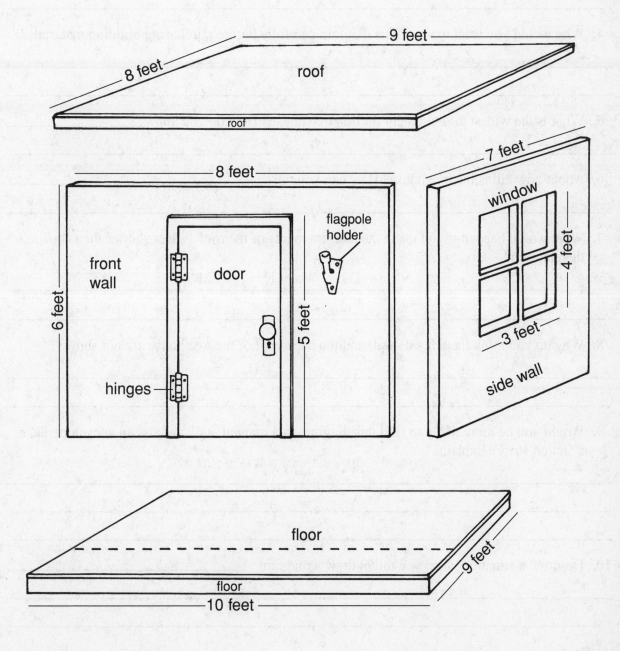

© Scott Foresman 6

Name _____

1. What is the purpose of this diagram? _____
_____

2. What else besides this diagram will you need to build a tree house? _____
_____

_____

3. What do the numbers on the diagram tell you? _____
_____

4. Why would you want to study this diagram carefully before purchasing building materials?
_____

_____

5. What is the widest measurement for this tree house? How do you know? _____
_____

6. About how tall is the tree house? How can you tell? _____
_____

7. What would happen if you made the measurements of the roof $1\frac{1}{2}$ feet shorter than shown in the diagram?
_____

_____

8. Why do you think the left side wall and the back wall of the tree house are not shown?
_____

_____

9. Would you be more likely to find this diagram in a manual, a dictionary, an encyclopedia, or a fiction story? Explain.
_____

_____

_____

10. Describe a situation when you might draw a diagram. _____
_____

_____

 Notes for Home: Your child examined a diagram that showed how to put something together.
Home Activity: Find a diagram that shows how to make something or how something works.
Take turns asking one another questions about what the diagram shows.

© Scott Foresman 6

Paraphrasing

- To **paraphrase** is to explain something in your own words.

- To paraphrase a piece of writing, first ask yourself what the author is trying to say. Then restate the ideas or description in your own words, without changing the meaning or adding opinions of your own.

Directions: Reread "A Lesson from the Master." Complete the table by paraphrasing portions of the story. Then answer the question below.

Passage	Paraphrase
Graybeard got to his feet. He lifted his thin arms over his head and stretched. Then he looked down at the boy. "Now it is time to begin," he said.	1.
The old man stopped him immediately, shaking his head briskly. "That is wrong. I have told you, always make your first sketch in charcoal. Black is better. And start with an outline of the body and the head."	2.
As he followed Graybeard's instructions Tao found he was drawing easier, faster. He smiled with a quick feeling of satisfaction. Just a few words from the master made a big difference.	3.
Graybeard nodded. "You are learning, my friend. It takes time, but you are learning."	4.

5. Why is it important not to add your own opinions when parapharasing a piece of writing?

_____

_____

Notes for Home: Your child read a story and used his or her own words to restate what happened in various parts of the story. *Home Activity:* With your child, read a paragraph from a story or article. Help your child use his or her own words to restate the ideas in the paragraph.

© Scott Foresman 6

Vocabulary

Directions: Choose the word from the box that best fits each definition. Write the word on the line.

Check the Words You Know

__ abandoned
__ alien
__ anxiety
__ improvise
__ themes
__ variations

_____ 1. altered or varied forms of something

_____ 2. deserted

_____ 3. compose music on the spur of the moment

_____ 4. uneasy thoughts or fears about what may happen

_____ 5. an imaginary creature from space

_____ 6. the principal melodies in pieces of music

Directions: Choose the word from the box that best complete each sentence. Write the word on the line to the left.

_____ 7. When I am worried, music helps me get rid of any feelings of _____.

_____ 8. Because I like melodies, I enjoy trying to identify the _____ in famous pieces of music.

_____ 9. Some people play many different _____ of the same basic tune.

_____ 10. Sometimes I play music written by others, but I also like to _____ my own music as I play my piano.

Write a Descriptive Paragraph

On a separate sheet of paper, write a paragraph about a strange new instrument that an alien taught you to play. Describe the instrument and the kinds of music you can play with it. Use as many vocabulary words as you can.

Notes for Home: Your child identified and used vocabulary words from "Tyree's Song."
Home Activity: Play some music that you and your child like. Use vocabulary words to discuss why people enjoy music.

© Scott Foresman 6

Paraphrasing

- To **paraphrase** is to explain something in your own words.

- To paraphrase a piece of writing, first ask yourself what the author is trying to say. Then restate the ideas or description in your own words, without changing the meaning or adding opinions of your own.

Directions: Reread the scene from "Tyree's Song" in which Tyree plays for the Argans. Then answer the questions below. Think about how you would paraphrase each sentence.

> I shut my eyes against all the furry faces and the star-clustered eyes and I tilted my head up toward the night sky, toward the real stars. Suddenly my song had found me. It was "Sweetwater," the song Jubal had played at that winter fête—but now I made it my own. I took the melody and I played it like an Argan, modeling my song after an Argan song about a lost child looking for its mother. All the months of frustration and loneliness poured out of me and I played like *I* was the lost, lonely child calling across the empty light-years of space to Mother Earth.

From SWEETWATER by Lawrence Yep. Text copyright ©1973 by Lawrence Yep. Used by permission of HarperCollins Publishers.

1. What does Tyree do first?

_____

2. What does Tyree mean by "my song had found me"?

_____

_____

3. In your own words, what emotions does Tyree feel as he plays?

_____

_____

4. Paraphrase the entire passage in two or three sentences.

_____

_____

_____

5. On a separate sheet of paper, paraphrase what happens on Tyree's first trip to Sheol.

Notes for Home: Your child restated events from story passages in his or her own words. *Home Activity:* Challenge your child to restate paragraphs from a favorite book in simpler form. Be sure your child includes the author's original ideas and opinions.

© Scott Foresman 6

1.	Ⓐ	Ⓑ	Ⓒ	Ⓓ
2.	Ⓕ	Ⓖ	Ⓗ	Ⓙ
3.	Ⓐ	Ⓑ	Ⓒ	Ⓓ
4.	Ⓕ	Ⓖ	Ⓗ	Ⓙ
5.	Ⓐ	Ⓑ	Ⓒ	Ⓓ
6.	Ⓕ	Ⓖ	Ⓗ	Ⓙ
7.	Ⓐ	Ⓑ	Ⓒ	Ⓓ
8.	Ⓕ	Ⓖ	Ⓗ	Ⓙ
9.	Ⓐ	Ⓑ	Ⓒ	Ⓓ
10.	Ⓕ	Ⓖ	Ⓗ	Ⓙ
11.	Ⓐ	Ⓑ	Ⓒ	Ⓓ
12.	Ⓕ	Ⓖ	Ⓗ	Ⓙ
13.	Ⓐ	Ⓑ	Ⓒ	Ⓓ
14.	Ⓕ	Ⓖ	Ⓗ	Ⓙ
15.	Ⓐ	Ⓑ	Ⓒ	Ⓓ

© Scott Foresman 6

Selection Test

Directions: Choose the best answer to each item. Mark the letter for the answer you have chosen.

Part 1: Vocabulary

Find the answer choice that means about the same as the underlined word in each sentence.

1. Darla thinks she saw an <u>alien</u>.
   A. a creature that is part animal and part human
   B. a person who makes others laugh
   C. a visitor from another country
   D. a creature from outer space

2. Ronnie was filled with <u>anxiety</u>.
   F. feeling of terror
   G. uneasy thoughts or fears about what might happen
   H. feeling of sadness or gloominess
   J. act of sharing someone else's sorrow or hardship

3. The performers began to <u>improvise</u>.
   A. make up music, poetry, or drama on the spur of the moment
   B. move together at the same rate
   C. take turns performing alone
   D. practice for a public performance

4. He used the same <u>themes</u> over and over.
   F. words repeated in a song
   G. ordered scales of notes
   H. combinations of musical instruments
   J. principal melodies in pieces of music

5. They played several <u>variations</u>.
   A. unusual musical instruments
   B. slight changes in tunes
   C. slow, sad songs
   D. humorous imitations of serious music

6. The town had been <u>abandoned</u>.
   F. deserted
   G. buried
   H. completed
   J. displayed for sale

Part 2: Comprehension

Use what you know about the story to answer each item.

7. This story takes place on—
   A. Earth.
   B. the moon.
   C. the planet Harmony.
   D. a space station.

8. Why did the Silkie colonists leave Sheol?
   F. They wished to return to Earth.
   G. They were angry with the Argans.
   H. Their homes were flooded.
   J. Argans drove them out.

9. When they first met, the Argan musician gripped Tyree with his—
   A. claws.
   B. magnetic force.
   C. jaws.
   D. suction pads.

10. In this episode, you can tell that the Argans and the Silkies—
    F. are alike in most ways.
    G. do not trust each other.
    H. all came from Earth.
    J. depend on each other.

11. "I moored my skiff to one of the pillars of the portico and splashed up the steps." Which is the best paraphrase of this sentence?
    A. I left my skiff near a pillar of the portico and went up the steps.
    B. I tied my boat to the porch and walked up the steps.
    C. I docked my skiff in front of the elegant mansion and went up the staircase.
    D. I steered my boat to a pillar and made my lonely way up the stairs.

GO ON

© Scott Foresman 6

12. "I had to trade twenty feet of my best nylon fishing line to Red Genteel, but he agreed to do my chores in the garden for that day while I napped." Which is the best paraphrase of this sentence?
    F. Red Genteel needed twenty yards of fishing line for the garden. He used it while I napped.
    G. Lucky for me, Red Genteel was willing to do my chores that day so long as I gave him a bit of fishing line.
    H. Red Genteel and I traded days for fishing, doing chores in the garden, and napping.
    J. In exchange for some fishing line, Red Genteel agreed to do my chores so that I could take a nap.

13. Which is a major theme in this story?
    A. True friendship can be found in unexpected places.
    B. Humans will live on faraway planets in the future.
    C. If you mistreat people, they will not go out of their way to help you.
    D. Music is the same everywhere.

14. When Tyree plays "Sweetwater" for the Argans, his song suggests that he—
    F. wants the Argans to like him.
    G. feels lonely.
    H. would prefer to be an Argan.
    J. is very nervous about performing.

15. What is the most important thing that Amadeus does for Tyree in this story?
    A. teaches him that he must let the music find him
    B. makes him feel that he is a very special person
    C. gets other Argans to accept him
    D. helps him understand the differences between Argan and human styles of music

© Scott Foresman 6

STOP

Author's Purpose and Theme

REVIEW

Directions: Read the passage. Then read each question that follows the passage. Choose the best answer to each question. Mark the letter for the answer you have chosen.

At the Movies

Movies are made up of pictures and sound. Actors speak their lines, but there is another important sound happening—background music. This music is known as a film's *score*. The score is as important as any other part of a movie because it helps provide the mood for a scene.

The score can add the extra "punch" to make a movie a success. Does the script call for feelings of awe or mystery? Sorrow or anger? Tension or joy? Filmmakers can provide a real sense of excitement or nervousness by adding music that has a quick rhythm. By emphasizing the mood, music can express the same emotions caught by the camera lens.

Music can also show changes in location. You can change from a quiet forest scene to a noisy city street with the help of different styles of music. Sometimes music can even replace the actors' dialogue!

Some film scores are written especially for movies. Many composers spend their whole careers writing scores for films. Other film scores are made up of popular songs or dance music that suits the characters and events in the film. This kind of score can be just as effective as one that was written for a movie.

Although it will never replace the camera as the filmmaker's favorite tool, music serves an important purpose in movie making. If the pictures are what make the meal, it is the music that provides the spice to flavor it.

1. The author wrote this passage to—
   A. provide an entertaining story.
   B. inform readers about careers in filmmaking.
   C. express an opinion about music in movies.
   D. persuade readers to watch more movies.

2. The main theme of the passage is that—
   F. movies have pictures and sound.
   G. music can replace dialogue in films.
   H. music can describe a location.
   J. music plays an important role in movies.

3. The author compared music to spice in a meal in order to—
   A. show the relationship between a film's music and its pictures.
   B. tell what kind of music is best.
   C. emphasize a need for music with quick rhythms.
   D. suggest that music appeals to an audience's sense of taste.

4. The author assumes that the reader—
   F. has heard music in movies.
   G. likes to go to action movies.
   H. likes movies set in big cities.
   J. believes that movies should be more exciting.

5. The author supports his or her opinions by—
   A. giving examples.
   B. quoting experts.
   C. making vague generalizations.
   D. explaining how music is recorded for movies.

© Scott Foresman 6

Notes for Home: Your child identified the theme of a passage and the author's purpose in writing it. *Home Activity:* Challenge your child to find examples of materials written for different purposes, such as editorials, advertisements, clothing care labels, and so on.

Phonics: Complex Spelling Patterns

Directions: Some words have letters that don't match the sounds we hear. Read the words in the box. Listen carefully to each sound. Then read the clues. Match the clues with the words. Write each word on the line.

privilege	miniature	acoustics	creature
ballet	ancient	mediocre	maneuver

_____ 1. This word has the letter *c*, but the *c* stands for a sound like *shut*.

_____ 2. This word has the long *u* sound, but the letters that represent the sound start with the letter *e*.

_____ 3. This word has the letter *a*, but you hear it as a schwa sound.

_____ 4. This word ends with the letters *-et*, but you say it with a long *a* sound.

_____ 5. This word has the letters *eat*, but it rhymes with the word *teacher*.

_____ 6. This word has the letter *g*, but the word sounds like it should be spelled with *dg*.

_____ 7. This word has the same ending sound as *father*, but it's spelled *re*.

_____ 8. This word has the long *u* sound, but the letters that represent the sound start with the letter *o*.

Directions: Read the words in the box. Then read each related word below. Write the word from the box next to its related word. Then circle the part of the word that is spelled differently from the related word.

creature	variation	decision	musician	competition	gratitude

9. music _____ **12.** create _____

10. vary _____ **13.** decide _____

11. grateful _____ **14.** compete _____

Directions: Choose one of the word pairs above. Use both words in one sentence.

15. _____

Notes for Home: Your child explored words in which the spelling did not match the sound. *Home Activity:* Read a short story with your child. Challenge your child to find words that have unusual spellings. Write them down to review after you read.

© Scott Foresman 6

Take Notes/Highlight

Taking notes about or **highlighting** key information in a text can help you understand and remember the text better. It can also help you organize information to study for a test or to include in a research report. There is no one right way to take notes. You might make a list, an outline, a story map, a word web, a table, or write a summary. When you highlight, you can circle, underline, or mark with special pens the important details in what you have read.

Directions: Read the passage and then read the questions that follow. Highlight details in the passage that will help you answer the questions, and then answer the questions.

Music has been around for thousands of years—perhaps as long as 30,000 years. Archaeologists—scientists who research and study objects from long ago—have found musical instruments that date back this long. In fact, it is possible that making music may even have developed before people learned to talk. It is believed that early music was used for religious purposes, as well as for entertainment, dance, and telling stories. Most cultures have developed musical instruments and specific musical traditions and styles.

In Europe, the first songs were really simple chants. Dots were written down, above or below a line, to remind the singer if the next note was higher or lower. It was not until the 1700s that the tradition of writing music notes on lined paper was developed.

In China, writings have been found dating back over 2500 years that refer to musical performances. In fact, much of the music in some cultures is the same today as it was centuries ago. The Japanese *gagaku* of the 8th century is a style of music that still exists today. The Chinese *guenzhen* of the 16th century is another style that can still be heard today in its original form. In fact, much of the music that we listen to today has components picked up from classical pieces of centuries before.

The many cultures of Africa also have a rich musical history. Traditionally, African music has been associated with drums, but it has also included a variety of instruments, such as bells, rattles, gongs, and even xylophones. A guitar-like instrument, called the *lamellaphone,* or "thumb piano" is made up of metal or bamboo strips strung across a board or box. The strips are plucked with the fingers. These rhythmic instruments give African music a sound of its own.

© Scott Foresman 6

1. Which specific continents or countries are discussed in the article? _____

_____

2. How long ago were some of the earliest musical instruments made?

_____

3. For what purposes has music been used? _____

_____

_____

4. Which facts would be useful in a report about written music? _____

_____

_____

5. What are two styles of Asian music that can still be heard today? _____

_____

6. What are the names of the instruments that are used in African music?

_____

_____

_____

7. How is this article organized? _____

_____

_____

8. Suppose you wanted to make a table to organize the information in this passage. Describe what your table might look like. What heads might your table have?

_____

_____

9. When you take notes, why is it important to write the names of the sources you have read?

_____

_____

_____

10. Why is it important to think about your questions of inquiry before you begin taking notes?

_____

_____

_____

Notes for Home: Your child read a nonfiction passage and highlighted key details to help him or her answer questions about it. *Home Activity:* Read a magazine or newspaper article with your child. Ask your child to highlight or take notes about important details in the article.

© Scott Foresman 6

Fact and Opinion

- A **statement of fact** can be proven true or false by reading, observing, asking an expert, or checking it in some way.

- A **statement of opinion** tells someone's belief, judgment, or way of thinking about something. It cannot be proven true or false, but it can be supported or explained.

- A valid statement of opinion is supported by facts or by the authority of an expert. A faulty statement of opinion is not.

Directions: Reread "Three Wondrous Buildings." Then complete the table. For each building, write one statement of fact and one statement of opinion from the article. One fact has been done for you.

The Taj Mahal	The Parthenon	Our Lady of Chartres
Fact: The Taj Mahal is in a small city in northern India.	**2. Fact:**	**4. Fact:**
1. Opinion:	**3. Opinion:**	**5. Opinion:**

Notes for Home: Your child read an article and identified statements of fact and opinion. *Home Activity:* With your child, watch a news program. Help your child identify statements of fact, as well as valid and faulty statements of opinion.

© Scott Foresman 6

Vocabulary

Directions: Match each word on the left with its definition on the right. Write the letter of the definition on the line to the left of the word.

_____ **1.** quarry

_____ **2.** architecture

_____ **3.** apprentices

_____ **4.** carver

_____ **5.** intricate

_____ **6.** masons

a. people who build with stones, bricks, and so on

b. sculptor

c. complicated; detailed

d. place for cutting stone from the earth

e. people learning a trade

f. art of designing buildings

Check the Words You Know
___ apprentices
___ architecture
___ carver
___ cathedral
___ intricate
___ masons
___ quarry

Directions: Read the newspaper article. Choose the word from the box that best completes each sentence. Write the word on the matching numbered line.

New Student Learns to Sculpt

Kelly was one of the **7.** _____ who was learning to sculpt stone. She was studying under a master **8.** _____ who was very well respected. She wanted to learn how to make beautiful, **9.** _____ designs. Someday, Kelly hoped to carve stones to be used in a **10.** _____ or church.

7. _____   **9.** _____

8. _____   **10.** _____

Write a Persuasive Argument

On a separate sheet of paper, write a persuasive argument telling why it is important to learn an art or a craft, such as drawing or woodworking . Use as many vocabulary words as you can.

Notes for Home: Your child identified and used vocabulary words from *Cutters, Carvers, and the Cathedral*. **Home Activity:** With your child, look at local architecture and talk about its special features, using the listed vocabulary words.

© Scott Foresman 6

Fact and Opinion

- A **statement of fact** can be proven true or false by reading, observing, asking an expert, or checking it in some way.

- A **statement of opinion** tells someone's belief, judgment, or way of thinking about something. It cannot be proven true or false, but it can be supported or explained.

- A valid statement of opinion is supported by facts or by the authority of an expert. A faulty statement of opinion is not.

Directions: Reread this description of a mason's job from *Cutters, Carvers, and the Cathedral.* Then answer the questions below. Think about how the statements of fact and statements of opinion are different.

Deep below the cathedral floor, "Jeep" Kincannon, the chief masonry draftsman, works in the architecture office. "To be a good mason, you must have a good sense of geometry," he says. "With the computer, I can produce the templates for the blocks that go into the cathedral. The masons use these templates, or patterns, to shape each block of stone." All the blocks are cut to fit into their specific places, and they rise one above the other into columns, arches, walls, and steeples.

From CUTTERS, CARVERS AND THE CATHEDRAL by George Ancona. Copyright © 1995 by George Ancona. By permission of Lothrop, Lee & Shepard Books, a division of William Morrow & Company, Inc.

1. What statement of opinion does Jeep Kincannon offer?

_____

_____

2. Is his statement valid or faulty? How do you know?

_____

3. What is a statement of fact about templates?

_____

_____

4. How might you prove this statement of fact true or false?

_____

5. On a separate sheet of paper, tell which of the jobs described in *Cutters, Carvers, and the Cathedral* seems the most difficult to you. Support your statement of opinion with facts or expert opinions from the selection.

Notes for Home: Your child distinguished between statements of fact and statements of opinion. *Home Activity:* Work together to identify facts and opinions in a newspaper article. Discuss how well the author's opinions are supported by the facts presented.

© Scott Foresman 6

Name _____

1.	Ⓐ	Ⓑ	Ⓒ	Ⓓ
2.	Ⓕ	Ⓖ	Ⓗ	Ⓙ
3.	Ⓐ	Ⓑ	Ⓒ	Ⓓ
4.	Ⓕ	Ⓖ	Ⓗ	Ⓙ
5.	Ⓐ	Ⓑ	Ⓒ	Ⓓ
6.	Ⓕ	Ⓖ	Ⓗ	Ⓙ
7.	Ⓐ	Ⓑ	Ⓒ	Ⓓ
8.	Ⓕ	Ⓖ	Ⓗ	Ⓙ
9.	Ⓐ	Ⓑ	Ⓒ	Ⓓ
10.	Ⓕ	Ⓖ	Ⓗ	Ⓙ
11.	Ⓐ	Ⓑ	Ⓒ	Ⓓ
12.	Ⓕ	Ⓖ	Ⓗ	Ⓙ
13.	Ⓐ	Ⓑ	Ⓒ	Ⓓ
14.	Ⓕ	Ⓖ	Ⓗ	Ⓙ
15.	Ⓐ	Ⓑ	Ⓒ	Ⓓ

© Scott Foresman 6

Selection Test

Directions: Choose the best answer to each item. Mark the letter for the answer you have chosen.

Part 1: Vocabulary

Find the answer choice that means about the same as the underlined word in each sentence.

1. He worked in a quarry.
   A. place where stone is dug or cut from the earth
   B. temporary structure for holding workers and materials
   C. place where stone or brick is stored for use in construction
   D. a large factory for building houses

2. Her father was a carver.
   F. person who designs buildings
   G. person who builds with bricks
   H. person who sculpts by cutting stone or wood
   J. person who transports stone blocks

3. The cathedral was in the capital city.
   A. an immense building
   B. a large room with a high ceiling
   C. a large or important church
   D. a place where people work with stone

4. The artist had several apprentices.
   F. people learning a trade or art
   G. areas set aside for keeping materials while working
   H. people who give aid or help
   J. styles or methods of working

5. My brother wants to study architecture.
   A. rocks of a particular area
   B. the art of making figures by carving, modeling, or casting
   C. the science of the forms of life represented by fossils
   D. the art of designing buildings

6. She was fascinated by the intricate designs.
   F. unusual
   G. complicated and detailed
   H. bold
   J. delicate and difficult to see

7. The masons had gone home for the day.
   A. people who draw diagrams
   B. people who build with stone or brick
   C. people who pound wedges into stone to separate ledge from seam
   D. people who operate saws

Part 2: Comprehension

Use what you know about the selection to answer each item.

8. Where does the stone for the Cathedral of Saint John the Divine come from?
   F. Indiana
   G. England
   H. New York
   J. Pennsylvania

9. What is dynamite used for in a limestone quarry?
   A. separating the ledge from the seam
   B. causing a section of ledge to crash to the ground
   C. uncovering a new section of the limestone seam
   D. finding fossils in the limestone

10. In the process of removing limestone from the earth, which step comes first?
    F. Small blocks are cut from the ledge.
    G. Drill runners drive holes into the base of the ledge.
    H. Rubber bags are inflated by hoses to push the ledge out.
    J. Saw runners cut blocks called ledges into the stone.

GO ON

© Scott Foresman 6

11. Which item states a fact?
    A. "To be a carver, you have to have a passion for it, to love it with all your heart."
    B. "The following Sunday, the Second World War broke out."
    C. "The breaker has to have a good 'lick' to hit those wedges just right."
    D. "But it is less important than the masons'. . . ."

12. In which of these sentences does the author state an opinion?
    F. "Construction on the cathedral has stopped for lack of funding."
    G. "Some of the figures portray leaders in the struggle for social justice, such as Nelson Mandela."
    H. "If the limestone took three hundred million years to form, a hundred years to build a monument to faith doesn't seem so very long."
    J. "Yet, services are held, concerts are performed, and festivals are celebrated."

13. The author uses quotations from actual workers in this selection to—
    A. give the reader a more vivid picture of what the work is really like.
    B. add humor to the selection.
    C. avoid having to restate what he has learned from them.
    D. make it seem as if the construction was completed long ago.

14. If you are very good at geometry, which of these jobs is most likely to suit you best?
    F. breaker
    G. stone carver
    H. drill runner
    J. masonry draftsman

15. Which of these workers uses the same tools he or she would have used 100 years ago?
    A. limestone quarrier
    B. stone mason
    C. masonry draftsman
    D. master carver

STOP

© Scott Foresman 6

Graphic Sources and Steps in a Process

Directions: Read the passage and look at the picture. Then read each question about the passage and picture. Choose the best answer to each question. Mark the letter for the answer you have chosen.

Building a Flower

Imagine a "Metallic Flower" rising into the sky in a field of old factories. Such a flower has grown into a reality in the form of Frank Gehry's Guggenheim Museum in Bilbao, Spain. The building's most striking feature is an immense roof constructed of curving, twisting metal that reminds people of a flower.

This building is a result of a process that began with an international competition. The competition invited leading architects to design a building that would blend with the Bilbao skyline and be different from all other buildings in the world. While Frank Gehry's winning design reminds some people of the unusual shape of New York City's Guggenheim Museum, it has elements all its own.

The roof's unusual sculpted curving shape required careful planning. First, Mr. Gehry built a wood and paper model of the museum. Next, he entered mathematical data about the curves of the model's walls and roof into a computer. Mr. Gehry said afterwards that the computer was essential to turning his designs into reality.

Roof of Guggenheim Museum in Bilbao, Spain

1. The first step in building the museum was to—
   A. invite Frank Gehry to design it.
   B. build the roof.
   C. use a computer to begin the design.
   D. hold an international competition.

2. The picture helps you understand—
   F. the shape of the roof.
   G. the location of the museum.
   H. how the computer software works.
   J. how Gehry's design was different from other designs.

3. Which picture would be of further help in understanding the article?
   A. a portrait of Frank Gehry
   B. a portrait of Solomon R. Guggenheim
   C. a picture of the Guggenheim Museum in New York City
   D. a picture of the city of Bilbao

4. What was the first step in moving from the design on paper to the actual building?
   F. looking at the Guggenheim Museum in New York
   G. assigning the job to Frank Gehry
   H. entering mathematical data about the curves of the walls and roof
   J. building a model of the design

5. Before Mr. Gehry was able to use the computer for help, he had to—
   A. win the competition.
   B. enter mathematical data about the curve of the roof and walls into the computer.
   C. invent a new computer program.
   D. name the roof "Metallic Flower."

Notes for Home: Your child analyzed a passage and a picture and identified the steps in a process. **Home Activity:** Describe a house or a room to your child. Encourage him or her to draw a picture of the house or room, based on your description.

© Scott Foresman 6

Word Study: Word Building

Directions: Read the word pairs below. Listen to how each word in a pair is different from the other. Underline the stressed syllable in each word, for example: **rectangle** and **rectangular.** Use a dictionary to check your work.

1. electric   electricians

2. history   prehistoric

3. specify   specific

4. restore   restorations

5. certify   certification

Directions: Read the letter below. It contains five related word pairs—a base word and a new word formed by adding a prefix or a suffix, for example: **electric** and **electricians.** Find each pair. Write each word in the correct column.

Dear Miguel,

I am having a great time helping to restore the old church in town. The restoration process is slow and tedious, but the people I work with dedicate as much time as necessary to the work. You'd be amazed at the decorations we've brushed off and cleaned. You know I've always been inspired by history. Well, some of the carvings we've found look almost prehistoric! We have to separate the very old workmanship from the new additions. This separation is very time-consuming. However, our dedication is paying off! Every day we marvel at how the carvers and cutters of long ago chose to decorate this amazing church. I wish you could see it!

Your friend,

Amelia

Base Word	**New Word**
6. _____	11. _____
7. _____	12. _____
8. _____	13. _____
9. _____	14. _____
10. _____	15. _____

Notes for Home: Your child compared the sounds of words with suffixes and prefixes to their base words. *Home Activity:* Read a magazine article with your child. Look for words that have been built from other words. Figure out the base word. Say the words to hear the sound changes.

© Scott Foresman 6

Technology: Order Form/Following Directions

An **order form** is a special chart with spaces to be filled in. It can be used to purchase merchandise or obtain other materials. Since order forms are often complex, it is important to **follow directions** carefully.

Suppose you wanted to order a book from an online bookstore. You might begin searching to see if the bookstore has the book you want to purchase. The computer screen could look like the one below. You type words in the boxes and click on the round buttons beneath the boxes. Then click "Search Now."

Welcome to Our Bookstore!

You can search by author, title, or subject.

Author [   ]

  ○ Exact Name   ○ Last Name   ○ Start of Last Name

Title [   ]

  ○ Exact Title   ○ Key Words   ○ Start of Title

Subject [   ]

  ○ Exact Subject   ○ Key Words   ○ Start of Subject

| **Search Now** | **Start Over** |

Directions: Use the computer screen above to answer these questions.

1. How would you find a book about architecture? _____

_____

_____

2. How would you find a book written by the architect Frank Lloyd Wright? _____

_____

_____

3. How would you find the book called *Understanding Architecture?* _____

_____

_____

© Scott Foresman 6

Once you have found the book you want, you might get an order form like the one below. To purchase a book, you would need to complete the order form and then click "Order Now." Never use a person's credit card without that person's permission. Never give information about a credit card unless you are sure that this information will be confidential.

Place Your Order Now

You have chosen the book:

Understanding Architecture: Its Elements, History, and Meaning

by Leland M. Roth

List Price: $28.00   Our Price: $22.40   You Save: $5.60 (20%)

Name [   ]

Address [   ]

City [   ]   **State** [   ]   **Zip Code** [   ]

Telephone Number   **E-mail Address**

[   ]   [   ]

Method of Payment   ○ Credit Card   ○ Bill Me

Credit Card Type [   ]

Credit Card Number [   ]

Order Now   **Start Over**

Directions: Use the computer screen above to answer these questions.

4. What would you do if you realized you had made a mistake typing in information or the book selected was not the one you wanted?

_____

_____

5. Why is it important to follow all directions carefully when filling out order forms?

_____

_____

Notes for Home: Your child learned about filling out an order form to order a book. *Home Activity:* Show your child different types of order forms and discuss how to fill them out. Help your child complete an order form to make an imaginary purchase.

© Scott Foresman 6